Instrument Development in the Affective Domain (2nd Edition)

Evaluation in Education and Human Services

Editors:

George F. Madaus, Boston College,
  Chestnut Hill, MA, U.S.A.
Daniel L. Stufflebeam, Western Michigan
  University, Kalamazoo, MI, U.S.A.

Other books in the series:

Instrument Development in the Affective Domain

Measuring Attitudes and Values in Corporate
and School Settings
(2nd Edition)

Robert K. Gable
University of Connecticut
Marian B. Wolf
Keilty, Goldsmith & Company

Foreword by
Joseph W. Keilty

Kluwer Academic Publishers
Boston/Dordrecht/London

Distributors for North America:
Kluwer Academic Publishers
101 Philip Drive
Assinippi Park
Norwell, Massachusetts 02061 USA

Distributors for all other countries:
Kluwer Academic Publishers Group
Distribution Centre
Post Office Box 322
3300 AH Dordrecht, THE NETHERLANDS

Library of Congress Cataloging-in-Publication Data

Gable, Robert K.
    Instrument development in the affective domain : measuring
attitudes and values in corporate and school settings / Robert K.
Gable, Marian B. Wolf. — 2nd ed.
        p.   cm. — (Evaluation in education and human services)
    Includes bibliographical references and index.
    ISBN 0–7923–9369–4 (acid-free paper)
    1. Affect (Psychology)—Testing.   2. Attitude (Psychology)—
Testing.   3. Values—Testing.   4. Psychological tests.   I. Wolf,
Marian B.   II. Title.   III. Series.
BF531.G23   1993
616.89—dc20
                                                                93–17662
                                                                        CIP

Printed on acid-free paper.

Printed in the United States of America

Contents

List of Figures

List of Tables

Foreword

There has been longstanding interest in affective characteristics in both educational and corporate environments. While each domain has produced its own set of theorists and researchers, the work of some, such as Bandura, has found a place in the literature of both areas. In each of these settings, theorists and researchers have agreed on the causal connections between such constructs as self-efficacy and perceived satisfaction and success, whether that success is measured by academic achievement or corporate quality and performance resulting in profitability.

Along with this interest, comes the need for the development of valid and reliable instruments to assess affective characteristics. It is clear that no matter whether your interest lies in the relationship between self-efficacy and academic success or employee satisfaction and corporate success, it is essential that the instruments used be carefully designed and tested to assure that they are measuring what they are intended to measure in a consistent manner. This work offers the theoretical perspective, modern psychometric techniques, real examples, and data needed to enable the instrument developer to produce such valid and reliable instruments.

While the development process changes very little as one goes from the educational to the corporate domain, the inclusion in this edition of specific corporate-based theories and research examples as a complement to the academic-based examples greatly enhances the relevance of this book for those of us concerned with the effects of affective variables in the workplace. For anyone involved with the development of instruments to measure these variables, this book should prove a necessary resource. With today's emphasis on quality, this book provides the road map and background to accomplish measurement with the certitude that quality demands.

Joseph W. Keilty
Executive Vice-President
Quality and Human Resources
American Express Company

Preface

The text was prepared for a graduate-level course in affective instrument development with a focus on the school-educational environment. A major change in this second edition is the inclusion of research on attitudes and values from the corporate domain. Self-efficacy has also been included as a major affective variable with implications for both educational and corporate worlds. The following methodological techniques have also been included in this edition: confirmatory factor analysis, causal modeling, Rasch latent trait techniques and generalizability theory. The techniques described, and the school and corporate environment data sets included, represent attempts over several years to prepare materials that would illustrate appropriate instrument-development techniques in the affective domain. The need for this text became apparent after witnessing several large-scale research projects that were hindered by inadequately prepared instruments. Researches in these projects were often unaware of the need to use appropriate procedures in developing affective instruments; furthermore, they could rarely, if ever, locate a comprehensive and readable text that could help. This text was developed to meet this important instructional need.

Chapter 1 discusses the importance of affective variables in school and corporate environments and presents conceptual definitions of major affective constructs such as attitudes, self-efficacy, and interests. Chapter 2 outlines and illustrates the domain-referenced approach for developing operational definitions (i.e., items) for the targeted conceptual definitions. Chapter 3 addresses the important area of scaling the affective characteristics in the context of Fishbein's expectancy-value model. The Thurstone, Likert, latent trait, and semantic differential techniques are included along with a section on normative versus ipsative measures.

Chapters 4 and 5 present the underlying theory and appropriate empirical techniques for examining validity and reliability evidence. Data gathered by the authors, using several different instruments, are included to illustrate each technique. Construct validity is examined using annotated SPSS[x] computer output for the Factor program to illustrate the exploratory technique of principal component analysis; and LISREL VII annotated output is presented to illustrate confirmatory factor analysis. Additional procedures described to examine construct validity include causal modeling and Rasch's latent trait analysis. Annotated output for the Reliability program is included for examining alpha internal consistency reliability. Actual item analysis and reliability data from the SPSS[x] Reliability program are also presented. Decision strategies are discussed and models for reporting the data analysis are illustrated. Readers should find these sections quite useful from an instructional viewpoint. For those interested in further study, several journal articles illustrating the techniques described are referenced at the end of each chapter. Finally, Chapter 6 reviews the steps in process of instrument development.

We would like to thank the University of Connecticut for granting the first author a recent sabbatical leave to work on the text, as well as the many graduate students whose penetrating questions have resulted in much rethinking, reworking, and we hope, clearer explanations.

Special appreciation is extended to Steve Owen, Bill Pilotte, and Elaine Slocumb for sharing their research with us. Particular thanks is due to Barbara Helms for her assistance in data analysis, preparation of tables, and the editing of the manuscript. Several graduate students at the Bureau of Educational Research and Service also helped. Steve Melnick, Marylou Kranyek, and Ching-Hui Chen assisted in the production of the references and the development of the index; Chris Murphy and Bob Garber proofread earlier versions. The comments of Marcy Delcourt, Gina Schack and John Rogers were most helpful. Finally, special thanks is extended to Marion Lapierre, Gail Millerd, Kathe Gable, and Bryon Harmon for their work on the final document.

RKG
MBW

Instrument Development
in the Affective Domain
(2nd Edition)

1 AFFECTIVE CHARACTERISTICS IN SCHOOL AND CORPORATE ENVIRONMENTS: THEIR CONCEPTUAL DEFINITIONS

School Environment

During the 1960s the cognitive domain received much attention from educators as proponents and critics argued the merits and evils of behavioral objectives, often utilizing the framework for the cognitive domain suggested in the *Taxonomy of Educational Objectives, Handbook I* (Bloom, 1956). In 1964, the *Taxonomy of Educational Objectives, Handbook II: The Affective Domain* (Krathwohl et al., 1964) was published but received little attention, in light of the debate over behavior objectives and the apparent national consensus that the primary aims of schooling were in the cognitive domain. In his article, "Assessing Educational Achievement in the Affective Domain," Tyler (1973) discussed the growing awareness in the late 1960s and early 1970s of the need for schools to attend to the affective domain when developing their learning goals and objectives.

Tyler suggested two prevalent views as explainations of why affective learning was not systematically planned as part of most school curricula. First, many educators felt that affective concerns such as "feelings" were not the business of the school, but rather the task of the home or church. The second view was that affective concerns were natural outgrowths (ends)

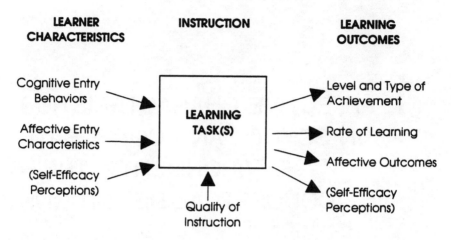

Figure 1–1. Adapted depiction of the major variables in the theory of school learning (from Bloom, 1976, p. 11).

of learning cognitive content and need not be included as separate objectives (means) to be addressed during the learning process. Fortunately, during the 1970s, affective objectives were recognized to be important as both ends and means in the overall school process, and were no longer considered as merely acceptable outgrowths of an emphasis on the cognitive domain. As a result, state-level, as well as school- and program-level, statements of goals and objectives included both cognitive and affective objectives.

The most recent emphasis on the cognitive domain surfaced mainly as a result of the continual decline in standardized test scores in the 1980s. Calls for increased emphasis in the cognitive area rang out loudly with publication of the report by the National Commission on Excellence in Education entitled "A Nation at Risk: The Imperative for Educational Reform" (Bell, 1983) and the report of the Carnegie Foundation for the Advancement of Teaching entitled "High School: A Report on Secondary Education in America" (Boyer, 1983).

While the cognitive domain receives increased attention, the affective area will remain firmly entrenched as an important aspect of the schooling process as well as an outcome of schooling. Bloom's (1976) adapted model of school learning, depicted in Figure 1–1, clearly suggests that during instruction learners approach any task with prior affective entry characteristics (e.g., attitudes, self-esteem, interests, and values), as well as cognitive behaviors. According to Bloom it is the dynamic interaction between these overlapping cognitive and affective domains during the instructional process that results in both cognitive learning outcomes and associated affective outcomes. These affective outcomes help guide future feelings about the course content and issues (attitudes), feelings of personal worth and success (self-esteem), desires to become involved in various activities (interests), and personal standards (values).

Bandura's (1986, 1989) research in the area of self-efficacy has added greatly to our understanding of Bloom's learner characteristics and learning outcomes. Later, we will note that the self-efficacy construct may be the most important construct described in this chapter, since it addresses the interplay of the cognitive, affective and behavioral domains. We will also describe the implications of the self-efficacy construct and research in the area of leadership training for educational administrators such as principals.

Corporate Environment

The importance of affective characteristics in the research on firm performance has been recognized for many years in the corporate setting. "Organizational Climate," a multidimensional organizational construct which encompasses such aspects as motivation, leadership, job satisfaction, and goal setting, is viewed as an important variable due to its relationship to firm performance. Hansen and Wernerfelt (1989) provide a brief review of some of this research.

Later, we will review Hansen and Wernerfelt's (1989) study of 60 Fortune-1000 firms, where in it was found that "organizational climate" factors explained twice as much of the variance in profit rates as did the usual economic factors. In addition, the importance of affective characteristics will be supported as we review the assessment of employee attitudes. Specifically, Ulrich, Halbrook, Stuchlik, and Thorpe's (1991) research regarding the role of employee and customer perceived "attachment" in creating a competitive advantage will be discussed.

Finally, the importance to the corporate environment of Bandura's self-efficacy construct, which addresses the affective as well as the cognitive and behavioral domains, will be reviewed. This topic will be given a comprehensive treatment due to its important contribution to human resources leadership-development programs. Understanding the causal influence of self-efficacy beliefs on leader behavior is necessary for the successful development, implementation, and evaluation of leadership-training programs.

	Negative		Neutral		Positive
Students	A	B	C	D	E

Figure 1–2. Direction and intensity of student attitudes toward microcomputers (Target) (Adapted from Anderson, 1981, p. 4).

In both educational and corporate settings, the accurate assessment of affective characteristics is dependent upon instruments that are both theoretically based and psychometrically sound. The purpose of this text is to assist in the selection and development of such instruments.

What are Affective Characteristics?

Anderson's book entitled *Assessing Affective Characteristics in the Schools* (1981) presents an in-depth theoretical and practical discussion of affective instrument construction. The author is indebted to Anderson for providing a clear perspective on the conceptual and operational definition of affective characteristics.

As described by Anderson, human characteristics reflect typical ways of thinking, acting, and feeling in diverse situations (Anderson, 1981, p. 3). While the first two areas reflect cognitive and behavioral characteristics, the third area reflects affective characteristics, which Anderson describes as "qualities which present people's typical ways of feeling or expressing their emotions."

Anderson states that all affective characteristics must have three attributes: intensity, direction, and target. The *intensity* attribute refers to the degree or strength of the feeling. For example, An individual's attitude toward working with microcomputers could be very strong, whereas another person's could be quite mild. The *direction* attribute reflects the positive, neutral, or negative aspect of the feeling. The final attribute, the *target*, identifies the object, behavior, or idea at which the feeling is being directed.

Figure 1–2 illustrates intensity, direction, and target attributes. Using again our microcomputer example, we see that the target of the affect is "working with a microcomputer." A hypothetical rating scale has been used to measure and locate the attitudes of five people toward microcomputers on a continuum which specifies negative and positive feelings (direction), as well as neutral (person C) and quite intense feelings (people A and E).

This example allows us to see the complexity of assessing affective characteristics such as attitudes toward microcomputers. The intensity of the individual's attitude is related to the individual's self-appraisal of capability or self-efficacy in this situation (see Lindia, 1992; Lindia and Owen, 1991; Murphy, Coover, and Owen, 1989).

Types of Affective Characteristics

Psychologists have identified numerous constructs that reflect affective characteristics. This volume will restrict the potential list to those variables that have been shown to be correlates of actual behaviors. We will begin with the construct of attitudes and move directly to a very popular and powerful construct, self-efficacy, which has been shown to be causally linked to several types of outcome behaviors in both school and corporate settings. Considerable emphasis will be placed on the theory and application of self-efficacy research because it provides us with the most comprehensive understanding of the interplay of cognition, affect, and behavior. Other constructs included in the chapter will be values, self-esteem, and interests. Prior to providing the mechanics of operationally defining these variables in the next chapter, it is important to have a clear understanding of the theory underlying each construct in the context of a school or corporate setting.

Attitudes

Kiesler, Collins, and Miller (1969) state that "the concept of attitude has played a central role in the development of American social psychology" (p. 1). The techniques of attitude measurement and scaling, as well as the theoretical and empirical issues of attitude change have received much attention dating back prior to World War II. Allport (1935) termed attitude as "the most distinctive and indispensable concept in contemporary social psychology" (p. 798) and offered the following definition:

> An attitude is a mental and neural state of readiness, organized through experience, exerting a directive or dynamic influence upon the individual's response to all objects and situations with which it is related. (Allport, 1935, p. 810)

However, no single definition of *attitude* has emerged over the years.

In a review by Severy (1974), two schools of thought regarding the structural nature of attitudes were described. The first school can be represented by Thurstone's definition of attitude as the intensity of positive or negative affect for or against a psychological object. A psychological object is any symbol, person, phrase, slogan, or idea toward which people can differ as regards positive or negative affect. (Thurstone, 1946, p. 39)

Proponents of this school of thought were known as "unidimensionalists," to denote their conception that attitudes are only *evaluative* (e.g., positive-negative or favorable-unfavorable) in perspective.

The second school of thought was supported by the *component* theorists, who conceived of attitudes on more than just an evaluative dimension. Wagner's definition illustrates this view:

An attitude is composed of affective, cognitive, and behavioral components that correspond, respectively, to one's evaluations of, knowledge of, and predisposition to act toward the object of the attitude. (Wagner, 1969, p. 7)

In a later volume, Triandis presented the following definition:

An attitude is an idea charged with emotion which predisposes a class of actions to a particular class of social institutions. (Triandis, 1971, p. 2)

This comprehensive definition also illustrates the component theorists' view that attitudes are composed of three components: cognitive, affective, and behavioral. The *cognitive* component is a belief or idea, which reflects a category of people or objects, such as microcomputers. The *affective* component represents the person's evaluation of the object or person, and is the emotion that charges the idea—that is, for example, feeling positive about working with the computer. Finally, the *behavioral* component represents overt action directed toward the object or person. It represents a predisposition to action, such as enrolling in an optional microcomputer-training course.

Several writers have combined common elements from the various definitions. In his article entitled "Attitude Measurement and Research," Aiken combines several definitions to state that

attitudes may be conceptualized as learned predispositions to respond positively or negatively to certain objects, situations, concepts, or persons. As such, they possess cognitive (beliefs or knowledge), affective (emotional, motivational), and performance (behavior or action tendencies) components. (Aiken, 1980, p. 2)

Campbell (1950) and Green (1954) also attempted to find some communality among the various attitude definitions. Campbell proposed that agreement was really present regarding the implicit operational definition of attitude and suggested that social attitudes are reflected by a "consistency in response to an object" (p. 32). Agreeing with this view, Green analyzed

Guttman's (1944) work in attitudes and stated that the "concept of attitudes implies a consistency of responses" (Green, 1954, p. 336). That is, the measurement of attitudes would consist of obtaining responses to a sample of statements about opinions from a sample of people. Whether these responses to the affective statements relate to cognitive or behavioral aspects of attitude can be determined through empirical studies. For example, Wicker (1969) reviewed 30 studies relating attitude to behavior and found the two to be not directly related. In reanalyzing the same data, Shaw (cited in Severy, 1974) focused on seven of the 30 studies which met his standards of appropriate measurement techniques. In these seven studies the relationship tended to be higher, and Shaw concluded that attitudes can lead to specific behavior given a particular situation and constraints. Thus, the cognitive and behavioral components of an attitude, as defined by Triandis (1971), are important consideration; however, behavior should be considered as a function of one's attitude in the context of the particular situation.

In this volume, consistency of responses to statements about ideas, people, and objects will be employed to reflect social attitudes. Emphasis will be placed upon the popular definition provided by Fishbein and Ajzen, which states that attitudes reflect

a learned predisposition to respond in a consistently favorable or unfavorable manner with respect to a given object. (Fishbein and Ajzen, 1975, p. 6)

Readers are encouraged to read Fishbein and Ajzen's (1975) book entitled *Belief, Attitude, Intention, and Behavior: An Introduction to Theory and Research*, which describes the *Expectancy-Value Model*. In this model, *attitudes* are distinguished from *beliefs* in that attitudes represent the individual's favorable or unfavorable evaluation (i.e., good–bad) of the target object, while beliefs represent the information the individual has about the object. Attitudes toward objects are determined by joining the product of the evaluation of a particular attribute associated with the target object and the subjective probability (i.e., belief) that the object has the attribute. Accordingly, the evaluation of the attribute contributes to the individual's attitude in proportion to the strength of his beliefs (see Fishbein and Ajzen, 1975, pp. 222–223). In Chapter 3 Fishbein's work will be further described as it forms the basis for the scaling of all of the affective characteristics described in this volume (e.g., attitudes, self-efficacy, self-concept, values and interest). Fishbein and Ajzen's work clearly parallels Anderson's summary which states that

attitudes are feelings that generally have a moderate level of intensity, can be either unfavorable or favorable in direction, and are typically directed toward some object (that is, target). The association between feelings and a particular target is learned. And, once learned, the feelings are consistently experienced in the presence of the target. (Anderson, 1981, p. 33)

School Environment. As discussed by Tyler, attitudes appropriately appear in most statements of educational objectives. In content areas such as social studies, the objectives usually pertain to "the development of objective attitudes toward alternate possible explanations of social phenomena and toward policies for dealing with social problems" (Tyler, 1973, p. 5). While such an objective has a cognitive component pertaining to the recognition of objectivity in dealing with social problems, the affective (emotional) component attempts to free the student from safe, familiar views and pro-motes exploration of new views. Several educational programs also include statements of attitude enhancement in their objectives. Typical statements begin with the phrase, "students should develop positive attitudes toward" and end with a particular target (e.g., computers, reading, math, learning, school, teachers, or special education students).

Examples of worker concerned with measures of attitudes in educational settings are the *Survey of Study Habits and Attitudes* (The Psychological Corporation), *Attitudes Toward School Subjects* (Gable and Roberts, 1983), *School Attitude Measure* (Dolan and Enos, 1980), *Attitudes Toward Computers* (Reece and Gable, 1982), *Adult-Attitudes Toward Computers Survey* (Coover and Delcourt, 1992), the Computer *Self-Efficacy Scale* (Murphy, Coover, and Owen, 1989), and the *Maslach Burnout Inventory* (business and educational forms; Consulting Psychologists Press). In addition, Lindia's *Student Computer Survey* (1992) assesses anxiety toward computers and interest in computers. Readers may also be interested in Woodrow's 1991 article, which describes and compares the following three attitudes toward computer instruments (in addition to the Reece and Gable scale noted above): *Computer Attitude Scale* (Gressard & Loyd, 1986); *Computer Use Questionnaire* (Griswold, 1983); and the *Computer Survey* (Stevens, 1980, 1982). Finally, we note the *School Situation Survey* (Helms and Gable, 1989), which assesses grade 4 through 12 students' perceptions of school-related sources (i.e., Teacher Interactions, Academic Stress, Peer Interactions, and Academic Self-Concept) and manifestations of stress (i.e., Emotional, Behavioral, and Physiological), and two additional instruments available from Consulting Psychologists Press: Folkman and Lazarus' *Ways of Coping Questionnaire* and Spielberger's *State-Trait Anxiety Inventory*.

Corporate Environment. In the corporate setting attitudes are often assessed using employee job satisfaction questionnaires. For several years researchers have examined the link between job satisfaction and job performance. According to Locke (1976), job satisfaction was often broken into events or conditions (e.g., work itself, pay, promotions, recognition, benefits and working conditions) and "agents" (e.g., supervision, coworkers, company, and management). More recent reviews have reported the consistent finding of a low relationship between job satisfaction and job performance. In a meta-analysis in this area, Iaffaldano and Muchinsky (1985) found the average satisfaction-performance correlations to be around .17. In a later more theoretically-driven meta-analysis, Podsakoff and Williams (1986) reported an average correlation of .27 in situations where *rewards were contingent on performance.* Thus, the reward contingency moderated the relationship of job satisfaction and job performance. Readers interested in a well-developed, path-analytic model, which addresses the conditions that moderate the satisfaction-performance relationship, are referred to the chapter by Katzell, Thompson, and Grizzo (1992) entitled "How Job Satisfaction and Job Performance Are and Are Not Linked."

Other researchers have studied employee satisfaction/dissatisfaction in the context of organizational factors such as communication flow, decision-making practices, leadership, goal setting, and emphasis on human resources (i.e., career development, pay, recognition). These dimensions of job satisfaction are important to assess, since they comprise the foundation of an important construct developed in the 1960s – namely, *organizational climate.* Hansen and Wernerfelt (1989) cite the later work of several authors (Field and Abelson, 1982; Glick, 1985; James and Jones, 1979; Schneider, 1975; and Steers and Lee, 1983) to support their claim that "climate" is still a major organizational concept. It "uniquely refers to a broad class of organizational and perceptual variables that reflect individual/ organizational interactions which affect individual behavior" (p. 401).

Hansen and Wernerfelt's (1989) study of 60 Fortune-1000 companies entitled "Determinants of Firm Performance: The Relative Importance of Economic and Organizational Factors" is important to this text as well as to the corporate world. It supports the need to assess employee attitudes and satisfactions using valid and reliable attitude instruments developed according to the theoretical framework of organizational climate. The study is important to the corporate world, given the goals and activities of human resource departments, because it has demonstrated that employee-perceived, organizational-climate factors explained approximately *twice the variance in firm profit rates* as did usual economic factors (i.e., various measures of firm assets).

We return to the importance of assessing employee satisfaction/dissatisfaction and to emphasis upon the continued recognition of employees as a most valuable company resource. The issue of employee turnover becomes an important consideration, in light of the fact that it has been shown to be the highest correlate of other work behaviors such as absenteeism, lateness, drug use, and sabotage (Fisher and Locke, 1992; see also Campion (1991), and Mobley, 1977). Schlesinger and Heskett's (1991) study of the relationship between employee training/development costs and retention (one indicator of satisfaction) is important in that it was conducted using a framework of the economics of customer service, taking into account the cost of turnover and the value of consistency in customer service. The authors cite Phillip's (1990) study at Merck & Co., which found that

> disruptions in work relationships and the transactional costs of getting employees on and off the payroll raised the total cost of employee turnover to 1.5 times an employee's annual salary. Further, the analysis concluded that, from an investment of 50% of an employee's salary in activities to eliminate turnover, Merck could reap a one-year payback. (p. 76)

Schlesinger and Heskett (1991) also report a 1989 study by Sears based on customer attitudes surveyed in 771 stores. This study documented the important relationship between employee turnover and employee composition and customer attitudes.

> In stores that were given relatively high customer-service ratings, 54% of the sales force turned over in a year, as compared to 83% at the poorer scoring stores. Second, customer satisfaction correlates directly with the composition of a store's sales force. The more a store relied on a continually changing group of part-timers (a staple in many service businesses), the lower the customer ratings it received. The higher its percentage of full-time and regular part-time workers, the more satisfied customers said they felt.

A further case for the relationship of employee attitudes and customer attitudes is supported in the Ulrich, Hallbrook, Stuelik, and Thorpe (1991) article entitled "Employee and Customer Attachment: Synergies for Competitive Advantages." The authors note that an outgrowth of the emphasis on managerial excellence/quality (e.g., Total Quality Management, Deming prize, Baldridge Award) has been a renewed emphasis on customers. Understanding the importance of and dedication to servicing customer needs is receiving much attention. Parallel to this movement is the continued human-resource emphasis on employee development, noted earlier. Ulrich et al. (1991) cite work by Schein (1985) and Wilkins (1984) that argues that the outcome of such an employee focus is increased "employee commitment, ownership, and dedication to the firm" (p. 89), known as "employee attachment." Ulrich et al. (1991) argue that such "employee attachment" is related to "customer attachment":

> As employees share and develop a greater unity around the values of a company, they come to embody the company in their professional demeanor. Customers who come in contact with employees who are highly devoted and unified in their professional outlook will likely be affected favorably by what they see. (p. 90)

The key to a company's attention to employee and customer attachment is Ulrich et al.'s contention that both result in the company's enhanced competitive advantage.

> HR practices may be used within a business to instill a shared mindset among employees. As employees share their mindset, they communicate and disseminate this mindset among customers. As customers come to share a common mindset with employees, an employee/customer attachment occurs which leads to competitive advantage. (p. 91)

While the role of employee and customer attitudes becomes clear in this context, we note that the foundation of assessment and research efforts in this area rests on accurate measurement of attitudes. Profiles obtained from questionnaires lacking validity and reliability will be both meaningless and inaccurate, and could lead to goal statements, action plans, and policy decisions that create a situation analogous to ships with the wrong cargo arriving at an incorrect destination. The intent of this text is to avoid these mistakes by facilitating the development of valid and reliable attitude questionnaires. An example of a comprehensive instrument development process can be found in Veiga's (1991) article describing the *Groups Behavior Profile*, a measure of the frequency with which individuals engage in self-limiting behavior in work groups (i.e., reduce their influence or contribution to the group's performance).

Self-Efficacy

In the previous section, we noted that attitudes were comprised of cognitive (beliefs), affective (evaluation), and behavioral (action) components. The interplay among these components becomes clear in the context of Albert Bandura's social cognitive theory, which is described in his highly recommended 1986 text, *Social Foundations of Thought and Action*, and in his 1989 article, "Human Agency in Social Cognitive Theory." While attitudes may, in fact, predispose behaviors in particular situations, Bandura argues that successfully modeled behaviors contribute to changes in attitudes. Of all the constructs described in this chapter, self-efficacy is perhaps the most important; it will receive a great detail of attention, because it is the basis for a **causal model**, analyzing human motivation, thought processes, and behavior. As stated by Bandura:

> The social portion of the (self-efficacy) terminology acknowledges the social origins of much human thought and action; the cognitive portion recognizes influential causal contributions of thought processes to human motivation, affect and action. (1989, p. xii)

Bandura defines self-efficacy as "people's judgments of their capabilities to arrange and execute courses of action required to attain designated types of performances" (1986, p. 391). Most simply, self-efficacy can be defined as one's perception of his/her ability to successfully perform a task or behavior: In effect, that is to say that those who believe they will succeed on a task are more likely to accomplish the task.

Corporate and School Environments.   Self-efficacy provides considerable implications for corporate and school environments in the area of leadership development. Designers of leadership-training programs need to be aware of the pervasive role of accurate self-perceptions in determining one's behavior toward personal development. People tend to avoid tasks or situations they perceive to be above their abilities, but will tend to expend more effort toward and persist longer in working to attain outcomes associated with high self-efficacy judgments (Bandura, 1977, 1986). People undertaking tasks that are above their capability can create functional problems for themselves as well as for their coworkers. On the other hand, accurate efficacy judgments, or even those a little above one's capability, can lead to healthy challenges and successes which contribute to personal development (Bandura, 1986, pp. 393–394). Readers are referred to the work of Gist (1987, 1992) for discussions of self-efficacy in the corporate realm, and to Leithwood (1992) and Leithwood, Jantzi, and Dart (in press) for the role of self-efficacy in developing "transformational-leadership" behaviors of school administrators.

Sources of Self-Efficacy Information.   People develop self-efficacy perceptions in a variety of ways. The sections that follow will discuss the primary sources described by Bandura. Special emphasis will be placed on aspects of self-efficacy that relate to corporate training and the school environment.

Previous Experience.   Previous experience (enactive attainment) is a strong source of self-efficacy information. Previous experience with mastering targeted behaviors (i.e., success influences success) could, in fact, be the most important source of self-efficacy judgments. People with high levels of self-efficacy with respect to the targeted behavior tend to view failures as situationally specific, or due to a lack of effort or poor strategy (Bandura, 1986, p. 399).

Physiological Cues.   Another way in which individuals develop accurate self-perceptions of efficacy is self-reading or physiological cues or anxiety arousal (e.g., nervousness, sweating while attempting a particular task). Self beliefs in capabilities regarding a particular situation, along with the cognitive ability to control aversive thoughts, will determine the level of stress and anxiety arousal. As noted by Bandura:

> The exercise of control over one's own consciousness is summed up well in the proverb: "You cannot prevent the birds of worry and care from flying over your head. But you can stop them from building a nest in your head." Perceived self-efficacy in thought control is a key factor in the regulation of cognitively-generated arousal. It is not the sheer frequency of aversive cognition but the perceived inefficacy to turn them off that is the major source of distress (Kent, 1987; Salkovskis and Harrison 1984; cited in Bandura, 1989, p. 1177).

Verbal Persuasion.   Persuasion from others is an important contributor to accurate self-efficacy. This feedback can be in the form of direct verbal feedback from others. An often employed feedback procedure is the use of well-designed questionnaires incorporated into an upward feedback system to provide the necessary evaluative reactions to performance that fit under Bandura's "persuasion from others" category. School principals are rated by teachers and corporate managers are rated by immediate subordinates to provide accurate assessments of leader behaviors. Such upward feedback systems consist of questionnaires that assess general dimensions, such as providing leadership, managing programs, managing conflict, problem solving, demonstrating integrity, and developing team-work. The key to these questionnaires is that the dimensions assessed are operationally defined by 50 to 70 specific observable behaviors. Some example items are:

- Sets clear goals and objectives,
- Allocates appropriate resources to support programs,
- Reacts appropriately in crisis situations,
- Encourages alternative approaches to complex problems,

- Communicates openly and honestly with others,
- Encourages individuals to work together as a team.

The ratings for these leader behaviors are attained using Likert-type response formats to quantify the **frequency** with which the leader exhibits the behavior, **agreement** that the behavior is exhibited, or **satisfaction** with the way the leader performs the behavior.

An important part of the successful incorporation of such feedback into leadership development programs is pre-training assessment with feedback to the leader profiling the ratings and periodic (e.g., 12 months) follow-up "second-generation" assessment. Changes in the targeted behaviors have implications for both the leader and the training curriculum (content and presentation). The initial feedback contributes to the leader's necessary awareness of behaviors; the second generation assessment provides crucial information regarding the success or failure of the changes in targeted behaviors. The first/second generation data also contribute to the evaluation of the overall leadership-development program.

While leadership development programs in corporate settings may include first- and second-generation assessments of manager behaviors, many neglect to emphasize to the leaders the importance of their actively seeking feedback subsequent to the training. Ashford and Tsui's (1991) review of the research in this area supports the potent role of leader self-regulated, active feedback seeking for developing leadership effectiveness. After commenting on "self-management" research, which focuses on the leader's control of more specific behaviors (e.g., getting to a meeting on time), the authors develop the "self-regulation" concept grounded in the control theory described by Carver and Scheier (1981) and the leader's task of minimizing the discrepancy between a goal/standard and his or her behavior, as discussed by Lord and Hanges (1987).

Ashford and Tsui's (1991) resulting self-regulation concept includes three sub-processes: standard setting, discrepancy detecting, and discrepancy reducing (p. 253). Such self-regulation is consistent with the importance Bandura attributes to feedback in developing accurate perceptions of self-efficacy. It is the active seeking of feedback from direct reports and colleagues that allows the leader to detect discrepancies between standards and behaviors. Thus, self-regulated feedback seeking becomes crucial in changing behavior to enhance leader effectiveness. In fact. Ashford and Tsui (1991) report research indicating that it is the active seeking of negative feedback (as opposed to positive feedback) from direct reports that results in increased **accuracy** of the leaders' understanding of their own behaviors, as well as in increasing the **perceptions of the leaders' overall**

effectiveness. These findings are supported by Goldsmith's (1992) study of the "Top 100" executives of a "Fortune-500" company. These leaders received feedback from their direct reports, developed action plans for improving behaviors, and periodically followed up with their direct reports to check on progress and to receive further assistance. Feedback-up data for these executives received 18 months later showed significant improvement in rated leader effectiveness.

Vicarious Experience. Observation and modeling of successful performances of targeted behaviors during skill training can raise one's self-efficacy for performing comparable tasks (Bandura, Adams, Hardy, and Howells, 1980). The role of such vicarious experiences in developing targeted behaviors has important implications for the activities designed for leadership-training programs. Building on accurate self-awareness developed through self-reading of physiological cues, feedback from others, and previous experience, the development/refinement of appropriate and new patterns of behavior (e.g., situational leadership skills) can be accomplished using competent models who successfully demonstrate the necessary behavior ("If they can do it, I can do it."). According to Bandura, a three-facet approach, consisting of modeling, guided enactment (i.e., coaching/role playing), and self-directed application (Rosenthal and Bandura, 1978), yields the most positive results. Successful modeling can enhance the self-beliefs of those having previous negative experiences with the targeted leadership behavior, and can offer positive reinforcement and refinements to the behaviors of those who already have confidence in their performance in the targeted skill areas. A heavy emphasis on successful skill practice (i.e., guided mastery of modeled behavior) will enhance the participants' self-efficacy for new behaviors in situations where little prior experience is available to evaluate personal competence (Bandura, 1986, pp. 160–161, p. 400).

It is necessary to emphasize that the modeled behavior must also be practiced following the training to strengthen the new skills under successful conditions. A weakness of many training programs is the lack of such follow-up activities. Participants typically attend a two-day training session, during which much information is presented, and under optimal conditions, modeling and guided role-playing activities are included. Following the training, the participants return to the work setting, essentially left on their own to successfully practice their new skills. Without periodic follow-up training and coaching/feedback, those struggling to successfully exhibit the new behaviors will have lower conceptions of self-efficacy and be less likely to continue to engage in the learned behaviors or persevere in light of continued experiences of failure. Unfortunately, this situation develops because many people engaged in leadership training place little emphasis on the third facet of Bandura's approach—namely, **self-directed practice/ application**. It is the successful use of the new or refined behaviors that contributes to the increased self-efficacy for performing the behaviors. It is clear that this self-regulated practice must take place in the framework described in our earlier discussion of Ashford and Tsui's (1991) work in the area of self-regulated feedback seeking—with emphasis upon negative feedback, which leads to more accurate self-perceptions and positive ratings of leader effectiveness.

Bandura's research with mastery modeling has contributed greatly to leadership-development programs. This work should be reinforced, given the critical role leaders play in the morale and productivity of an organization. Bandura reviewed Latham and Saari's (1979) work with mastery-modeling techniques designed to enhance corporate manager competencies. Videotape modeling was used to demonstrate targeted skills (e.g., recognize good work, enhance interest, change work habits to enhance competence). The keys to the process were the use of guided role-playing (i.e., modeling, successful practice, and instructive feedback). In another corporate world study, improved supervisory skills developed through modeling were associated with improved organizational climate and performance (i.e., reduced absenteeism and turnover) and higher productivity (see Porras, Hargis, Patterson, Maxfield, Roberts, and Bies, 1982).

School Environment.   Several researchers contend that self-efficacy beliefs are causally related to such school-related variables as academic achievement, academic motivation, occupational interests, and career choices. Earlier in the description of Bloom's theory of school learning (see Figure 1–1), we listed self-efficacy (e.g., academic or study skills) as a major student entry characteristic and learning outcome. Support for this position is found in Schunk's (1991) highly recommended article entitled "Self-efficacy and Academic Motivation." This is consistent with the work of Owen and Froman (1992) in the area of academic self-efficacy and its role in the educational setting. The concept of a self-fulfilling prophecy is drawn upon in the discussion of how successful school experiences will enhance self-efficacy.

Since we know that efficacy beliefs influence choice of activities, effort, expenditure, persistence, and task accomplishment (all important attributes for self-regulated learning), successful learning experiences should lead to enhanced probability of future success. Schunk (1981) has reported that elementary-school students' mathematics self-efficacy beliefs are related to achievement in mathematics. Owen and Froman's review of academic self-efficacy also suggests that these beliefs are clearly influenced by the school environment and may show gender differences. Studies are reviewed to support the gender-typed nature of selected achievement behaviors (e.g., females in mathematics).

Further theoretical support of the importance of self-efficacy as a relevant school-related variable is found in Lindia's review of student self-efficacy studies regarding use of computers. In this study, gender and ability-level differences were reported (i.e., males had higher interest in computers and higher levels of computer self-efficacy; higher-ability math students had higher self-efficacy scores (Lindia, 1992). Readers are encouraged to review Owen and Ramirez's (1991) work in developing a measure of study-skills self-efficacy at the college level. The theoretical framework for the instrument was drawn from Zimmermann's (1989) concept of self-regulatory academic behaviors, Schmeck, Ribich, and Ramanaiah's (1977) individual learning preferences, and Mahoney and Thoreson's (1974) model of self-control.

Owen and Froman's (1992) review of academic self-efficacy also included support for the gender-typed nature of subsequent patterns of occupational interests and career choice (p. 6). This position is consistent with studies by Hackett and Betz (1981), reported by Bandura (1986, p. 431) that describe a causual model of career development. It is proposed that occupational pursuits are influenced by beliefs of cognitive and social competency which are fostered by institutional and social practices (see Bandura 1986, p. 431; 1989, p. 1178). Betz and Hackett (1981, 1983) found that college-age males had similar efficacy beliefs for traditional male and female vocations; females had high efficacy beliefs for positions traditionally held by women, but low self-efficacy for the requirements and functions of male-dominated jobs. In fact, Bandura (1986) reports that higher self-efficacy beliefs result in more diverse consideration of career options and higher levels of interest in careers (p. 432). Consistent with this theory, Collins (1982) reports that self-efficacy beliefs were better predictors of career interests than verbal and quantitative ability.

Finally, we note the research in the area of perceived self-efficacy in physical and mental health. Froman and Owen (1991) have reported concerning the development of the *School Health Efficacy Questionnaire* which addresses adolescent health beliefs in the areas of Physical Health (e.g., such daily routines as getting enough sleep and eating a balanced diet) and Mental Health (e.g., avoiding anxiety-provoking situations, controlling academic anxiety). As noted by Froman and Owen, enhanced self-efficacy perceptions in the life-style and choice areas should be an achievable goal of school-based health education programs.

Measuring Self-Efficacy. As we noted in earlier sections, instruments assessing self-efficacy beliefs have been developed in several areas. Lindia (1992) developed the *Student Computer Survey* which included a set of items assessing self-efficacy to perform computer tasks. Alpha reliability for a sample of sixth graders was .96; stability reliability for a 16-week period was .52 (see also Lindia and Owen, 1991). Owen and colleagues have successfully developed instruments to measure self-efficacy beliefs in such areas as college academics (Owen and Froman, 1988), college-level study skills (Owen and Ramirez, 1991), adults' capability for computer use (Murphy, Coover, and Owen, 1989), and adolescent social skills (Owen, Smith, and Froman, 1989). In addition, readers are encouraged to review Smist's (1993) description of her development of the *Science Self-Efficacy Questionnaire.*

As suggested by Bandura (1986), Owen (1989) emphasizes that self-efficacy refers to relatively specific beliefs about behaviors, not consequences (p. 1). An example is Owen and Ramirez's (1991) *Study Skills Self-Efficacy Questionnaire*, containing 47 items (i.e., behavioral descriptions) responded to on a 5-point Likert Scale. For this instrument, respondents are asked to rate their confidence in doing the things described by the items. Four sample items identifying study-skill behavior, along with the self-efficacy dimension each represents, are listed below. Note that the Likert-response format used by Owen and Ramirez is labeled on either end, but does not include rating anchors for the middle response options. We will discuss various response-option issues in Chapter 3.

Rate your confidence using this scale:

$$\begin{array}{ccccc} \textbf{A} & \textbf{B} & \textbf{C} & \textbf{D} & \textbf{E} \\ \textbf{QUITE} & \longleftarrow & \text{-----------} & \longrightarrow & \textbf{VERY} \\ \textbf{A LOT} & & \textbf{CONFIDENCE} & & \textbf{LITTLE} \end{array}$$

Spending more time studying than most of my friends (study routines).

Storing detailed information in my memory (memorization).

Taking tests that ask me to compare different concepts (conceptual skills).

Praising myself for doing a good job studying (self-motivation).

Most relevant to the later sections of this text is the notion that respondents are asked to rate their *confidence* in performing relatively specific behaviors that are clear and understandable. Readers are encouraged to obtain Owen's (1989) paper entitled "Building Self-Efficacy Instruments" for a discussion of the problem and for considerations in measuring self-efficacy. Other useful suggestions and illustrations can be found in Bandura's work (1986, Chapters 1 and 9) as well as in Owen and colleagues' work, cited earlier in the section.

Values

In his book *Beliefs, Attitudes, and Values*, Rokeach (1968) argues that the concept of values is the core concept across all the social sciences. In a later book entitled *The Nature of Human Values and Value Systems*, Rokeach defines a value as

> an enduring belief that a specific mode of conduct or end-state of existence is personally or socially preferable to an opposite or converse mode of conduct or end-state of existence. (Rokeach, 1973, p. 5)

Clarifying the difference between an attitude and a value, Rokeach states that an attitude refers to an organization of several beliefs around a specific object or situation, whereas a value refers to a simple belief of a very specific kind:

> This belief transcends attitudes toward objects and toward situations; it is a standard that guides and determines action, attitudes toward objects and situations, ideology, presentations of self to others, evaluations, judgements, justifications, comparisons of self with others, and attempts to influence others. (Rokeach, 1973, p. 25)

Other writers have referred to value as "the importance or worth attached to particular activities and objects" (Aiken, 1980, p. 2); "preferences for life goals and ways of life" (Nunnally, 1978, p. 589); "a belief upon which a man acts by preference" (Allport, 1961, p. 454); and as a "conception of the desirable—that is, of what ought to be desired, not what is actually desired—which influences the selection of behavior" (Getzels, 1966, p. 98). The Getzels, Rokeach, and Tyler definitions of a value were summarized by Anderson in a most informative manner as follows:

> First, values are beliefs as to what should be desired (Getzels), what is important or cherished (Tyler), and what standards of conduct or existence are personally or socially acceptable (Rokeach). Second, values influence or guide things:

behavior (Getzels); interests, attitudes, and satisfactions (Tyler); and a whole host of items, including behavior, interests, attitudes, and satisfactions (Rokeach). Third, values are enduring (Rokeach). That is, values tend to remain stable over fairly long periods of time. As such they are likely to be more difficult to alter or change than either attitudes or interest. (Anderson 1981, p. 34)

The target, direction, and intensity of values can also be identified. According to Anderson, the targets of values tend to be ideas. However, as the definition offered by Rokeach implies, the targets could also be such things as attitudes and behavior. The direction of a value could be positive or negative (or right/wrong, important/unimportant). Finally, the intensity of values can be referred to as high or low, depending on the situation and the value referenced.

School Environment.   In this text work/career-related and human/interpersonal values will be described. Work values refer to satisfactions that people desire in their future work, such as economic returns, altruism, and independence. Super's *Work Values Inventory* (1970) will be discussed as an instrument for assessing work-value orientations for high-school students. In a similar area, Super's *The Values Scale* (1989, Consulting Psychologists Press) can be used to assess intrinsic and extrinsic life/career values. The *Rokeach Value Survey* (1989, Consulting Psychologists Press) is an example of an instrument that assesses how important certain values are as guiding principles in one's life. Interpersonal values represent values that people consider important in their way of life, such as support, leadership, conformity, and benevolence. Gordon's *Survey of Interpersonal Values* (1960) will be discussed in a later chapter, since it is still used in both the educational and business worlds to assess interpersonal values.

The important role of values in an educational program is discussed by Tyler in his monograph entitled "Assessing Educational Achievement in the Affective Domain." In this work, Tyler uses a definition of values that indicates their role in influencing interests, attitudes, and satisfactions by stating that a value is

> an object, activity, or idea that is cherished by an individual which derives its educational significance from its role in directing his interests, attitudes, and satisfactions. (Tyler, 1973, p. 7)

In arguing that there are sound, aesthetic, and good-health values that are appropriate as objectives of schooling, Tyler says that

> Since human beings learn to value certain objects, activities, and ideas so that these become important directors of their interests, attitudes, and satisfactions, the school should help the student discover and reinforce values that might be

meaningful and significant to him/her in obtaining personal happiness and making constructive contributions to society. (Tyler, 1973, p. 6)

As examples of such appropriate objectives for student, reflecting underlying values, Tyler lists the following Citizenship objectives approved by lay panels for the National Assessment of Educational Progress:

1. show concern for the well-being and dignity of others,
2. participate in democratic civil improvement, and
3. help and respect their own families. (Tyler, 1973, p. 6)

Corporate Environment. The study of the "culture" of an organization has received much attention over the last several years (see for example, Deal and Kennedy, 1982; Schein, 1985). Smircich (1983) has summarized several definitions of organizational culture as follows:

> Culture is usually defined as social or normative glue that holds an organization together (Siehl & Martin, 1981; Tichy, 1982). It expresses the values or social ideals and the beliefs that organization members come to share (Louis, 1980; Siehl & Martin, 1981). These values or patterns of belief are manifested by symbolic devices such as myths (Boje, Febor, & Rowland, 1982), rituals (Deal & Kennedy, 1982), stories (Mitroff & Kilmann, 1976), legends (Wilkins & Martin, 1980), and specialized language (Andrews and Hirsch, 1983) (from Wiener, 1988, p. 535).

Values are central to these definitions of organizational culture, because the shared set of core values, in fact, forms the operational definition of the culture. Examples of selected organizational values from companies such as American Express, Contel, Kodak, Weyerhauser, Southwestern Bell, and Texaco are as follows:

People:	Treat people with respect and dignity.
Customers:	Listen to internal and external customers to understand and meet their needs.
Quality:	Create an environment that fosters a continuous quest for quality.
Teamwork:	Promote open communication that gives everyone a sense of personal involvement in corporate performance.

Integrity: Maintain high standards of open communication where actions are consistent with words.

Good Citizenship: Encourage involvement in local communities.

Noting that Fishbein and Ajzen (1975) discuss values as antecedents to behavior, it is important for businesses to understand and articulate their corporate values. Such shared core values influence the organization's decision making (i.e., strategy formulation and implementation), as well as its response to quickly changing business conditions and immediate crises (e.g., Johnson & Johnson's reaction to the Tylenol scare a few years ago). Many writers also argue that corporate values shared by employees contribute to overall organizational effectiveness. For example, consider a corporate value in the area of customer service where "satisfying customer needs is a top priority." This value would pertain to collective efforts to meet the needs of both internal (i.e., colleagues) and external customers. Living this value with a goal of exceeding customer expectations would contribute to efficiency and productivity within the organization, which would, in turn, result in more satisfied customers and enhanced profits (see the earlier discussion of the article by Ulrich et al., 1991).

Since a value is a "standard that guides and determines action" (Rokeach, 1973, p. 25), it is important to know if the company and businesses and departments within the company are indeed "walking the talk." Well-designed questionnaires administered to a large cross section of employees, along with appropriate interview and focus-group activities, can contribute to the articulation of corporate values. Information obtained from assessments of corporate values serves as a profile of current status and sets the direction for goal statements and action plans for developing needed change. Second generation follow-up assessments are beneficial for evaluating the efforts at change and for plotting a future course of action.

Self-Concept

An early comprehensive definition of self-concept was presented by Coopersmith as follows:[1]

> ... the evaluation which the individual makes and customarily maintains with regard to himself; it expresses an attitude of approval or disapproval, and indicates the extent to which the individual believes himself to be capable, significant, successful, and worthy. In short, self-esteem is a *personal* judgement of

worthiness that is expressed in the attitudes the individual holds toward himself. It is a subjective experience which the individual conveys to others by verbal reports and other overt expressive behavior. (Coopersmith, 1967, pp. 4–5)

After integrating features of several definitions such as Coopersmith's, Shavelson et al. (1976) state that in broad terms self-concept "is a person's perception of himself" (p. 411). The perceptions are formed through experiences with the environment, with important contributions coming from environmental reinforcements and significant people in one's life (i.e., self-concept is learned). Shavelson et al. further identify seven features critical to defining this complex construct. Self-concept organized, multifaceted, hierarchical, stable, developmental, evaluative, and differential. Interested readers are encouraged to read this important discussion. In a later article, Shavelson, Bolus, and Keesling (1980) present the results of administering six self-concept instruments to seventh- and eighth-grade students. Covariance structure analysis supported the contention that self-concept is causally predominant over achievement.

Similar to the other affective characteristics identified in this volume, the target, direction, and intensity of self-concept can be identified. The target of self-concept is usually the person but could also be areas such as the school (i.e., academic self-concept); the direction can be positive or negative; and the intensity can range on a continuum from low to high.

The self-concept construct has received considerable attention from educators due to renewed emphasis on affective outcomes of education and the reported relationships between affective and cognitive measures. Purkey's (1970) book entitled *Self-Concept and School Achievement* was an important early volume, as it supported the relationship between self-concept and achievement and inspired much additional interest and research in examining the relationships between the affective and cognitive domains. Readers are referred to the Shavelson et al. (1976) article, which reviews several self-concept studies and provides a comprehensive discussion of the validity of self-esteem construct interpretations, and to Byrne's (1990b) article entitled "Methodological Approaches to the Validation of Academic Self-Concept: The Construct and its Measure." Byrne's article provides much information regarding the methodology of validating self-concept instruments. Examples of self-concept instruments include Coopersmith's *Self-Esteem Inventory* (1967, 1989; now available from Consulting Psychologists Press in children and adult forms), *Michigan State Self-Concept of Ability* scale (Brookover et al., 1965); *Piers-Harris Children's Self-Concept Scale* (Piers and Harris, 1964); and the *Tennessee Self-Concept Scale* (Fitts, 1965).

Several school programs include objectives pertaining to enhancing self-concept. Typical statements read as follows: Students will develop positive feelings of self-worth. Students will evidence positive perceptions of self in relation to peers (or school achievement—i.e., academic-self or family-social relations).

Interest

Interest measurement grew out of the early graduate-school work by Cowdery, who reported the differential interests of lawyers, physicians, and engineers (cited in DuBois, 1970). On the basis of this work in the early 1900s, interest measurement became a focal point of vocational guidance through the extensive contributions of such researchers as E.K. Strong and F. Kuder. Defining interests as "preferences for particular work activities" (Nunnally, 1978), most inventories developed during the 1900s have item content that reflects occupational and work activities and employ the "Like/Dislike" rating instructions.

Examples of popular interest inventories are the *Kuder General Interest Survey* (grades 6–12) and the *Kuder Occupational Interest Survey* (high school and beyond), available from Science Research Associates; and The *Ohio Vocational Interest Survey II* and the *Strong Interest Inventory*, available from Consulting Psychologists Press. We also note that since 1990 The Psychological Corporation's *Differential Aptitude Tests* (fifth edition) assessment has included the *Career Interest Inventory*, which addresses students' educational goals, interest in various school subjects and school-related activities, as well as in various fields of work. Interested readers are referred to Zytowski's (1973) book *Interest Measurement* and Dawis' (1980) excellent article entitled "Measuring Interests" for discussions of the history and techniques of interest measurement.

Similar to other affective characteristics examined in this volume, interests can be described with regard to their target, direction, and intensity. The targets of interests are activities; the direction can be described as interested or disinterested; and the intensity can be labeled as high or low. Interests with high intensity would tend to lead one to seek out the activity under consideration.

According to Tyler, school objectives in the area of interests are quite justified when the school activity involved "can contribute to the individual's development, social competence, or life satisfaction" (Tyler, 1973, p. 4). These objectives should be designed to develop interests for future learning in a wide variety of major fields of knowledge so that the student desires to pursue several activities that will assist in building a "more comprehensive and accurate picture of the world" (p. 4). Furthermore, Tyler suggests that appropriate school affective objectives in the interest area should broaden student interest to learn important things from several fields as well as deepen student interest to attend to a few special content areas. Typically statements of educational objectives reflecting student interests would read as follows: Students will develop interest in listening to music. Students will develop an interest in reading.

Relationships Among the Affective Characteristics

This chapter has examined the conceptual definitions of affective characteristics selected on the basis of their relevance to the school experience. The characteristics are attitudes, self-efficacy values, self-concept, and interests. In general terms, attitudes were described as feelings toward some object; self-efficacy was referred to as a self-appraisal of capability; values reflected beliefs; self-concept represented perceptions of self; and interests reflected preferences for particular activities.

Clarification of the similarities and differences among the constructs was obtained through Anderson's (1981) discussion of their target, direction, and intensity attributes. It should be emphasized that the constructs selected in this volume are clearly not independent. While many writers may disagree with respect to the criteria for a taxonomy, it appears that some general statements can be offered. Values and a related value system can be considered as central to one's overall personality. Manifestations of one's values may be seen in one's interests and attitudes. Some would say that interests and attitudes are quite similar in that attitudes are targeted toward objects and that interests really reflect attitudes toward tasks or activities, while self-efficacy reflects a perceived ability to perform a task or activity. Clearly, one's self-concept also interacts in light of an overall value system and could be called an attitude toward self. This discussion could go on further and become more confusing. Instead, we will follow the lead of many writers and use different labels for the constructs in this volume. It should be noted that the instrument development techniques to be described in later chapters are equally applicable to all of the constructs.

In selecting an affective characteristic for measurement, instrument developers should carefully consider the theory underlying the construct. Only with a clear conceptual understanding can one proceed to create valid operational definitions (i.e., items) for each affective characteristic. Chapter 2 will describe how these operational definitions can be developed.

Note

1. Coopersmith actually employed the term "self-esteem." Many writers distinguish among such terms as self-concept, self-esteem, and self-perception. In this volume no such distinction is made.

Additional Readings

Ajzen, I. (1985). From intentions to actions: A theory of planned behavior. In J. Kuhl and J. Beckmann (Eds.), *Action control* (pp. 11–39). Berlin: Springer–Verlag.

Bandura, A. (1988a). Self-efficacy conception of anxiety. *Anxiety Research*, I, 77–98.

Bandura, A. (1988b). Organizational applications of social cognitive theory. *Australian Journal of Management*, 13, 137–164.

Dawes, R.M. (1972). *Fundamentals of attitude measurement.* Now York: Wiley.

Gist, M.E. (1989). The influence of training method on self-efficacy and idea generation among managers. *Personnel Psychology*, 42, 787–805.

Henerson, M.E., Morris, L.L., and Fitz-Gibbon, C.T. (1978). *How to measure attitudes.* Beverly Hills: Sage.

Insko, C.A. (1967). *Theories of attitude change.* Englewood Cliffs, NJ: Prentice-Hall.

Kent, G. (1987). Self-efficacious control over reported physiological, cognitive and behavioral symptoms of dental anxiety. *Behaviour Research and Therapy*, 25, 341–347.

Ringness, T.A. (1976). *The affective domain in education.* Boston: Little Brown.

Sackmann, S.A. (1992). Cultures and subcultures: An analysis of organizational knowledge. *Administrative Science Quarterly*, 37, 140–161.

Schwessler, K.F. (1982). *Measuring social life feelings.* San Francisco: Jossey-Bass.

Shavelson, R.J., Burstein, L., and Keesling, J.W. (1977). Methodological considerations in interpreting research on self-concept. *Journal of Youth and Adolescence*, 14, 83–97.

Shavelson, R.J., and Stuart, K.R. (1980). Application of causal methods to the validation of self-concept interpretations of test scores. In M.D. Lynch et al. (Eds.), *Self-concept: Advances in theory and research.* Boston: Ballinger.

Thurstone, L.L. (1928). Attitudes can be measured. *American Journal of Sociology*, 33, 529–544.

Thurstone, L.L. (1931). The measurement of social attitudes. *Journal of Abnormal and Social Psychology*, 26, 249–269.

Thurstone, L.L., and Chase, E.J. (1929). *The measurement of attitudes.* Chicago: University of Chicago Press.

Wylie, R.C. (1979). *The self-concept: Theory and research on selected topics.* Lincoln: University of Nebraska Press.

Wood, R., and Bandura, A. (1989). Social cognitive theory of organizational management. *Academy of Management Review*, 14, 361–384.

Woodrow, J.E.J. (1991). A comparison of four computer attitude scales. *Journal of Educational Computing Research*, 7, 165–187.

2 CONSTRUCTING AFFECTIVE INSTRUMENTS

In Chapter 1, conceptual definitions of selected affective characteristics were presented. This chapter will review a practical framework, described by Anderson (1981), for operationally defining the affective variables.

The content and construct validity of the affective measures are extremely dependent on the existence of appropriate *operational* definitions, which directly follow from the theoretically based *conceptual* definitions. In a later chapter procedures for examining the content and construct validity of the instrument will be described. In this chapter we will address a situation often confronted during program evaluation or research activities: knowing, from a theoretical perspective, what you want to measure (e.g., attitude toward school subjects or leadership behaviors), but not being sure how to develop your own instrument, if no applicable instruments are available.

Operational Definitions

After the theory concerned with the affective characteristic has been thoroughly reviewed, the next step is to generate the perceptions, attributes, or behaviors of a person with high or low levels of this characteristic. Anderson (1981) illustrates two similar approaches to this task—namely, the domain-referenced approach and the mapping-sentence approach. The domain-referenced approach, modeled after Hively's (1974) work in developing domain-referenced achievement tests, is highly recommended for this task. When carefully implemented, the procedure leads to clear operational definitions of the affective characteristics, which properly follow from the conceptual definitions. Resulting instruments can then be used to generate data that permit valid inferences regarding an individual's location on the intensity continuum underlying the affective characteristic. Several instruments end in failure from a psychometric point of view due to a lack of clear correspondence between the intended conceptual and the actual operational definition employed. We will address this validity issue further in a later chapter.

The Domain-Referenced Approach

In the domain-referenced approach to affective scale construction described by Anderson (1981), the *target* and *direction* of the affective characteristic are first addressed, and then the *intensity* aspect is considered. It is proposed that Anderson's technique be adapted to also include a statement of the a priori, judgmentally-developed categories which the clusters of statements are intended to represent.[1]

Table 2–1 illustrates the domain-referenced approach employed to develop the *Gable-Roberts Attitude Toward School Subjects Scale* (Gable and Roberts, 1983). The activity column specifies the process to be followed in operationalizing the affective characteristic attitude toward school subjects. The second column contains the target object domain for the affective characteristic. Finally, the last column specifies the domain or content categories which the instrument developers intended to build into the instrument on an a priori basis, as a result of the literature review.

In this example of attitude toward school subjects (Table 2–1), the instrument was designed to cover several different subjects, so the general target was listed as "subject." Readers should note that the target could be further broken into such areas as numbers and algebra.

An Illustration

School Environment.   To illustrate how the domain-referenced approach can be employed, the example in Table 2–1 will be discussed. In step 1, the

Table 2-1. Steps for Developing an Operational Definition for Attitude Toward School Subjects[a]

Step	Activity	Target	Verb	Directional Adjective	A Priori Category
1	Indicate domains for attitude toward school subjects	The object is "school subjects"	Verbs that express feelings or forms of verb "to be"	Adjectives expressing favorable or unfavorable attributes of school subjects	General Interest, Usefulness, Relevance
2	Generate examples of domains for attitude toward school subjects	Subject	like, enjoy, fascinate, hinders, develop, is, are	boring, fun, exciting, waste, interesting, accurate, good, bad, valuable, beneficial, relevant, useful, dull	
3	Select one example from each domain	Subject	is	interesting	General Interest
4	Generate a statement	The subject	is interesting.		
5	Develop transformations of the statement	I feel the subject is a real bore. The subject is not very interesting. I really enjoy the subject. The subject fascinates me. I look forward to my class in the subject.			
6	Select another example for the domains	Subject	develop	good	Usefulness
7	Generate a statement	The subject helps me to develop good reasoning ability.			
8	Develop transformations	The subject	teaches me to be accurate. is beneficial to everybody who takes it. gives students ability to interpret situations they will meet in life. is of great value to me.		

[a]Adapted from Anderson (1981) to develop the Gable-Roberts Attitude Toward School Subjects Scale (Gable and Roberts, 1983).

developers first identified the attitude target "school subjects." Based upon the review of literature, interviews of teachers, and the theoretical base underlying the program being evaluated or the other variables in the study, the a priori categories were then selected. In this example, the developers wished to build three categories of items into the attitude measure: General Interest, Usefulness, and Relevance. With the target and categories in mind, the developers then described a class of applicable verbs and directional adjectives. In step 2, the target object, "Subject," was selected and applicable lists of verbs and adjectives were generated, keeping in mind the category (e.g., General Interest) of statements that were selected on an a priori basis. Step 3 was quite simple. As one example from each domain was selected (e.g., target: subject; verb: is; adjective: interesting; category; general interest), so that a draft statement could be listed in step 4 (e.g., The subject is interesting.).

Step 5 is a crucial step, since it involves developing several statements that are semantic transformations of the first statement. These transformations must reflect the domain attributes selected for the first statement. The easiest type of transformation is a rather direct reuse of essentially the same words. For example, the original statement would read "The subject is interesting"; the transformations would pick up on the word *interest* to yield statements such as "The subject does not interest me" or "I have no interest in the subject." In addition to these somewhat direct transformations, it is recommended that different words from the adjective and verb lists be selected to yield similar transformations within the same a priori content category. Examples of such statements from the General Interest category would be: "I really enjoy the subject" and "I find the subject to be a real bore."

The later importance of developing good transformed statements lies in the fact that all of the resulting statements should, in this example, reflect the a priori category of General Interest. It is hoped that content similarities among these statements will lead later respondents to provide internally consistent responses to the items that have been clustered on an a priori basis into the category "General Interest" (see the discussion of consistent responses underlying the definition of attitudes in Chapter 1). For example, students really liking the subject should tend to agree with the statements listed in step 5 of Table 2–1: "The subject is interesting" and "I really enjoy the subject"; they should tend to disagree with the statement "I find the subject to be a real bore." To the extent that the respondents consistently rate the statements in this manner, the categories built into the instrument on an a priori basis will tend to emerge in the later data analysis to be factors or constructs measured by the instrument. Inconsistencies in responses will tend to lower internal consistency reliabilities and result in meaningless (invalid) scores from the instrument. This discussion of validity and reliability will be suspended until a later chapter. The point here is that this early stage in the instrument development process, where the domains are specified and several statements generated, is a most crucial aspect of the overall instrument-development process. Treat it seriously, take lots of time and be creative!

Table 2–2 illustrates the use of the domain-referenced approach for developing the *Gable-Roberts Attitude Toward Teacher Scale* (Gable and Roberts, 1982). Readers may wish to see how the statements and their transformations were generated. For further examples, see Anderson (1981) where the technique is illustrated for the areas of "attitude toward mathematics" and "interest in teaching."

Corporate Environment. Finally, we illustrate the use of the domain-referenced approach for developing a feedback-up questionnaire for direct report and colleague ratings of manager behavior (i.e., agreement or satisfaction with the manager's ability to perform the behavior, or the frequency with which the manager exhibits the behavior). The domain of content for such feedback-up systems comes from the company's statement of corporate values. These values, which reflect the organization's culture, often have labels such as leadership, quality, people, customers, good citizenship, integrity and teamwork. The purpose of such a feedback-up questionnaire is to provide information for manager self-improvement, as well as to assess the extent to which the company and subgroups within the company are living the stated corporate values.

Table 2–3 presents an illustration of the process of developing a feedback-up form addressing three categories of corporate values: Leadership, Quality, and People. As in Tables 2–1 and 2–2, applicable verbs and directional adjectives were listed for the target object (manager). Steps 3, 4, 7, and 8 contain statements operationalyzing the appropriate corporate value, as well as transformations of each statement.

Item Content Sources

But where do all these targets, verbs, adjectives, and categories come from? As noted earlier, a well-done literature review will be a rich source of content. The theoretical work behind the affective characteristic, as well as studies using Osgood's work with the semantic-differential technique, may be a rich source of adjectives. (See Osgood, Suci, and Tannenbaum, 1957,

Table 2–2. Steps for Developing an Operational Definition for Attitude Toward Teacher[a]

Step	Activity	Target	Verb	Directional Adjective	A Priori Category
1	Indicate domains for attitude toward teacher	The object is "teacher"	Verbs that describe teaching activities, express feelings, forms of verb "to be"	Adjectives expressing favorable or unfavorable teacher attributes	Presentation of Subject, Interest in Job, Interest in Students, Teaching Techniques
2	Generate examples of domains for attitude toward teacher	Teacher	is, motivates, makes, fails, succeeds, like, help, lacks, assign, test, yell, discipline	cheerful, boring, fun, interesting, successful, pleasant, enthusiastic, structured, liberal, conservative, hurried, vague, strict, fair	
3	Select one example from each domain	Teacher	makes	fun	Presentation of Subject
4	Generate a statement	This teacher	makes learning fun.		
5	Develop transformations of the statement	This teacher	does not make learning fun. fails to stimulate interest in the subject. is not interesting to listen to in class. is generally cheerful and pleasant. is successful in getting the point across.		
6	Select another example from the domains	Teacher	is	structured	Teaching Technique
7	Generate a statement	This teacher	is too structured.		
8	Develop transformations of the statement	This teacher	has no structure in the lectures. assigns too much homework. tests too frequently. tries to cover too much material in too short a time. disciplines too strictly.		

[a]Adapted from Anderson (1981) to develop the *Gable-Roberts Attitude Toward Teacher Scale* (Gable and Roberts, 1982).

Table 2–3. Steps for Developing an Operational Definition for Perceptions of Corporate Values

Step	Activity	Target	Verb	Directional Adjective	A Priori Category
1	Indicate domains for perceptions of manager behavior reflective of corporate values	The object is "manager"	Verbs that decide manager behaviors	Adjectives expressing favorable or unfavorable manager attitudes	Leadership, Quality, People
2	Generate examples of domains for manager behavior	Manager	establishes, is, demonstrates, gives, communicates, makes, helps, assigns, avoids, creates, takes, ensures, treats	clear, positive, specific, effective, honest, self-confident, quality, new, creative, different	
3	Select one example from each domain	Manager	establishes	clear	Leadership
4	Generate a statement	This manager	establishes clear priorities.		
5	Develop transformations of the statement	This manager	provides specific direction and supervision.		
			concentrates on achieving what is not important		
6	Select another example from the domain	Manager	communicates	clear	Quality
7	Generate a statement	This manager	communicates clear quality standards.		
8	Develops transformations of the statement	This manager	avoids compromising quality. focuses on continuous quality improvement. takes responsibility for achieving quality performance. uses resources to ensure quality products.		

p. 43.) Applicable verbs will, of course, depend on the target you have selected. For example, the "attitude toward teacher" illustration in Table 2-2 leads one to focus on verbs that will describe typical behaviors of teachers. The literature on teacher evaluation (see for example Brophy and Good, 1974; Good and Brophy, 1978) will assist in generating the necessary verbs.

The most useful technique, though, is the interview/observation process. After identifying the attitude target and the group to be administered the instrument (e.g., school subjects; high-school students), spend considerable time talking with students about how they feel about school subjects. Through tape recordings and notes, you should be able to find several applicable verbs, adjectives, and even possible categories suggested by the students. Finally, a group of graduate students or teachers can serve as excellent resource people for this task. Tell them exactly what you are doing and brainstorm lists of verbs and adjectives. Also, give these individuals a sheet of paper with a definition of the a priori category and the first generated statement at the top and ask them to generate as many alternate ways to say the same thing as possible. If you are fortunate, you will have access to a group of graduate students in gifted education. These tasks are viewed by gifted folks as a real challenge to their creativity and can be the answer to your need for several parallel statements.

In the corporate world, a computerized search of relevant journals will provide a rich source of information (see, for example, *Academy of Management Review*, *Academy of Management Journal*, *Human Resource Development Quarterly*, *Human Resource Planning*, *Strategic Management Journal*, *Administrative Science Quarterly*, and *Organizational Behavior and Human Performance*). This literature search should be followed by several focus-group sessions with Human Resource people. If the literature search and group activities are comprehensive, there will be no shortage of categories and statements for the questionnaire.

Summary

In this section we have reviewed a procedure for generating operational definitions for affective characteristics. Once the target and a priori categories are specified, appropriate verb and adjective domains are developed in light of the domain categories the developer desires in the instrument. By selecting from these domains, developers are then able to link the target and adjectives with verbs to generate sentences that become the statements or items on the instrument. If this process is successful, the conceptual definitions underlying the affective characteristic will be operationally defined. During the later stage of content validation in the instrument development process, the relationship between the operational and conceptual definitions will be supportive of the content validity of the instrument (see Chapter 4). If the operational definitions are poorly constructed, it is doubtful the instrument could have much content validity. Later empirical examinations of construct validity and internal consistency reliability would most likely also be quite depressing to the developer.

Note

1. Later, after response data are gathered using the instrument, these categories could become the constructs measured by the instrument.

3 SCALING AFFECTIVE CHARACTERISTICS

In Chapter 1 we noted that affective characteristics can be described as having intensity, direction, and a target. A framework was described for developing statements for an affective instrument by carefully sampling from a universe of content. After developing such statements, we typically obtain the responses of selected individuals to these statements and claim that we have measured the intensity and direction of their affect toward the particular target object.

Measurement

The basis of the above activities is the process we call *measurement*. As Wright and Masters (1982) have noted, measurement begins with the concept of a continuum on which people can be located with respect to some trait or construct. *Instruments* in the form of test items are used to generate numbers called *measures* for each person. It is important to realize that the test items are also located on the continuum with respect to their direction and intensity. Variations of judgmental and empirical techniques are used to scale the items. Some scaling procedures calculate numbers called *calibrations*, which indicate the location of an item on the underlying affective continuum. During the measurement process, people are measured by the items that define the trait underlying the continuum. That is, people are located on this abstract continuum at a point which specifies a unit of measurement to be used to make "more or less" comparisons among people and items. According to Wright and Masters, the requirements for measuring are:

1. the reduction of experiences to a *one dimensional* abstraction (i.e., continuum),
2. *more or less* comparisons among persons and items,
3. the idea of *linear magnitude* inherent in positioning objects (i.e., people) along a line, and
4. a unit determined by a *process* which can be repeated without modification over the range of the variable. (Wright and Masters, 1982, p. 3)

The process, which can be repeated without modification, is actually the measurement or *scaling model* used to describe how people and items interact to produce measures for people. Several such scaling models have received much attention over the last 60 years, with particular emphasis during the last 20 years. In this chapter we will describe some models that have been utilized for scaling affective variables. Differences among the models with respect to the process used for calibrating the items and locating people on the continuum underlying the affective construct will be discussed. The techniques to be presented include Thurstone's (1931a) *Equal-Appearing Interval* technique, Likert's (1932) *Summated Rating* technique, *Latent Trait Theory* reported by Wright and Masters (1982), and Osgood's *Semantic Differential* technique (Osgood, Suci, and Tannenbaum, 1957). Finally, we will illustrate a procedure, suggested by Fishbein and Ajzen (1975), for combining belief and probability components to measure attitudes. Following the description of the attitude scale techniques, the chapter will conclude with a discussion of the properties of ipsative and normative scales.

All of the scaling techniques will be presented in the context of Fishbein's Expectancy-Value Model for measuring attitudes (Fisbein and Ajzen, 1975). While Fishbein's model addresses the affective-characteristic attitudes, it can be generalized to the other characteristics described in chapters 1 and 2—namely, self-concept, values, and interests.

SCALING AFFECTIVE CHARACTERISTICS

Fishbein's Expectancy-Value Model

As we noted in Chapter 1, Fishbein has argued that attitude should be measured by a procedure that locates the individual on a bipolar evaluative dimension with respect to some target object (Fishbein and Ajzen, 1975). This attitude scaling process takes place in the framework of an expectancy-value model. To scale people using the expectancy-value model, Fishbein distinguishes between attitudes and beliefs. Whereas *attitudes* are described as the individual's favorable or unfavorable evaluation (i.e., good/bad) of the target object, *beliefs* represent the information the individual has about the object. In this context, then, the belief links the target object to some attribute. For example, Table 2–2 contained operational definitions for "attitude toward teacher." In step 4 of the table, we developed the statement: "This teacher makes learning fun." This statement is, in fact, a *belief* that links the *target object* "teacher" to the *attribute* "*makes learning fun*." A person's attitude, then, is a function of his beliefs at a given time and is based upon the person's total set of beliefs about the target object and the evaluations of attributes associated with the object (see Fishbein and Ajzen, 1975, chs. 3 and 6).

Fishbein's model for scaling peoples' attitudes is based upon the relationships between beliefs about a target object and attitude toward that object. In this model, different beliefs and evaluations of the target object are combined in a summative manner to produce an index representing the overall attitude toward the target object. The integration process described by Fishbein (Fishbein and Ajzen, 1975, p. 29) is presented here as Equation 3.1,

$$A_O = \sum_{i=1}^{n} b_i e_i \qquad (3.1)$$

where A_O is the overall attitude toward some object, O; b_i is the belief i about O (i.e., the subjective probability is that O is related to attribute i); e_i is the favorable evaluation of attribute i; and n is the number of beliefs. As stated in Chapter 1, an individual's attitude toward some object is determined by forming the product of that individual's favorable/unfavorable evaluation of each attribute associated with the target object and his/her subjective probability that the object has the attribute, then summing these products across the total set of beliefs. Thus, the evaluation of the attribute contributes to the person's attitude in proportion to the strength of his/her beliefs (Fishbein and Ajzen, 1975, pp. 222–223).

In this chapter we will describe some attitude scaling techniques, all of which arrive at a single attitude score based upon responses to statements of beliefs. All the techniques yield attitude scores that represent the person's location on a bipolar evaluative dimension with respect to the target object. For all procedures attitude scores are obtained from the product of beliefs, b, about the object and evaluations, e, of the attributes of the object. One difference among the procedures represents the relative weights placed on the beliefs (b) and the evaluations (e) of the respective attributes in developing the attitude score. Another difference lies in the properties of the individual items. Depending on the technique employed, items selected for inclusion in the instrument are based upon different criteria, which results in selecting items with different item-characteristic curves or tracelines. (These terms will be made clear in a later section.)

In the sections that follow, we will clarify and illustrate the similarities and differences among the attitude scaling techniques. Each technique will be described in the context of Fishbein's expectancy-value model.

Thurstone Equal-Appearing Interval Scale

The Thurstone technique was originally developed by Thurstone and Chave (1929) and has been described by Thurstone (1931a) and Edwards (1957) (see also Anderson, 1981; Fishbein and Ajzen, 1975; Nunnally, 1978; Thurstone, 1927, 1928, 1931b, 1946). Employing the expectancy-value model, the Thurstone technique begins with a set of belief statements (i.e., attributes) regarding a target object. These statements are then located (i.e., calibrated) on the favorable/unfavorable evaluative dimension through a judgmental procedure that results in a scale value for each belief statement. In the context of Fishbein's expectancy-value model, specified in equation 3–1, the favorable/unfavorable evaluations (e) of the belief statements or attributes are obtained from an independent set of judges whose ratings are used to place the statements on the evaluative continuum. The values of e can then range from the highest to lowest value used in the judges' rating procedure (e.g., 1–5, 1–11, etc.). On the other hand, when later respondents select individual attributes as being characteristic of the target object, they are actually specifying the values of b or the probability that the target object possesses the stated attribute. The values of b in the Thurstone technique are 0 if the statement is not selected and 1 if the respondent selects the statement as a characteristic of the target object.

Prior to describing the steps in the Thurstone procedure, we need to mention Thurstone's early use of paired comparisons. After the set of items had been scaled by the judges, items were paired with other items with similar scale values; and sets of paired comparisons were developed. In some cases, each item was paired with all other items from other scales on the instrument, and respondents were asked to select the item from the pair that best described the target object. The Edwards Personal Preference Schedule (Edwards, 1959) illustrates the use of such paired comparisons. The problem with this procedure is that a large number of paired items is needed to measure the affective characteristic—for k items, $k(k - 1)/2$ pairs would be necessary. As a result, Thurstone (1931a) developed the successive interval and equal-appearing interval techniques for measuring affective characteristics. The equal-appearing interval procedure has proven to be the most popular and will be described in the next section. Readers wishing to study the paired comparisons and successive interval techniques are referred to Edward's (1957) book *Techniques of Attitude Scale Construction*.

With this overview in mind, we now proceed to detail the two phases involved in developing an attitude instrument using Thurstone's Equal-Appearing Interval Technique.

Phase I: Item Selection

Using the procedures described in Chapter 2, a large set of items (e.g., 30–50) is constructed to operationally define the affective characteristic. A group of judges *very similar to the future respondents* to the instrument is then asked to rate the items *with respect to the extent that the items describe the affective characteristic*. It is essential that the judges realize that they are not agreeing or disagreeing with the items. Rather, they are assisting in the quantification of the intensity (i.e., favorable/unfavorable) of the statement. That is, the items are being calibrated or scaled in such a way that the ratings of the judges will result in locating the item on the psychological continuum underlying the affective characteristic.

For example, consider the scale developed by Kahn (1974) for evaluating university-faculty teaching. Thirty-five items were developed which described the process of teaching (see Table 3–1). A sample of approximately 300 college students responded to the form in Table 3–1 by indicating *how characteristic the statement was regarding the quality of teaching*. Note that the respondents were not asked to rate their particular teacher. Instead, they were assisting in scaling the item pool with respect to the degree of teaching quality exhibited in each item. While this form employed

Table 3–1. An Illustration of the Judges' Rating Form for the Thurstone Technique[a]

"Teaching Quality Survey"

No doubt you have been asked many times to rate your instructor. We are not now asking you to do the same thing, but rather to help define the **IMPORTANCE OF VARIOUS TEACHER CHARACTERISTICS.** For each of the items, please assign a rating in accordance with your judgement:

(1) Highly uncharacteristic of a good teacher.
(2) Usually uncharacteristic of a good teacher.
(3) Usually characteristic of a good teacher.
(4) Highly characteristic of a good teacher.

Rating

1. Gives specific reading assignments. _____
2. Reports test and quiz scores promptly. _____

3. Displays enthusiasm for his subject. _____
4. Relies heavily on class discussion. _____

5. Relies heavily on lecture. _____
6. Defines scope and content of course. _____

7. Displays considerable knowledge of the subject. _____

8. Encourages student initiative. _____
9. Fair to students. _____

Rating

19. Digresses from topics under discussion. _____
20. Elicits student experiences for illustrative purposes. _____

21. Is available to students outside of classroom. _____

22. Open to suggestions from students for discussion, class, or individual projects. _____
23. Lecture style is difficult to follow. _____
24. Has expectations of students unrelated to course content. _____

25. Lectures complement rather than follow reading assignments. _____

26. Uses pertinent audio/visual presentations. _____

10. Relates content of his course to other subject matter. ———
11. Is interested primarily in his subject. ———
12. Is interested primarily in his students. ———
13. Varies level (abstraction) of his presentation. ———
14. Employs humor and anecdotes. ———
15. Makes use of examples and illustrations. ———
16. Responds to individual student needs and problems. ———
17. Meets classes punctually. ———
18. Prepares and organizes his presentations. ———

27. Defines expectations for grading purposes. ———
28. Generates enthusiasm in class. ———
29. Evokes student interest in subject. ———
30. Maintains liveliness in discussions and presentations. ———
31. Lectures directly from notes. ———
32. Uses his knowledge of individual students' strengths in developing the course. ———
33. Responds to individual exams and term papers. ———
34. Discusses evaluation of exams and term papers. ———
35. Lectures reflect current developments. ———

You need not identify yourself. However, we would appreciate the following information:

Class Standing (please circle) Freshman Sophomore Junior Senior Masters 6th Year Doctorate
Sex (please circle) Male Female

---

[a]Developed by Kahn (1974).

a 4-point scale, the original work of Thurstone (1931a) employed an 11-point scale. The only guideline for the number of scale points is that the response format must result in adequate variability. It appears that less than 11 points would achieve this goal.

After the judges' data are obtained, the distribution of the judges' responses to each item is generated so that the mean or median response can be obtained. It is this value that represents the scale value (i.e., weight) for each item on the psychological continuum underlying quality teaching. In addition to the scale values, the interquartile range is calculated for each item, to represent a measure of variability in the judges opinions. This statistic, called the *criterion of ambiguity,* is used to screen out items on which the judges disagree with respect to the degree of affect contained in the item. The criterion of ambiguity represents the first criterion by which items are selected (i.e., items that are equally spaced and nonambiguous).

It is also important that the calibration of the items results in scale values that have generality beyond the particular sample of judges used to locate the items on the continuum. According to Thurstone,

> If the scale is to be regarded as valid, the scale values of the statements should not be affected by the opinions of the people who help construct it. This may turn out to be a severe test in practice, but the scaling method must stand such a test before it can be accepted as being more than a description of the people who construct the scale. At any rate, to the extent that the present method of scale construction is affected by the opinions of the readers who help sort out the original statements into a scale, to that extent the validity or universality of the scale may be challenged. (Thurstone, 1928, pp. 547–548)

For this reason Kahn (1974) sampled several groups of college students and compared the scale values for different subgroups of judges on the basis of sex and level of program (undergraduate, masters, doctorate). The process of scaling the items continued until stable scale values were found.

Once the scale values are found to be stable across groups of judges, the actual item selection takes place. If there are 50 items, and you desire a 25-item instrument that adequately spans the psychological continuum, simply select every other item. The result is actually two parallel forms of the measure. Careful selection of the scale values results in what Thurstone called an *equal-appearing-interval scale* (Edwards, 1957). In the Kahn (1974) example, 20 items were selected from the items in Table 3–1. The items selected and their scale value weights are presented in Table 3–2. Note that the weights have been included in the table but would not appear in the actual form.

Table 3-2. An Illustration of the Respondents' Rating Form for Thurstone Technique

Instructor Evaluation

As a basis for continuing efforts at improvement, your instructor and the department are concerned with gauging the quality and appropriateness of instruction. Your cooperation in furnishing information is essential for this purpose.

Please Note:

A. YOUR RESPONSES WILL BE ANONYMOUS AND WILL NOT AFFECT YOUR GRADE IN ANY WAY.

B. SOME OF THE ITEMS ARE LESS APPROPRIATE FOR CERTAIN KINDS OF COURSES THAN THEY ARE FOR OTHERS. THEREFORE, CONSIDERING THE TYPE OF COURSE (LECTURE, SEMINAR, PRACTICUM) fiLL IN THE RESPONSE POSITION PERTAINING *ONLY* TO THOSE ITEMS YOU JUDGE TO BE APPROPRIATE DESCRIPTIONS OF YOUR INSTRUCTOR.

Weight	No.	Item	
3.169[a]	1.	Lectures reflect current developments in the field	☐
2.649	2.	Defines expectations for grading purposes	☐
2.404	3.	Meets class punctually	☐
2.112	4.	Uses knowledge of individual student's strengths in developing the course	☐
3.377	5.	Maintains liveliness in discussions and presentations	☐
3.887	6.	Generates enthusiasm in class	☐
1.989	7.	Relies heavily on class discussion	☐
3.324	8.	Responds to individual student needs and problems	☐
3.039	9.	Defines scope and content of course	☐
2.254	10.	Elicits student experiences for illustrative purposes	☐
3.064	11.	Prepares and organizes presentations	☐
3.707	12.	Encourages student initiative	☐
2.999	13.	Responds to individual requests for supplementary meterials	☐
2.749	14.	Is interested primarily in students	☐
2.704	15.	Varies level of abstraction of presentation	☐
2.164	16.	Gives specific reading assignments	☐
2.334	17.	Uses pertinent audio/visual presentations	☐
1.502	18.	Digresses from topics under discussion	☐
-0.035	19.	Lectures directly from notes	☐
2.294	20.	Relates content of course to other subject matter	☐

[a]Note that the weights would not appear on the actual form.

Phase II: Locating People on the Continuum

Once the items have been scaled, the location of people on the continuum proceeds as respondents actually rate the target object with respect to the affective characteristic. In our example using the instructions in Table 3–2, respondents merely indicate which of the 20 attributes their teacher exhibits. The score for the teacher rated is then the mean or median of the scale values for those items selected. For example, a respondent checking items 1, 5, 6, 8, and 12 would actually give the instructor a rating of $(3.169 + 3.377 + 3.887 + 3.324 + 3.707) \div 5 = 3.49$; whereas if items 7, 16, 18, and 19 were checked the rating would be $(1.989 + 2.164 + 1.502 - .035) \div 4 = 1.41$. Clearly, the first rating is higher, since the student felt the teacher exhibited characteristics *previously judged* to indicate good teaching.

After obtaining the scale values of a target group, one final analysis will represent the second criterion for selecting items in the Thurstone technique. This procedure, developed by Thurstone and Chave (1929), is called the *criterion of irrelevance* and has been described by Thurstone (see Edwards, 1957, pp. 98–101) and Fishbein and Ajzen (1975, p. 70), and illustrated by Anderson (1981, pp. 243–248). The procedure is not often used but should gain support in that it examines the relationship between the judges' ratings of favorable/unfavorable affect in each item during Phase I and the respondents' scale values obtained after administering the items in Phase II.

The purpose of the analysis is to identify items that yield responses that appear to represent factors other than the affective characteristic being measured. By employing the criterion one assumes that items with particular scale values will be selected by people whose attitudes are located near the scale value on the evaluative continuum. Fishbein and Ajzen (1975, p. 70) and Anderson (1981, pp. 243–247) have illustrated the use of item tracelines or characteristic curves to represent the relationship between the proportion of people or probability of agreeing with a particular item and the item-scale value. Figure 3–1 contains a modified version of Fishbein and Ajzen's tracelines for three items with low, median, and high scale values (i.e., unfavorable, neutral, and favorable items). The horizontal axis represents possible attitude scores, and the vertical axis indicates the proportion of people selecting the item and obtaining the respective attitude scores. In practice, the values on the horizontal axis would represent ranges of attitude scores around the 11 points (e.g., 2.5–3.4). After generating the traceline for each item the criterion of irrelevance is examined by considering the peak of the curve in relation to the location of the item on the evaluative dimension (i.e., the scale value). Items passing the criterion of irrelevance will exhibit tracelines that peak at the scale-score category

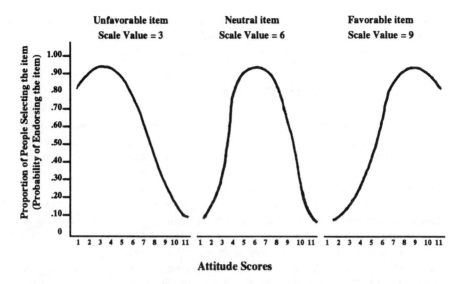

Figure 3–1. Hypothetical trace lines for three Thurstone items with different scale values (Adapted from Fishbein and Ajzen, 1975, p. 70).

containing the item's scale value. When this happens, we conclude that the item will most likely be selected by people whose attitudes are near the scale value on the attitude dimension, and the item is retained for the final form of the instrument.

Prior to leaving this section, we note that for Thurstone scales we do not expect a high correlation between the obtained attitude score and the selection of items. This is the case since the relationships between item selection and scale values depicted for the three items in Figure 3–1 are curvilinear in nature, with the shape of the traceline differing for items with different scale values. Therefore, in the Thurstone technique, items, are not selected on the basis of the relationship between item endorsement and the attitude score. In a later section, we will note that the opposite is true for the Likert technique.

Some researchers have shied away from developing Thurstone scales. It is true that the procedure is time-consuming in that different subgroups of judges can result in different scale values for the items. This variability in judges' opinions means the weights are unstable and suspect for future use. Nunnally (1978) suggests that the more easily constructed summative (Likert and semantic differential) rating scales tend to be more reliable. It is recommended that researchers using the Thurstone technique place much emphasis on the stability of the scale values across subgroups of judges and select another procedure if stability is not present. Those wishing to review several Thurstone scales are referred to Shaw and Wright's (1967) book *Scales for the Measurement of Attitudes*.

Likert's Summated Rating Techniques

Likert's (1932) method of summated ratings has been appropriately popular. According to Nunnally (1978), the Likert scales have been frequently used because they are relatively easy to construct, can be highly reliable, and have been successfully adapted to measure many types of affective characteristics. Instruments employing Likert's technique contain a set of statements (i.e., items) presented on what has been called a "Likert response format." The 5-point strongly agree/strongly disagree format is commonly employed. Responses are then summed across the items to generate a score on the affective instrument. Examples of Likert scales discussed in earlier chapters include the *Gable-Roberts Attitude Toward Teacher Scale* (Gable and Roberts, 1982) and the *Work Values Inventory* (Super, 1970).

With respect to Fishbein's expectancy-value model (see Equation 3–1), we note that the evaluation (e) of the favorable/unfavorableness (i.e., positive/negative) of the statement or attribute with respect to the target object is initially determined by the instrument developer and not by an independent set of judges as was the case for the Thurstone procedure. While a group of judges could later examine the items, they do not assist in scaling the statements on the evaluative dimension, as was the case in the Thurstone technique. Thus, the values of e in Equation 3–1 are set at –1 and +1 for negative and positive item stems; the value of b takes on the values of the selected response format. For example, a 5-point strongly agree/strongly disagree format would yield values from 1 to 5 for b. In responding to the items, people are actually locating themselves on the underlying affective continuum through their intensity and direction ratings. People are thus scaled on the items by summing their item-level responses across the items defining the characteristic. (Note that negative item stems should first be reverse scored so that the scoring process takes place in the same direction for all items.)

Item Selection

The development of a Likert scale begins with the selection of a large number of items (i.e., belief statements that represent operational definitions

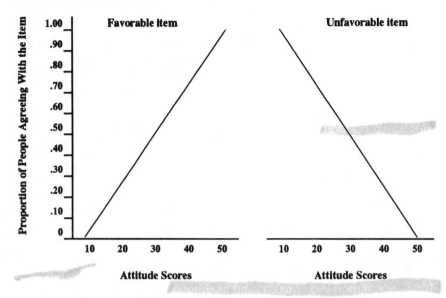

Figure 3–2.   Hypothetical trace lines for two Likert items (Adapted from Fishbein and Ajzen, 1975, p. 72).

of the affective characteristic). Approximately 10–12 items should be initially written for each judgmentally derived affective category specified during the content-validity stage. After the items are reviewed during the content-validity phase, a pilot study should be conducted where a representative sample of people (6–10 times as many people as there are items) respond to the pilot form. Item-analysis, alpha-reliability, and factor-analysis procedures can then be carried out as described in Chapters 4 and 5.

The criterion for item selection used by Likert was the *criterion of internal consistency*, which results in eliminating items that do not relate to the affective characteristic being measured. Theoretically, this criterion specifies that people with higher overall attitude scores should tend to agree with favorable or positive items and disagree with unfavorable or negative items.[1] Fishbein and Ajzen (1975) illustrate the resulting tracelines for two items meeting the criterion of internal consistency. A modified version of their illustration is presented in Figure 3–2. Consider a 10-item attitude scale that employs a 5-point agreement response format. The possible range of scores from 10 to 50 is indicated on each baseline in Figure 3–2. The vertical axis represents the probability of endorsing the item or the proportion of people agreeing with the item at various attitude-score intervals. Operationally, this reduces to the correlation of the item score with the total attitude score. Readers will note, contrary to the Thurstone technique, that the tracelines for the favorable and unfavorable items are linear, and the correlation between item endorsement and the attitude score is the criterion used for item selection.

Response Formats

The response format for the items should be consistent with the intent of the rating form. Since several different formats are available, one has to select the format that best provides the information desired so that the instructions and item phrases can be written to be consistent with the response format. For example, do you want to know if respondents *agree* with the items, or how *frequently* they have experienced the event described by the item? To facilitate this decision, Table 3–3 presents several popular response formats for the following intensity areas: agreement, frequency, importance, quality, and likelihood. There are certainly several variations on these response formats, but the ones listed appear to be the most popular, especially the formats listed in bold italic type.

If you decide to use a less-popular format or develop your own format, a pilot study may be needed to validate the ordered nature of the response options. Since the scaling of people will involve assigning ordered numbers to the options, there must be no question that the rank order of the options is correct and that the intervals between the options can be assumed to be equal. If there is any doubt, have a group of about 15 judges independently rank the response options and discuss the intervals between the options. Confusion at this point will severely restrict the later assessment of reliability and validity of the instrument, as well as the choice of parametic versus nonparametric statistics, to be used in the analysis of data.

Number of Steps in the Response Format

Several opinions have been expressed regarding the number of steps to use in the Likert response format. As illustrated in Table 3–3, several different formats have been employed by researchers. The decision is important in that using too few steps will result in failing to illicit the fine discriminations of which the respondent is capable, while using too many steps could create confusion and frustration. Thus, the number of steps to be used may differ across various instruments and should be made on the basis of both practical and empirical considerations.

Table 3–3. Response Formats Used for Rating Agreement, Frequency, Importance, Quality, and Likelihood[a]

AGREEMENT

Strongly Agree	Agree Strongly
Agree	Agree Moderately
Undecided	Agree Slightly
Disagree	Disagree Slightly
Strongly Disagree	Disagree Moderately
	Disagree Strongly

Agree	Agree Very Strongly
Disagree	Agree Strongly
	Agree
	Disagree
	Disagree Strongly
	Disagree Very Strongly

Agree	Yes
Undecided	No
Disagree	

Completely Agree	Disagree Strongly
Mostly Agree	Disagree
Slightly Agree	Tend to Disagree
Slightly Disagree	Tend to Agree
Mostly Disagree	Agree
Completely Disagree	Agree Strongly

FREQUENCY

Very Frequently	*Always*
Frequently	*Very Frequently*
Occasionally	*Occasionally*
Rarely	*Rarely*
Very Rarely	*Very Rarely*
Never	*Never*

Always	Almost Always
Usually	To a Considerable Degree
About Half the Time	Occasionally
Seldom	Seldom
Never	

A Great Deal	Often
Much	Sometimes
Somewhat	Seldom
Little	Never
Never	

Always
Very Often
Sometimes
Rarely
Never

Table 3-3. (Cont.)

IMPORTANCE	LIKELIHOOD	QUALITY
Very Important *Important* *Moderately Important* *Of Little Importance* *Unimportant*	*Like Me* *Unlike Me*	
Very Important Moderately Important Unimportant	To a Great Extent Somewhat Very Little Not at All	
	Almost Always True *Usually True* *Often True* *Occasionally True* *Sometimes But Infrequently True* *Usually Not True* *Almost Never True*	
Very Good Good Barely Acceptable Poor Very Poor	True of Myself Mostly True of Myself About Halfway True of Myself Slightly True of Myself Not at All True of Myself	*Extremely Poor* *Below Average* Average *Above Average* *Excellent*
	True False	Good Fair Poor
	Definitely, Very Probably Probably Possibly Probably Not Very Probably Not	

[a]Most popular formats are in bold type.

From a *practical* viewpoint, a greater number of steps in the scale will necessitate a higher level of thought for making fine discriminations between the scale anchor points. If respondents become annoyed or generally confused by the large number of gradations used, they could become careless and provide you with unreliable data. It is, therefore, important to consider the context of the items, as well as the training, age, educational level, motivation, and cognitive level of the respondents when selecting the number of steps to be used.

From an *empirical* viewpoint, several researchers have examined the issue of the optimal number of rating scale steps. Whereas Cronbach (1950) cautioned that the number of steps issue was also a validity issue, most researchers have focused on the reliability of the data obtained. As Nunnally (1978) and Guilford (1954) have noted, the reliability of the scale should increase as a function of the number of steps employed. This view has been supported in studies reported by Garner (1960); Finn (1972); and Komorita and Graham (1965). According to Nunnally, increasing the number of steps from 2 to 20 generally increases reliability rapidly at first, levels off around 7, and increases little after about 11 steps. These findings are consistent with research reported by McKelvie (1978) and Jenkins and Taber (1977). McKelvie found that 5-point or 6-point scales were most reliable. A larger number of categories appeared to have no psychometric advantage and fewer than five categories could result in a lack of response discrimination. On the other hand, Komorita (1963) found that the reliability of a dichotomous format was not significantly less than the reliability of multistep scales. Similarly, Matell and Jacoby (1971) developed 18 different Likert scale formats (2 points to 19 points) for use with a 60-item modified version of the Allport-Vernon-Lindzey *Study of Values* (1960). Both internal consistency and stability reliabilities were found to be independent of the number of steps employed in the rating format. These findings were consistent with those reported by Komorita and Graham (1965). Likewise, concurrent validity information obtained through additional self-ratings of each *Study of Values* domain category indicated that validity, as defined in the study, was independent of the number of scale points. In another study, Comrey and Montag (1982) compared the factor analysis (construct validity) results of 2-point and 7-point response formats used on the *Comrey Personality Scales*. While the factor structure was found to be similar for the two formats, higher factor loadings reflecting higher intercorrelations among the variables were found for the 7-point scale. Comrey also reports that other researchers have reported differences in factor structures when dichotomous and multistep formats have been employed for the Rotter *I-E Scale* (Joe and John, 1973), the *Personal Orientation Inventory* (Velicer,

DiClemente, and Corriveau, 1979), and the Eysenck *Personality Questionnaire* (Velicer and Stevenson, 1978). On the basis of these studies, Comrey (1982) concluded that the 7-point format for personality inventories allows for distinctions by respondents and for more precise measures of the underlying factor structure.

It appears that, while some researchers might disagree, there is little empirical support for the use of 2-point response formats. Using such formats may make responding and scoring easier, but could result in a loss of meaningful information. For example, although Coopersmith's (1967, 1989) popular *Self-Esteem Inventory* has always employed the 2-point (Like Me/Unlike Me) response format, several studies have reported low-scale alpha reliabilities and factor structures that fail to support Coopersmith's suggested scoring scheme (see, for example, Glover and Archambault, 1982). On the basis of the research reported, the reliability and validity issues seem to be best served through the use of from five to seven response categories.

A related issue is the use of an odd or even number of steps in the response format. An odd number results in an "undecided" or "neutral" category which allows the respondent to avoid committing to either a positive or negative direction. Proponents of its use suggest that no significant differences are found in scale scores for the same respondents using both types of scales and that the selection of a neutral rating is no more ambiguous in meaning than the selection of any of the other categories (Dubois and Burns, 1975; Ory and Wise, 1981). On the other hand, Doyle (1975) notes that not using a neutral point forces more thought by the respondent and possibly more precise discriminations. Consistent with this view, Ory and Wise found that significant pre/post attitude treatment differences were found for respondents to a 4-point scale, while no differences were found for another group randomly assigned to respond to a 5-point format.

While we would like to think that we know what respondents mean by "strongly agree" or "disagree," we should not be so quick to describe the meaning and appropriate scoring for the "undecided" or "neutral" response category. The center point of the Likert scale could indicate ambivalence (i.e., mixed attitudes toward the target object), indifference (i.e., little concern for the target object), lack of understanding of the item, or a form of refusing to answer.

There is simply no definitive answer to the question of using a neutral point in response format. If you are concerned that respondents may not be responding to the middle category to represent a neutral attitude, you can follow the technique described by DuBois and Burns (1975) to examine this issue. Essentially, the procedure involves the plotting of the respond-ent's mean scale scores (vertical axis) for each separate response category (horizontal axis; SA, A, U, D, SD). If the middle category is a true neutral response, the plot of means should be in a relatively straight line (upper left to lower right), and the standard deviations (dispersion) of the scores around the means at each response category should be similar. While some researchers may wish to examine this issue empirically during the pilot stages of a new instrument, Nunnally (1978) does not consider this issue to be of great importance and concludes that it may best be decided on a situational basis in the context of the item content and nature of the respondents. We do note, though, that an empirical examination of pilot data would certainly add to an informed decision for a particular set of items. In fact, Nunnally's advice seems to be a little outdated in light of the capability of the DuBois and Burns (1975) procedure. In a later section on latent trait methodology a discussion of a most powerful and informative procedure for empirically examining the use of the neutral point will be presented.

Response Format Definition

After selecting the number of steps to use in the response format, the labeling of the response categories becomes an issue. In the previous section, Table 3–3 presented several examples of all-category defined formats. Dixon, Bobo, and Stevick (1984) have reviewed several studies where different techniques were used to label the response categories. Tech-niques consisted of various combinations, such as labeling all categories versus labeling only categories at the end of the response continuum, verbal versus numerical labels, and vertical versus horizontal labels. The influ-ence of the formats on the results of the study was mixed; in some studies differences were noted and in other studies no differences were present. For data gathered by Dixon et al. (1984), no differences in perceptions of locus of control were found between the end-defined and all-category defined versions of a control scale for college students. The end-defined format was associated with higher standard deviations than the all-category defined format.

The labeling of the response format categories appears to be an open question from an empirical point of view. It seems important to consider the age and educational level of the respondents in the context of the cognitive complexity of the rating task. Pilot studies of different formats are always good insurance during the process of instrument development.

Positive and Negative Item Stems

In Chapter 2 we discussed the development of operational definitions for the affective characteristics that were the item stems to be included in the instrument. Prior to and after the content-validity study, it is important to consider the issue of positive and negative item stems. Will you use all positively stated *items*, negative items, or a set of mixed items? Prior to the 1980s, the research in this area did not offer a definitive answer to this question. During the 1980s and early 1990s, though, the issue received appropriate attention, and the findings have emerged quite consistently across respondent age levels.

The research in this area focuses on the topic of *response* sets, or response styles, which Cronbach defined as "any tendency causing a person consistently to make different responses to test items than he would have had the same content been presented in a different form" (Cronbach, 1946, p. 476). For example, individuals may tend to select the "neutral" category on a 5-point "agree/disagree" response continuum, "true" on a "true/false" continuum, or simply agree with most statements. Cronbach (1950) states that such response sets are possible on affective instruments that contain ambiguously stated items, employ a disagree/agree response continuum, and require responses in a favorable or unfavorable direction.

Efforts at identifying response sets have been mixed, though, since a true response set must represent a reliable source of variance in individual differences, be an artifact of the measurement procedure, and be partially independent of the affective characteristic measured (Nunnally, 1978). While it has proved difficult to isolate response sets that consistently meet these criteria, Rorer's (1965) review of the response set literature supports the view that item content relates to a response set that represents a reliable source of response variance. Researchers have spent much time studying such areas as social desirability (i.e., giving socially accepted responses) and acquiescence (i.e., tendency to agree). The forced-choice item format has been suggested to assist in dealing with social desirability. In a later section on ipsative versus normative scores, we will note that the forced-choice format may only partially address the tendency to give socially accepted responses.

The college-student and adult-based research on the response set labeled "acquiescence" or "agreement tendency" has been reviewed by Nunnally (1978), who feels that it may not be an important response set given his three criteria for the definition of a response set. He does conclude, however, that the issue can be mostly eliminated by constructing the instrument to have a balanced number of "positive" and "negative" items. Prior to the 1980s researchers tended to accept this advice for respondents of all ages and educational levels and routinely proceeded with data gathering. It was quite common to see affective instruments with a mix of positive and negative item stems. More recently it has become quite clear that "negated" item stems can pose conceptual problems for some respondents and a variety of measurement problems that are often ignored in the interpretation of results. Research reported in the 1980s and 1990s clearly indicates that Nunnally's advise is inappropriate, especially for younger students.

The problems with negation of item stems can best be understood through Pilotte's discussion of schema theory and linguistics as follows:

> Schema theory (Rosch, 1973, 1975) suggests that information is processed by matching it to prototypes or exemplars of existing knowledge structures. These exemplars guide the interpretation and inferences associated with the incoming sensory stimuli (Soloway, Anderson, & Ehrich, 1988). Nummedale (1987) has proposed that conceptual difficulty may arise from attempting to process statements in which the exemplars have been implicitly or explicitly negated. Wason (1980) stresses that negative information may be harder to process because interaction with the environment is in terms of "things" rather than "not things". (Pilotte, 1991, pp. 2, 6–7)

Pilotte further clarifies the role of schema theory in the following section:

> Language is a tool used for systematic communication; consequently, the use of language activates schemata. Sentences are composed of phrases which can be further decomposed into smaller parts of speech. The same information can be supplied by a simple sentence or by an equivalent transformed form. Evans (1982) notes that linguistic propositions and transformational markers become the coded instruction for the generation of meaningful sentences. Similarly, Fillenbaum (1966) discusses a simple sentence as a kernel plus a transformational tag, which are held independently of each other. An example of this theory employs the sentence: "The door is not closed," wherein the tag would be negation.
>
> The linguistic complexity is further complicated when evaluative adjectives like "good" are employed. Such adjectives may be referred to as syncategorematic, since the adjective itself must be defined in terms of the noun it modifies; e.g., "good chair" really conveys a different meaning for the word "good" than would "good nurse" (Miller, 1978). Reversing an item using a word considered to be a polar opposite may cause additional confusion resulting from "scalar properties" like hot/cold. In the example, hot/cold, a substance may not be hot; however, this does not necessitate its being cold. Hot/cold sets up a continuum on which one can locate the substance. A second type of reversal uses contraries which are exclusive, e.g., open/closed. In this case the object is either open or it is not. Clark and Chase (1972) argue that a sentence like "A isn't above

B" is representative of many different visual models which may include "A is below B," "A is next to B," or "A is front of B." They conclude that negative statements indicate what is not and that this rarely defines a unique image.

This transformational complexity involved in negating a sentence using the word "not" or by using a polar opposite seems to support Evans (1982) remark that negatives are more complex than affirmatives. Evans (1982) cites the asymmetrical nature of some adjective pairs as a possible source of confusion. He discussed the different underlying assumptions associated with the two questions: (1) "How good is John?" and (2) "How bad is John?", where the second question assumes that John is bad. Anderson (1983) reaffirms this relationship when discussing the sentence "John is not a crook," which supposes that it is reasonable to believe that "John is a crook" but negates it. In analyzing the four possible responses to the question, "How are you feeling?", Anderson (1983) states that even though "I am not sick" and "I am well" convey the same information, it is confusing to be told "I am not sick," since this presupposes that this person is usually ill. Evans (1982) concludes "the difficulty of negation seems to be characteristic of thought rather than language" (p. 30). Later, Evans (1983) stated that since it is not the logical information that is changed but the linguistic expression, then it is the linguistic expression which becomes crucial when interpreting any statement. (Pilotte, 1991, pp. 30–33)

Studies by Benson and Hocevar (1985), Benson and Wilcox (1981), Campbell and Grissom (1979), Melnick and Gable (1990), Pilotte and Gable (1990), Schriescheim and Hill (1981), and Wright and Masters (1982) provide us with appropriate caution and suggest that the instrument developers should pilot different versions of an instrument to ascertain if the ratio of positive and negative item stems is associated with different reliability and validity information. Using latent trait theory Wright and Masters (1982) found that the positive and negative attitude toward drug items did not measure the same construct. In the Benson and Wilcox (1981) study, all positive, all negative, and balanced instruments were randomly administered to 622 grade 4–6 students to measure attitude toward a court-ordered integration plan. For this age level, the mixed form was associated with lower alpha reliabilities at all grade levels (total group: mixed = 0.65; other forms = 0.78) suggesting that the grade 4–6 students responded more inconsistently to the mixed form. Also, it was found that younger (grade 4) students marked significantly more positive responses for the positive stems than the other forms and more negative responses for the negative form. On the other hand, the older students (grade 6) responded equally across all three forms.

The later study by Benson and Hocevar (1985) furthered the analysis of these data by examining the factor structure (construct validity) of the three forms; different factor structures were found. Combining the results of both studies led Benson and Hocevar to recommend that attitude instruments for elementary school students should use all positively stated items.

Support for this recommendation for high-school respondents was found in a study of 270 grade 9–12 students by Pilotte and Gable (1990), where computer anxiety was defined as follows:

> An unpleasant, emotional state marked by worry, apprehension and attention associated with thinking about, learning about, using, or being exposed to a computer. Verbs expressing feeling and forms of the verb "to be" were used in item construction along with directional adjectives that express worry, concern, panic, lack of confidence, or lack of comfort, thus assuring that consideration was given to both the target, computer anxiety, and the direction, wording that is indicative of anxiety. (p. 54)

Three forms of a computer-anxiety scale were examined to ascertain if the items for each form defined a single construct or two different constructs. Form A contained 9 items (e.g., I feel threatened by computers) reflecting computer anxiety that were responded to on a 5-point Likert agreement scale. Form B contained a parallel set of items devised by negating each item on the original form (e.g., I do not feel threatened by computers.), and Form C contained mixed-positive and negative items. Each student responded to one of the three forms. Alpha Internal consistency reliability estimates for the three forms were as follows: A—Computer Anxiety, .95; B—Negated Computer Anxiety Items, .87; and C—Mixed Items, .73. A confirmatory factor analysis using LISREL VI (Jöreskog and Sörbom, 1984) was employed to determine if the positive and negative item stems were measuring the same construct. The covariance matrix for the students' responses was input and a two-factor solution specified such that items reflecting computer anxiety were forced to load on one factor and the reverse scored items on the other. The analysis clearly indicated that factor invariance was not found between Form A (all items indicative of computer anxiety) and Form B (all items indicative of a lack of computer anxiety). The analysis of the mixed form yielded a correlation between factors of .24. While not statistically significant, a two-factor structure was considered to provide a better fit of the data.

In a later study of 2236 grade 9–12 students from three high schools, Pilotte (1991) further investigated differences between positive and negative item stems using nine forms of a computer-anxiety scale. The first form was created through several judgmental item reviews followed by principal-component and alpha-reliability analyses that resulted in a single-factor, ten-item scale. The eight additional forms were then developed to acertain if the items or their explicit and implicit negations defined the same construct. First, the differences between positive and negative item stems were studied using three forms of the scale to ascertain if the negation of an item produced a parallel item, and to determine if factor invariance could be claimed. Second, two forms containing an equal mix of items and their explicit negations were analyzed to determine if a one-factor or two-factor model provided a better fit. Similarly, two forms consisting of an equal mix of items and their implicit negations were also analyzed. Third, the differences in item reliabilities and overall LISREL estimates of instrument reliability were assessed to determine if negating an item reduces its reliability.

Pilotte reported his findings as follows:

Factor Invariance. A **LISREL** measurement model was developed for the original scale for use with the **LISREL** multiple groups procedure to test for factor invariance between the items worded to reflect computer anxiety and their negations. The multiple groups analysis indicated that there were significant differences between both the factor loadings and the measurement errors when the original scale items were compared to those items negated by polar opposites. However, for the items negated using "not," differences were found between factor variances and the measurement errors. A comparison for the entire sample and the subsample of students reporting English as the primary language in the home yielded comparable results.

Item Equivalence. A second analysis was undertaken to test the equivalence of the items and their negated counterparts involving scales that were composed of an equal number of items from the original form and one of the negated forms. Prior research in language, cognition and psychometrics has demonstrated that the negation of an item may not produce a parallel item (Clark & Chase, 1972; Gillieron, 1984; Givon, 1978; Wason, 1959, 1962, 1980), may not produce highly correlated items (Campbell, Seigman, & Rees, 1967), and may produce items that are not closely related to the prototype (Rosch, 1973, 1975). Other researchers have documented the emergence of a "negative" factor when affective scales were written to include mixed item stems (Benson & Hocevar, 1985; Bolton, 1976; Marsh, 1987; Schriesheim & Hill, 1981; Wright & Masters, 1982).

A one-factor and a two-factor model for two forms, which consisted of an equal mix of items from the original scale and the scale formed by negating each item with the word "not," were compared to determine if a negative factor would emerge. A highly significant chi-square difference between these models indicated that the negated items formed a distinct factor. Similarly, a one-factor and two-factor model for two forms, which consisted of an equal mix of items from the original scale and the scale formed by negating each item using a polar opposite, were compared. The highly significant chi-square difference between these models also indicated the emergence of a "negative" factor. Again, an analysis of the subsample of students reporting English as the primary language spoken within the home yielded similar results. These results suggest that high-school students interpret items worded to reflect computer anxiety and their negations in different ways. Further, they indicate that the differences in factor structures are not confounded by the primary language issue. The inclusion of two versions of each "mixed" form also reaffirms the differences as negation-related rather than as unique to the specific item chosen for inclusion on the form.

Implicit vs *explicit negation.* The study also examined if explicit and implicit negation resulted in parallel items. A measurement model was developed for the scale where all items were negated using their polar opposites (i.e., implicit negation) and then compared to the form in which the negation was accomplished using the word "not" (i.e., explicit negation). LISREL multiple groups procedures were performed for the entire sample as well as for the subsample of students reporting English as the primary language spoken within the home. These analyses revealed that the factor loadings and measurement error were different for the two types of negation. To determine if students interpreted the two types of negation differently, one- and two-factor models for the two scale forms were also compared. Since the single-factor hypothesis was rejected, and since there were differences in factor structure for the two-factor models, as well as differences in the formation of the factors themselves—one corresponding to implicit and the other to explicit negation of the items—it appears that high-school students interpret explicit and implicit negation differently.

Item variance. The variance for each item on the original form was compared to the variance of the negated items on explicit and implicit negated forms with the F-max test to ascertain if the negation resulted in an increase in the item's variance as reported for elementary-school students (Benson & Hacevar, 1985). A significantly larger variance was found for 6 of the 10 items on the explicit negation form and three of the 10 items on the implicit negation form.

Item means. A multivariate comparison of item means was also performed to determine if respondents rated the negated item closer to the neutral point on the Likert-type scale than the positively worded items from which they were formed. The hypothesis of equal item means was rejected and the *post hoc* analysis indicated that 9 of the 10 item means on the explicit negation form were scored closer to the neutral position while all of the items on the implicit negation form were scored closer to the neutral point. This can be interpreted as another indicator that the high-school student interprets the statement worded to reflect computer anxiety and its negations differently.

Item reliabilities. The equivalence of item reliabilities across the forms was examined using the squared multiple correlation of each item with its latent variable and the variance of the errors of measurement from the LISREL program, which estimate the disturbances that "disrupt the relationship between the latent and observed variables" (Bollen, 1989). The latent trait, computer anxiety, accounted for more than 50% of the variance of 9 of 10 items on the original form, but could account for more than 50% of the variance for only five items on either the explicit or implicitly negated forms. This indicates that more of the trait, computer anxiety, could be explained by the items on the original form than the items on either of the negated forms where the results appear confounded with the issue of negation. In addition, the error variances were higher for the items on both negated forms, which indicated that the items written to indicate computer anxiety were better aligned with the construct than either of the two negations (Pilotte, 1991, pp. 101–106).

Melnick and Gable (1990) examined the use of negative item stems on the 47-item *Parent Attitudes Toward School Effectiveness* survey, which assesses six dimensions of school effectiveness. Responses to four pairs of parallel items (i.e., one positive and one negative item) were examined to create two groups of parents: N = 1636 who *consistently* responded to the item pairs (i.e., "Strongly Agree" or "Agree" on one item followed by "Strongly Disagree" or "Disagree" on the negated version of the item), and N = 476 who were *inconsistent* in their responses to the item pairs (i.e., "Agree" or "Disagree" with both positive and negative versions of the stem pair). Analysis of the total set of 47 items reflecting the six-school effectiveness dimensions indicated that: 1) The group that was consistent in its responses had significantly higher means on all six scales than the group that was inconsistent; 2) Alpha internal consistency reliabilities were higher for the consistent group on all but one scale than for the inconsistent group; and, 3) In every case, the consistent group had a significantly higher education level than the total sample.

In summary, the studies reported in this section clearly indicate that negated item stems are challenging in a cognitive sense especially for younger respondents and those with lower education levels, and can result in lower item- and scale-level reliabilities, as well as lack of proper definition and support for the targeted constructs being assessed. It is quite clear that Nunnally's suggestion of using a balanced number of positive and negative item stems should not be routinely employed in constructing attitude instruments. It appears that, for especially young students, it is important to pilot and analyze different versions of instruments prior to assuming that the mixed item stems have dealt with the acquiescence response set.

Proximity Effect

Related to this issue of positive and negative item stems is the tendency to respond in a similar manner to adjacent (i.e., prior) items—this has been called a proximity effect. Schurr and Henrikson (1983) discovered a proximity effect for a low-inference classroom observation scale for one sample of respondents. Reece and Owen (1985) extended the work of Schurr and Henrikson by examining the existence of the proximity effect for data from different low- and high-inference instruments and negative items and seven different samples of grade-school through college students. Through the use of regression techniques, the authors found substantial variation in proximate effects across the instruments and suggested that additional study was needed to examine the circumstances that produce large proximate effects. It should be clear at this point that the existence of a large proximity effect would most likely result in contaminated factors during a study of construct validity and in inflated estimates of alpha internal-consistency reliabilities. Support for this latter statement was found by Melnick (1993). An attitude measure with items grouped by dimension was administered to 350 school administrators; a version with items randomly placed was given to 369 administrators. The alpha reliabilities of the dimensions tended to be higher for the form with the grouped items.

Latent Trait Models

Cognitive Instruments

During the last several years, latent trait techniques have received considerable attention in the construction of *cognitive achievement* tests. These techniques have become quite popular for describing the probability that a person with a given ability level will pass an item with given item parameters. During the phase of item calibration, three possible item parameters can be estimated from the response data: difficulty, discrimination, and chance-success level. A feature and an assumption of the latent trait models is that the estimated parameters are *sample-free*—i.e., the same regardless of the sample of people employed. In addition, once the items have been calibrated, a subset of the items can be used to measure a person's trait level. Thus, the latent trait model also produces *item-free* trait measurement. A measurement model yielding both sample-free and item-free measurement has been crucial in selecting test items and creating parallel forms for longitudinal comparisons in several statewide achievement testing programs.

The early work with latent trait models for dichotomously scored achievement tests (i.e., correct/incorrect) was carried out by Rasch (1966) in the 1950s and has been popularized by Wright as described in an excellent source entitled *Best Test Design* (Wright and Stone, 1979). The Rasch model is a one-parameter model which assumes that items differ only in terms of item difficulty. For more detailed reading in this area, readers are referred to Hambleton and Swaminathan's 1984 text entitled *Item Response Theory: Principles and Applications*, and to several issues of the following journals: *Journal of Educational Measurement, Applied Psychological Measurement*, and *Applied Measurement in Education*.

Affective Instruments

While the various latent trait models have received considerable attention from psychometricians in the area of achievement testing, few people are aware that several additional models are available. These models are simple extensions of Rasch's Dichotomous Model (1966) and are applicable to other response formats. In this section, we will present the work of Wright and Masters as described in their book *Rating Scale Analysis* (1982). Specifically, the rating-scale model described by Andrich (1978a, 1978b, 1978c) and Masters (1980) will be presented in the context of scaling (i.e., calibrating) items and measuring people's affective characteristics with items employing Likert-response formats. Before we proceed, it is important to review some key features of the Thurstone and Likert approaches to measuring attitudes.

The last two sections have described the Thurstone and Likert techniques for scaling attitude statements. As noted by Andrich (1978c) Thurstone's law of comparative judgment was primarily concerned with the affective properties of the items (i.e., their ability to arouse affect). Thurstone's time-consuming process featured the use of the judges' ratings to obtain scale values (i.e., item calibrations) that quantified the extent to which the statements described the affective characteristic. While this process allowed the instrument developer to locate and order the *statements* along the affective continuum, Andrich (1978c, p. 666) points out that the process has no "direct consequence" for the quantification of a *person's* attitude. Indirectly, a person's attitude was measured by using the median of the scale values of the statements endorsed. On the other hand, the popular version of Likert's procedure does not include a formal process of scaling the statements along the affect continuum. Instead, the developer hopefully selects statements that span the affective continuum, and the respondent selects a successive integer from successive response categories (e.g., Strongly Disagree (1), Disagree (2), Undecided (3), Agree (4), Strongly Agree (5)). Thus, the Likert technique quantifies a *person's* attitude while having no "direct consequence" for the scaling of *statements*.

These comments are not meant to negate the use of the Thurstone or Likert scaling techniques. Rather, they are intended to provide strong support for the use of latent trait models that can address the features of both the Thurstone and Likert techniques. One such model, the Rasch model, can be used for Likert-type, successive-integer response formats to quantify both the affective nature of a *statement* and the attitude of the *person* responding. This technique has direct consequences for both *statements* and *persons*, since parameter estimates are estimated for both statements and people.

Our discussion of the Rasch latent trait technique will address the following four topics and questions:

1. *Item calibration*: Where is each statement (item) located on the affective continuum?
2. *Measuring people*: Where is each person located on the affective continuum?
3. *Item Fit*: How well do the statements (items) fit the model?
4. *Person Fit*: How well do the people fit the model?

Since the technique is not well understood by many affective instrument developers and will be frequently used in the near future, the description will be presented in some detail. Interested readers are referred to papers by Johnson, Dixon, and Ryan (1991), and Masters and Hyde (1984), which illustrate the use of the Rasch latent trait model for Likert scaling.

Calibrating Items for Measuring People

The Likert response format has been used extensively for affective instruments. The typical 5-point agree continuum consists of ordered response alternatives such as:

Strongly Agree   Agree   Undecided   Disagree   Strongly Disagree
5   4   3   2   1

According to Wright and Masters (1982, p. 48), "completing the kth step" represents the selection of the kth step over the $(K-1)^{th}$ step on the response continuum. (Note that a 5-point response format has four steps, such as 1–2 = 1 step, 2–3 = 1 step, etc.). Given this format, a person selecting the "agree" option has chosen "disagree" over "strongly disagree" and "undecided" over "disagree," but has not chosen "strongly agree"

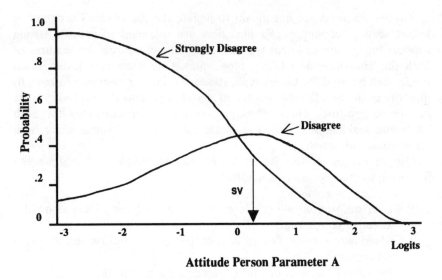

Figure 3–3. Strongly disagree and disagree category probability curves for a hypothetical item.

over "agree." These ordered steps in the response format represent the relative difficulties in responding to the item and are assumed to be constant across all of the items.

Given this assumption, the Rating Scale Analysis model is run on a computer program called CREDIT which employs one of several (e.g., PROX, PAIR, CON, UCON) procedures for estimating the item parameters (i.e., scaling the items) and the person parameters (i.e., measuring people). If the UCON procedure is employed, the person and item parameters are estimated simultaneously. To be more specific, the procedure estimates a position for each person on the affective-variable continuum being measured (i.e., person parameter), a scale value for each item (i.e., item parameter), and m (e.g., 4) response thresholds for the $m + 1$ (e.g., 4 for a 5-point Likert agreement scale) response categories employed. Figure 3–3 contains these values for the item characteristic curves, which are called *ogives*, for a hypothetical attitude item. For ease of illustration only the "strongly disagree" and "disagree" curves are included for the 5-point scale. (Note that for the Rasch Dichotomous Model employed in achievement tests only one such curve exists per item.) The purpose of this curve is to estimate the probability of person n responding "strongly disagree" (i.e., 1) rather than "disagree" (i.e., 2) on this item as a function of the person's affective characteristic parameter A, and an item scale value parameter SV, which dictates the transition from responding "strongly disagree" to responding "disagree" on the item (see Wright and Masters 1982, pp. 55, 128, 130). The values marked off on the horizontal axis represent units called *logits* from the logistic scale, varying from -3 to $+3$. (The logistic scale can be converted to the normal curve using a conversion factor.) High logit values are associated with items with which it is easy to agree (i.e., low difficulty and a high attitude score); low values with items with which it is easy to disagree (i.e., high difficulty and low attitude score). Once the item characteristic curves for an item have been centered on their scale value, we can estimate the probability of any person selecting any one of the response alternatives. To do this, we locate the person's attitude estimate in logits (provided in the computer output) on the horizontal axis and project a vertical line to the height of one of the curves, then read off the probability value from the vertical axis. For example, in Figure 3-3, a person with an attitude estimate of -1 logits has a .35 pobability of disagreeing and a .65 probability of strongly disagreeing with this item. Further, the average scale value in logits for a set of items will always equal zero. After calculating the standard deviations (S) of the scale values in logits, we can determine the probabilities of selecting each response option for people with attitude raw score levels of $\bar{X} + S$, $\bar{X} + 2S$, $\bar{X} - S$, and $\bar{X} - 2S$.

Item Fit

Earlier we noted that the rating-scale model attempts to locate the items on the affective continuum. On the basis of peoples' responses to the items, scale values were generated for this purpose. A feature of the procedure is a test of whether each item fits the rating-scale model. This t-test statistic reflects the extent to which the responses support the existence of continuum underlying the affective characteristic. Items not fitting the model can then be discarded from the item set. The item fit statistic is extremely important in instrument development as an item-analysis procedure. In Chapter 4 we will illustrate the depth of information available from the statistic in the framework of construct validity. Response patterns will be examined in light of patterns expected by the mathematical model. Clearer understanding of the respondents' perceptions of the item content should result.

The item-fit statistic can also be used to generate empirical evidence for the question of including the "neutral" or "undecided" response option on a Likert scale (see our discussion of this topic in the previous section on Likert scaling). Masters and Hyde (1984) examined the response options for a set of attitudes toward school items. For an item not fitting the Rasch model, four attitude groups representing low to high attitudes were created so that the proportions of students in each group responding "disagree," "undecided," and "agree" could be calculated. These proportions were then plotted along with the Rasch model probability of selecting each option to study the nature of an item's misfit with the model. For one of the misfitting items, more students than expected (based on the model) selected the "neutral" option. Thus, the misfit of this item could be attributed to a use of the "neutral" response, suggesting that it is not another point on an ordered continuum.

Person Fit

The CREDIT computer program also provides useful information regarding the extent to which people fit the hypothesized model. People whose responses are inconsistent with the statement difficulty ordering can be easily identified for follow-up study of their response frequencies, as well as other cognitive and affective characteristics.

Wright and Masters (1982) also illustrate how the analysis of *person fit* can be used to examine the *response styles*, or sets, which result when not all people use the response options in the same way. That is, some people may tend to select extreme responses, "agree" responses, or the "true" option for various rating scales. The common practice is to include both positive and negative item stems to help control for the possibility of a response style. Wright and Masters (1982, Ch. 6) provide an interesting illustration of how the rating-scale model analysis of "person fit" can be used to ascertain if the positive and negative items really measure the same affective characteristics. Ten positive and 10 negative attitude, toward drugs items were compared for 75 students. The person-fit analysis indicated that the positive and negative item stems did not provide consistent information regarding a person's attitude and should not be combined into a 20-item instrument. Since the goal was to locate each person on the affective continuum, differences in response styles would present a problem for the combined 20 items. Whereas most developers tend to routinely combine the items, the rating-scale model and UCON procedure provide the necessary empirical support for using a combination of positive and negative items.

Regarding Fishbein's expectancy-value model (Fishbein and Ajzen 1975), the evaluation (*e*) of the favorableness/unfavorableness of the items is initially examined by the developer and then empirically determined as the items are placed (calibrated) on the attitude continuum on the basis of the response data. The belief values (b) initially take on the values of the response scale employed and are then used to locate (i.e., measure) people on the affective characteristic using the latent trait model.

In summary, this section has described some of the features of using latent trait techniques for developing and analyzing affective instruments. The purposes of the techniques were to locate items on a continuum of an affective characteristic and then measure people on the characteristic. The Rating Scale Analysis measurement model was identified for use in conjunction with the UCON procedure for calibrating items and measuring people as well as for examining item and person fit to the model.

Readers are encouraged to read Wright and Masters (1982) book, *Rating Scale Analysis*, for a detailed discussion of the available techniques. Their description of the analysis of the attitude toward drugs items (Ch. 6) is particularly recommended, since it illustrates the technique in the context of data tabled from the CREDIT computer program. The *Rating Scale Analysis* book ($24) can be obtained from the MESA Press, University of Chicago, Department of Education, 5835 South Kimbark Avenue, Chicago, IL 60637.

Before leaving this section, we should note that the Rasch model is called a one-parameter model, since it employs only difficulty estimates (scaled values that represent the "difficulty" of agreeing with the statement). The response thresholds or steps on the response continuum are estimated once and used for all of the statements, and the discriminations at all thresholds are assumed equal. Readers interested in a more complex measurement procedure can examine Samejima's (1969) two-parameter, graded-response model described by Koch (1983). In this model different threshold and discrimination values are estimated for each item. The good news is that Andrich (1978a) and Koch (1983) have demonstrated that both the Rasch one-parameter model (difficulty) and the graded-response, two-parameter (difficulty and discrimination) model can be successfully employed to conduct attitude measurement for Likert-response format scales. The focus in this text will be on the Rasch model. Later, in Chapter 4 the use of the Rasch latent trait model for examining construct validity will be examined (see Gable, Ludlow, and Wolf, 1990).

Semantic-Differential Scales

The semantic differential is a technique that scales people on a set of items called *scales* anchored or bounded on each end with bipolar adjectives.[2]

The rated target is called a *concept* and appears at the top of the set of scales. A sample concept and scale is presented in Appendix A.

The development of the semantic differential technique is credited to Charles Osgood (1952) and is described in the book entitled *The Measurement of Meaning* (Osgood, Suci, and Tannenbaum, 1957). As the title implies, Osgood's research focused on the scientific study of language and the meaning of words. The assumption was that much of our communication takes place through adjectives. That is, we commonly describe teachers as good or bad, fair or unfair, hard or easy; athletes as fast or slow, strong or weak; and school subjects as useful or useless, valuable or worthless. Theoretically, the semantic differential scales bounded by these bipolar adjectives can be represented as a straight-line or geometric *semantic space*. The scales pass through the origin of the semantic space and, as several scales, they form a multidimensional geometric space. When individuals rate a concept on a scale, they are effectively differentiating the meaning of the concept. That is, they are expressing the *intensity* and *direction* of affect they feel is associated with the bipolar adjective scale in relation to the targeted concept.

In Osgood's (Osgood et al., 1957) original work 20 different concepts (i.e., target objects) were rated (i.e., differentiated) by 100 people using 50 sets of bipolar adjectives. After collapsing the data across people and concepts, a 50 × 50 matrix of intercorrelations of scales was generated so that a factor analysis could be performed. The purpose of this analysis was to identify the minimum number of orthogonal dimensions necessary to provide a parsimonious description of the relationships among the scales. In other words, the aim was to explore the common meanings of the adjectives across the 20 different concepts (i.e., the measurement of meaning). As a result of these studies, Osgood identified several dimensions of the semantic space. Three consistently identified dimensions were: evaluative, potency, and activity. Examples of the bipolar adjective pairs defining the dimensions are listed in Table 3–4.

Since Osgood's early work in 1957, several researchers have used the semantic differential technique to scale people with respect to affective characteristics. In the fields of psychology and education, most researchers have concentrated on the evaluative dimension as a measure of attitude toward the stated concept. Interested readers are referred to an excellent volume by Snider and Osgood (1969), which contains discussions of the theory and development, as well as illustrations of several applications of semantic differentials.

Analogous to the Likert technique Equation 3–1 of Fishbein's expectancy-value model takes on the values of −1 and +1 for the evaluation of

Table 3–4. Typical Semantic Differential Bipolar Adjective Pairs

Evaluative	Potency	Activity
good-bad	large-small	fast-slow
beautiful-ugly	strong-weak	active-passive
pleasant-unpleasant	rugged-delicate	excitable-calm
positive-negative	heavy-light	busy-lazy
sweet-sour	thick-thin	quick-slow
valuable-worthless		hot-cold
kind-cruel		
happy-sad		
nice-awful		
honest-dishonest		
fair-unfair		

the favorableness/unfavorableness of the attribute (i.e., e) and the values of the response format employed (e.g., 1–5 or 1–7) for the belief (i.e., b) that the target object or concept rated has the attribute described by the bipolar objectives.

Item Selection

In developing a semantic differential, the first step is to identify the concept or target object you want to measure. Following this, a careful review of all possible bipolar adjective pairs is necessary. Osgood et al. (1957) list the 50 pairs from Osgood's original work (p. 43), as well as several adjective pairs identified through a series of factor analyses carried out in the context of a thesaurus study (pp. 51–61). Additional sources to be examined include Snider and Osgood's book entitled *Semantic Differential Technique* (1969) and Chapter 33 of Kerlinger's *Foundations of Behavioral Research* (1973). Finally, the APA and AERA journals can be perused for studies utilizing various semantic differential scales.

Given a comprehensive list of bipolar adjective pairs, the task is to first select appropriate ones for differentiating the targeted attitude, self-concept, or value concept. In most applications the adjectives will most likely represent the evaluative dimension.[3] Within the evaluative dimension, though, there may be several subdimensions or factors defined by clusters of adjectives. The next step is to select about 10 adjectives that seem logically interrelated. Measuring another evaluative dimension for the same concept would necessitate using another set of about 10 logically interrelated adjectives. The result would be one concept to be rated on 20 bipolar adjective pairs or scales. These scales are then mounted on a single sheet of paper below the concept to be rated. For college students, Osgood suggests the use of a 7-step scale, whereas a 5-step scale may be more appropriate for elementary students (Osgood et al., 1957, p. 85). A set of clear instructions, including examples, is then written and the pilot form of the instrument is completed. An illustrative semantic differential developed by Pappalardo (1971) for measuring the concept "Me as Guidance Counselor" is presented in Appendix A. Note that the form contains 25 scales, several of which are evaluative scales and a few of which serve as potency and activity marker scales.

Analysis of the Semantic Differential

After the semantic differential has been constructed, it is necessary to pilot the form on a representative sample of about 6–10 times the number of people as scales used. The pilot group should be very similar to the group for which the future research is targeted. Clear instructions and clear understanding of the process are necessary to achieve data of good quality.

Given the pilot data, the next step is to conduct a factor analysis as well as item and reliability analyses.[4] The factor analysis (see Chapter 5) will identify the dimensions measured within the set of scales; the item analysis and reliability analysis (see Chapter 4) will further assist in determining which items best relate to the identified dimensions as well as the alpha reliability of the dimensions. If the sample size is smaller than desired, you may wish to run the item analysis first to weed out items with high or low means and low variance prior to the factor and reliability analyses. These techniques are illustrated in Pappalardo's (1971) study, where 25 scales were factored for 161 educational counselors and two evaluative dimensions were derived. Factor I (alpha reliability = .94) was called "Counseling Role," as it was defined by such scales as valuable/worthless, sharp/dull, and good/bad; Factor II (alpha reliability = .90) was defined by such scales as insensitive/sensitive, unpleasant/pleasant, and unfair/fair and was called "Facilitative Role." In another study, reported by Gulo (1975), 676 university students rated the concept "Professor" on about 50 bipolar adjectives. Subsequent factor analysis generated eight dimensions, some of which were as follows: Teaching Dynamism (interesting, colorful, progressive, and active), Acceptance (positive, approving, optimistic, sensitive, and motivated), and Intellectual Approach (objective, aggressive, and direct). The point of these examples is that if only a few scales are included, and they are not homogeneous in meaning, it is possible that the resulting factor structure would produce factors defined by too few scales to generate adequate reliability levels. Thus, it is important to carefully construct the set of bipolar adjective scales so that the clusters of homogeneous scales result in the desired dimensions in the factor analysis.

The semantic-differential technique employs the same *criterion of internal consistency* as the Likert technique for item selection. To meet the criterion, a scale (i.e., item) must correlate well with the attitude score. The resulting item characteristic curves or tracelines are linear in nature as illustrated by the Likert technique tracelines presented earlier in Figure 3–2.

Scoring

After appropriate revisions, the semantic differential will be ready for administration to the research sample. At this point, it is essential that you consider how you will score the form, as this area has caused much confusion and misuse by users of the semantic differential. Lynch (1973) suggested three ways in which semantic differentials may be scored by computing: mean scores on each scale, mean scores on each dimension, and the D statistic. The mean scores on each scale technique has been used to compare two concepts (How I See Myself versus How My Teachers See Me) on a scale-by-scale basis. The problem with this technique is that the scales were selected on the basis of their relationship to some larger dimension of meaning. Common-sense interpretations of the scales, one at a time, ignores the multidimensional nature of the set of adjective pairs as perceived by the respondent. A better approach, then, is to score the scales in a summative manner by creating means on each dimension identified through the factor analysis. Comparisons of pre/post differences or between two concepts for the same dimensions can be carried out with the simple t-test model.

A final technique involves a form of profile similarity, through the use of the generalized distance formula known as the D statistic. Osgood (Osgood et al., 1957) suggested that this statistic be used as a multidimensional measure for quantifying similarity in meaning as it allows us to combine ratings across scales and dimensions to form an index of connotative judgment. The formula can be represented as

$$D^2 = \sum_{i=1}^{n} d_i^2 \qquad (3.2)$$

where D is the distance between the profile of the two concepts, d_i^2 represents the squared difference in the ratings of the two concepts on the ith bipolar adjective scale. The summation indicates that these squared differences are summed across the number of scales, n, used to rate the two different concepts. Simply, this index represents the sum of the squared distances between two concept profiles and can be readily used as a dependent variable representing profile similarity (i.e., small values mean close profiles). Lynch (1973) mentions several studies where this scoring technique has been used for a multidimensional comparison of two concepts. The dependent variables formed in this manner represented such areas as identification (Myself versus My Teachers), idealization (Myself versus How I'd Like to Be), and empathy (How I Fell about Handicapped People versus How I Feel about Non-handicapped People).

In summary, the semantic differential has the potential for being a very valuable technique for scaling people on the evaluative dimension of meaning, since the ratings can be utilized as a generalized index of attitudes toward selected concept targets. It is essential, however, that the scales be carefully selected to represent the desired evaluative dimensions and that a sensible technique be used to score the resulting data. Many researchers are confused by the results of a semantic differential and dismiss the procedure when the problem is not the procedure but the development and understanding of its application.

Fishbein's Expectancy-Value Model: An Illustration

In this chapter we have described how the expectancy-value model provides the framework for standard attitude scaling techniques. An instrument developed by Norton (1984) provides an interesting illustration of how the model can be operationalized using a modified version of Likert's technique. *The Sports Plus Attitude Scale* (SPAS) was designed to measure the attitudes toward physical education of grade 5–8 students. The first step in developing the *SPAS* involved identifying the attributes relevant for student attitudes toward sports. A review of literature, as well as an open-ended questionnaire that asked students about their likes, dislikes, and beliefs with respect to physical education, provided the input for developing the statements.

A pilot study was then conducted where 129 grade 5–8 students first *evaluated each attribute* (*e*) on a 7-point bipolar (i.e., good/bad) evaluative dimension which was bounded by the adjectives "good" (7) and "bad" (1) and included the descriptors "rather good" (6), "slightly good" (5), "don't

Table 3–5.   Sports Plus Attitude Scale

	Physical Scale[a]
Evaluative Attributes	*Belief-Probability Statements*
Endurance	By running during physical education, I will increase my endurance.
Physical Fitness	Physical education does not improve my fitness. (–)
Speed	When I play games during gym. I run faster.
Sports Skill	Skill drills do not make me a better player. (–)
Strength	If I take gym, I will get stronger.

[a]Statements followed by (–) were negative statements which were reverse scored. From Norton (1984).

know" (4), "slightly bad" (3), and "rather bad" (2). The next step involved *obtaining measures of belief strength* (b) which represented the probability that the target object (i.e., physical education) had the stated attribute. To obtain the belief probabilities, Norton (1984) developed another rating form that contained modified versions of the statements used for the initial evaluations of the attributes. These statements were rated on a 7-point scale which ranged from "agree" (7) to "disagree" (1) and included the descriptors "mostly agree" (6), "slightly agree" (5), "don't know" (4), "slightly disagree" (3), and "mostly disagree" (2). Associated with each of the 7 points on the belief scale was a probability that the target object had the attribute. For the 7-point agree/disagree scale the probabilities were as follows: 1.00, .83, .67, .50, .33, .16, and 0. Table 3–5 contains the five statements used for the Physical Education scale in their evaluative and belief (i.e., probability) forms. For example, the students were asked to rate "endurance" on the good/bad scale (e) and the statement, "by running during physical education, I will increase my endurance," on the belief (b) scale.

A student's attitude toward physical education (i.e., the target object) was estimated by multiplying that student's evaluation (e) of each attribute by the belief/probability (b) that the target object had the attribute. Summing the resulting products across the five items yielded a scale score which represented the student's attitude toward physical education as measured by the *SPAS* Physical Scale. Table 3–6 contains a handy chart developed by Norton (1984) for scaling each person using the expectancy-value technique. The row labels represent the 7-point good/bad evaluation (e) rating scale; the column designations list the belief/probability values associated with the 7-point agree/disagree belief (b) rating scale. To

Table 3–6. Table for Calculating Attitude Scores from Evaluation and Belief Ratings[a]

		Agree 7	Mostly agree 6	Slightly agree 5	Belief (b) Probabilities Don't know 4	Slightly disagree 3	Mostly disagree 2	Disagree 1
		1.00	.83	.67	.50	.33	.16	0
Good	7	7.	5.81	4.69	3.5	2.31	1.12	0
Rather good	6	6.	4.98	4.02	3.0	1.98	.96	0
Slightly good	5	5.	4.15	3.35	2.5	1.65	.8	0
Don't know	4	4.	3.32	2.68	2.0	1.32	.64	0
Slightly bad	3	3.	2.49	2.01	1.5	.99	.48	0
Rather bad	2	2.	1.66	1.34	1.0	.66	.32	0
bad	1	1.	.83	.67	.5	.33	.16	0

Evaluations (e)

[a]From Norton (1984).

illustrate the use of the matrix, consider two students. Student 1 evaluates endurance as "good" (7) and "slightly agrees" (5) with the belief "by running during physical education, I will increase my endurance." Student 1 receives an attitude score of 4.69 for this statement. Student 2 exhibits a lower attitude for this particular statement, since the evaluation of "slightly bad" (3) and the belief of "mostly disagree" (2) yield an attitude score of only .48.

As we noted earlier, the item-level attitude scores are summed across the items defining the respective scale. To examine the construct validity of the instrument, factor analysis can also be employed to explore or confirm the item/scale assignments used on the instrument. After such an examination, Norton (1984) reported, the pilot version of the *SPAS* contained three meaningful factors labeled Physical, Emotional, and Social. Alpha reliabilities for these three scales were found to be .75, .77 and .77, respectively. Later development of the final version of the *SPAS* included adding new items to define a fourth factor.

In summary, this section has described techniques for attitude scaling which were developed by Thurstone (1931a, b), Likert (1932), Osgood (Osgood et al., 1957), and Fishbein (Fishbein and Ajzen, 1975). Some recent developments in attitude scaling using latent trait models, as described by Wright and Masters (1982), were also discussed. The techniques were described in the framework of Fishbein's expectancy-value model used to arrive at a single attitude score which represented a person's location on a bipolar evaluative dimension with respect to a target object. Each technique resulted in an attitude score by summing the product of an evaluation of the favorableness/unfavorableness of the attribute stated in the item and the person's belief that the target object is described by the stated attribute. One difference among the techniques was found in relation to how the relative weights were determined and implemented for the evaluation and belief components. Whereas the Thurstone technique employed a separate set of judges to judgmentally determine the location of each item on the *evaluative* dimension, the latent trait, the Likert, and the Osgood semantic-differential procedures allowed the developer to specify the favorableness/unfavorableness (positive/negative) aspect of the statement, and, as such, employed evaluation (e) weights of +1 or −1 in equation 3.1. Further, for the *belief* (b) component of equation 3.1, Thurstone's technique employed weights of 0 and 1 depending on whether or not the respondent selected the statement as a characteristic of the target object. The latent trait, Likert, and semantic-differential techniques employed weights that reflected the response continuum employed in rating the belief that the statement described the target object (e.g.,

5 = strongly agree, 4 = agree, 3 = undecided, 2 = disagree, and 1 = strongly disagree). In a similar manner, the Thurstone technique classified nonendorsement (i.e., selection) of an item as having no relation to the attitude score. On the other hand, the latent trait, Likert, and semantic-differential techniques record the disagreement with a negatively stated item and include the item in the calibration process leading to the attitude score. A final difference described among the techniques was the different item characteristic curves or tracelines resulting from the method of item selection employed.

In selecting an attitude-scaling technique readers should note that techniques attempt to estimate a person's location on a bipolar evaluative dimension with respect to the target object for some affective character-istic. The affective characteristics can include the variables described in Chapters 1 and 2—namely, attitude, self-efficacy values, self-concept, and interests. We now turn to a consideration of the properties (ipsative or normative) of affective instruments that result from the manner in which items are presented in the instrument.

Ipsative Versus Normative Scale Properties

In the previous sections we discussed ways for scaling items and measuring people. Related to this scaling issue is a decision regarding whether the instrument will have ipsative or normative measurement properties. This is a fairly serious decision because the ipsative and normative properties are associated with important practical and psychometric differences. In the sections that follow, we will examine these differences for ipsative and then for normative scales. The definition of each type of scale will be followed by examples of well-known instruments. Finally, we will discuss the practical and psychometric implications associated with ipsative and normative scales.

Ipsative Measures

Cattell (1944) employed the term *ipsative* to describe forced-choice measures that yield scores such that an individual's score is dependent on his/her own scores on other scales, but is independent of and not compar-able with the scores of other individuals (Hicks 1970). The term ipsative (Latin *ipse* = he, himself) was chosen to represent scale units relative to the individual's scores on the other scales on the instrument. This is the case, since *any individual's scores across the scales on the instrument will always sum to the same constant value.* When this is the case, the instrument can be termed "purely ipsative." Variations on the ipsativity of instruments can result in "partially ipsative" instruments, but this discussion will focus on "purely ipsative" measures.

The *Edwards Personal Preference Schedule* (Edwards, 1959) is a good example of a forced-choice format that results in an ipsative measure. The *EPPS* consists of 135 distinct items presented as 255 pairs of items or 450 separate items which yield 15 scale scores. Each scale is defined by nine different items. Eight of the nine items are used three times, and one item is used four times, to yield a total score for each individual of 210 and a maximum scale score of 28. Respondents select one item from each of the 225 item pairs and one point is given to the scale represented by the item. The use of triads on the *Kuder Occupational Interest Survey* (Kuder and Diamond, 1979) and Gordon's *Survey of Interpersonal Values* (1960) illustrates another forced-choice format. In the triad case, each item represents a different scale on the instrument. One of the three items is selected by the respondent as the most applicable (e.g., an interest inventory) or important (e.g., a value-orientation instrument), and one of the remaining two is selected as least applicable or important. Scoring of the triads is usually *2* for most, *1* for blank, and *0* for least. Variations of this scoring system are certainly possible.

An important feature of an ipsative system employing matched pairs or triads is the attempt to deal with biased responses that reflect social desirability (i.e., giving socially acceptable, usually positive, responses) and faking (i.e., intentionally untrue responses). The word *attempt* is appropriate, because it is quite difficult for any self-description instrument to obtain measures that are independent from socially desired or possibly faked responses when the person clearly wishes to portray a certain image through the responses. Actually, the presence of socially desirable responses can be empirically studied, but, as Nunnally (1978) has stated, the techniques are often quite complex. To empirically examine the presence of reliable variance due to socially desired responses, it is necessary to take into account the three components of social desirability: a person's actual state of adjustment, the individual's knowledge of his/her own personal characteristics, and frankness in revealing what the individual knows about himself/herself (Nunnally, 1978, p. 662). Quantifying these areas has proven to be quite difficult for researchers. In some cases, scales specifically designed to measure social desirability—e.g., the Marlowe-Crowne *Social Desirability Scale* (Crowne and Marlowe, 1960)—are administered along with a target instrument, and correlations between the two measures are obtained. Low correlations are supposed to indicate the absence of socially desired

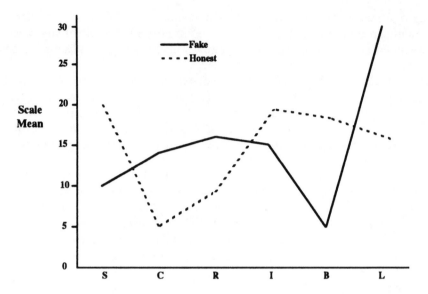

Figure 3–4.   Honest and faking profiles for *SIV* data from 20 education students.

responses in the target instrument. While these attempts are a step in the right direction, they do not fully address the three components of social desirability identified by Nunnally.

The point is that it is difficult to develop instruments that are free from socially desirable or faked responses. Consider, for example, Gordon's (1960) *Survey of Interpersonal Values (SIV)*, which employs 30 triads to measure the following interpersonal values: Support, Conformity, Recognition, Independence, Benevolence, and Leadership. Respondents are asked to consider each triad and select the statement that is "most important" and the statement that is "least important" to their way of life. Several large businesses have used the *SIV* to screen applicants for managerial positions so that potential leaders can be identified. But even the forced-choice format on the *SIV* cannot eliminate socially desirable responses. To support this claim consider the two *SIV* profiles presented in Figure 3–4. Twenty senior-level, teacher-education students took the *SIV* that resulted in the profile labeled "honest." As expected, the prospective teachers were found to be high on Support and Benevolence; and, as typical college students, they were also high on Independence. During the same session the students were given new *SIV* forms and asked to respond as if they were applying for a job in the competitive business world and wanted to give the appearance of a "good manager candidate." The "fake" condition profile clearly indicates that the group is now highest on Leadership, followed by high emphasis on Recognition and Independence. Thus, when people are threatened or simply desire to present a particular image, even the forced-choice format cannot eliminate faked responses.

Practical Considerations

A serious problem with ipsative measures results from the fact that the sum of each person's scores across all scales is the same as any other person's. The implications of this from a practical (e.g., counselor's) viewpoint are different from those for the test developer. The counselor can use such ipsative scores to compare a person's score on one scale with that person's score on another scale but should not compare the scores with other people's scores in a normative sense, since high scores on one scale for an individual must result in low scores on another scale if the scales add to the same total score. At the same time, the counselor must realize that the scoring system has arbitrarily produced some high scores and some low scores, since an individual will appear above or below his or her own average or perhaps near average on all scales, but cannot be high or low on all scales. The use of such an ipsative system is often heartening to high-school counselors and job counselors who find most people to be high in some areas and low in others so that discussions follow easily.

This point can be illustrated by looking again at the "honest" profile in Figure 3–4. The six scales (30 triads) on the *SIV* will always result in 90 total points for each person. Consider the average score to be a horizontal line at 15 on the profile, and note that the ipsative nature of the scale results in an interesting restriction. For all points above the average, an equal number must be present below the average, since the scores all add to 90. The *SIV* was cleverly developed in that it generally reflects two different sets of value types: those people high on Leadership, Independence, and Recognition versus those people high on Support, Conformity and Benevolence. Profiles for individuals or groups tend not to be flat, and *SIV* users are happy. While these are practical considerations, there are some serious psychometric implications resulting from ipsative instruments.

Psychometric Consideration

Clemans' (1966) work in the area of ipsative measures has provided much insight into this area. He has clearly demonstrated that when one correlates

Table 3–7.   Intercorrelations Among SIV Scales[a]

	S	C	R	I	B	L
Support		−.09	.40	−.23	−.12	−.52
Conformity			−.38	−.38	.39	−.45
Recognition				−.30	−.37	−.02
Independence					−.44	.06
Benevolence						−.41
Leadership						

[a]From SIV manual (Gordon, 1960).

the scores on ipsative scales, the resulting intercorrelation matrix will have a larger number of low and negative correlations, because the column sums of the initial covariance matrix must always equal zero (see Clemans, 1966, p. 25).[5] This is a most important consideration for the test developer who is attempting to examine the interrelationships among the concepts measured by the instrument. The correlations partially reflect the nature of the ipsative scoring system and not necessarily the underlying relations between the scales. For example, Table 3–7 contains the intercorrelations among the six scales on the *SIV* reported in the *SIV* manual (Gordon, 1960). Note that there are several negative correlations which, Gordon notes, are "due to the interdependence among the scales resulting in the forced-choice format" (p. 5).

A related problem lies in the area of validating scores on the instrument using regression and multiple-correlation procedures. The presence of multiple correlations where sums of validity covariances between the specified criterion and ipsative variables equals zero can result in sleepless nights for the ipsative test developer. In fact, Clemans says that the ability to predict a specified criterion is not increased by deleting one variable from the ipsative see (Clemans, 1966, pp. 30–33).[6] But as convincing as Clemans' argument is mathematically, much actual test data is yet to be analyzed.

Another psychometric restriction of ipsative instruments is the inappropriateness of factoring the scales on the instrument to examine construct validity (Clemans, 1966; Guilford, 1952). Since the aim of factor analysis is to generate dimensions or constructs which parsimoniously describe the scale covariations, it is not methodologically sound to factor a matrix whose entries partially reflect the psychometric virtues of ipsative scales rather than the true conceptual interrelationships among the scales. In fact, Clemans (1966) illustrates that under some conditions, the ipsative covariance matrix contains the same "variance information" as the residual matrix that results from taking out the first centroid from a normative intercorrelation matrix. If the information gained or lost can be measured by variance, the fact that the first centroid, like the first principal component, accounts for maximum test variation, clearly indicates that the problem of "variance information" is missing in an ipsative matrix.

The area of reliability has also been noted as a problem for ipsative measures (Hicks, 1970). Studies by Scott (1968) and Tenopyr (1968) suggest that the interdependence of the scale scores resulting from the ipsative technique can seriously limit the alpha internal-consistency reliabilities of the ipsative scales as compared to normative scales.

In summary, we have described some of the properties of ipsative scales resulting from the use of forced-choice, paired comparison and triad formats. While the forced-choice format may assist in controlling for response bias in some situations, from a practical and psychometric viewpoint, several problems have been identified that suggest much caution in and justification for the use of such scales.

Normative Measures

Normative scales are more popular than ipsative scales, since they are generally easier to construct and tend to present fewer practical and psychometric problems. On a normative scale, individuals respond to each item separately (i.e., no pairs or triads), with the result that there is no fixed total score across the scales included in the instrument. That is, individuals could have all high scores or all low scores across the scales, since the only restriction is set by the possible score range associated with the response format.

Examples of normative scales are Super's *Work Values Inventory* (1970), Coopersmith's *Self-Esteem Inventory* (1967, 1989) and the *Gable-Roberts Attitude Toward Teacher Scale* (1982).

Practical Considerations

From a practical viewpoint, normative instruments can be easier to develop. Score interpretations could be more difficult, though, if an individual has all high-scale or all low-scale scores, suggesting that the individual probably did not distinguish well among the various items. Such scores could also indicate that the choice of concepts to be measured has resulted in flat profiles. If possible, try to include different types of concepts such that most respondents will display variability in their mean-scale scores.

It is also easier for respondents to fake on normative instruments when they are threatened or stand to gain from presenting a false description of themselves. Coopersmith (1967, 1989) attempted to deal with the issue of faking on the *Self-Esteem Inventory* by including "lie" items with specific determiners such as "always" and "never" (e.g., I am always happy). These items are keyed to a "lie" scale, whose norms can be established to ascertain if some respondents are selecting too many of the lie-scale items as self descriptions. In the end, however, it is quite obvious that both ipsative and normative instruments can be faked. Self-assessments are only as accurate as the individual wishes them to be for a particular purpose. If the situation is nonthreatening and the goal is enhanced self-understanding, the presence of faking should be low.

Psychometric Considerations

From a measurement viewpoint, normative instruments are clearly preferred over ipsative ones. The simple reason is that validity evidence gathered through correlational, regression, or factor-analytic techniques is not hindered by the restrictions set by ipsative properties. That is, obtained relationships among variables can be considered to reflect relationships among the concepts being measured; they are not partially due to the ipsative scoring system.

In summary, normative scales can be easier to construct; they also allow one to avoid the measurement problems associated with ipsative scales.

An Illustration

McMorris (1971) developed normative and ipsative forms of a set of occupational values items (see Appendix B). Note that the footnote in Table 3–8 indicates that each instrument contains 9 items measuring 3 occupational values areas: Favoritism (FAV), Intellectual Laziness (LAZ), and Greed (GRD). Also included are the item/scale assignments.

Appendix B contains the normative form for the 9 items, which are rated on a 5-point Likert scale where 1 = "unimportant" and 5 = "very important." Note that individuals actually rate all items using any points on the Likert scale; the scale score is formed by summing the responses to the appropriate items (e.g., FAV = item 1, 6, and 8).

Table 3–8. Occupational Values Inventory

Means, Standard Deviations, and Correlations
N = 40

	Mean	SD	NFAV	NLAZ	NGRD	IFAV	ILAZ	IGRD
NFAV	7.0	2.0	(.45)					
NLAZ	6.8	2.2	.17	(.54)				
NGRD	6.1	2.6	.60	.18	(.75)			
IFAV	3.2	1.3	.41	.01	.05	(.45)		
ILAZ	2.8	1.5	-.33	.35	-.36	-.59	(.59)	
IGRD	3.1	1.3	-.04	-.45	.36	-.32	-.57	(.55)
SOCD	4.2	.8	.32	.18	.31	.06	-.06	.01

Note: Part N (Normative)—3 items/scale, each scored 1–5.
Part I (Ipsative)—3 triads, scored 0–2.

	Item #
FAV–Favoritism	1, 6, 8; 10, 15, 17
LAZ–Intellectual Laziness	2, 4, 9; 11, 13, 18
GRD–Greed (Unethical Remuneration)	3, 5, 7; 12, 14, 16
SOCD–Social Desirability	19

The ipsative scale was developed using triads where one item from each scale is included in the triad. For example, in the first triad, items 10, 11, and 12 represent the FAV, LAZ, and GRD scales, respectively. Respondents were asked to select a "most" and "least" important statement for each triad. The "most," "blank," and "least" responses were scored 2, 1, and 0, respectively. Thus, consistent with the forced-choice technique, respondents carefully consider the three statements but are only allowed to indicate the one that is "most" important. A final question was also presented after the three triads in a quick attempt to quantify the extent that socially desirable responses could be present.

Forty undergraduate education students responded to both forms. After the scale scores were generated, means, standard deviations, and correlations were calculated for display in the multitrait-multimethod matrix presented in Table 3–8. While Campbell and Fiske's (1959) original discussion of the multitrait-multimethod matrix was based upon using different methods of measurement (i.e., paper survey and peer ratings), displaying the correlations in this manner facilitates our discussion. Employing the strategy to be discussed further in Chapter 4, we see some interesting patterns in the correlations. The Underlined values in the diagonal represent validity coefficients (homotrait-multimethod or same-trait measured by two methods). At first glance these validity coefficients seem low, but each needs to be considered in light of the alpha reliabilities for the respective scales, which appear in parentheses in the main diagonal. The low number of items used for both the normative and ipsative scales appears to have resulted in low reliability levels, except for the normative GRD scale. Later, in Chapter 5, we will note that the maximum validity coefficient is the square root of the product of the reliabilities of the two scales. For example, while the correlation between IFAV and NFAV was .41, the maximum correlation possible was $\sqrt{(.45)(.45)}$ or .45. On the other hand, the maximum correlation possible between the NGRD and IGRD scales is approximately .64 (i.e., $\sqrt{(.75)(.55)}$) and the correlation reported is only .36. Thus, for these scales the normative and ipsative measures using the same items are not highly related. We also noted that the diagonal validity values are higher than their row and column counterparts in the dashed-line triangles (multitrait-multimethod). But it is difficult to interpret the values in the dashed triangles, since they partially represent the ipsative scales which reflect both the occupational-values content and the ipsative-scale properties.

The solid triangles contain the scale intercorrelations (multitrait-homomethod) for the normative and ipsative forms. For the normative form, it makes sense that those individuals with high scores on Greed tended to also score highly on Favoritism ($r = .60$), while the Intellectual Laziness scale was found to have low correlations with Favoritism ($r = .17$) and Greed ($r = .18$). While these correlations make conceptual sense; the correlations from the ipsative scales in the solid triangle are negative and make little sense. This is consistent with Cleman's (1966) statements reviewed earlier regarding ipsative measures.

Finally, the correlations between the scale scores and the indication of social desirability (SOCD) (item 19) are presented in the bottom row of Table 3–8. Consistent with the opinions of proponents of ipsative measures, the ipsative version appears to result in scores that are less related to socially desirable responses in this nonthreatening situation.

In summary, this example, using normative and ipsative forms for the same set of items, has illustrated some of the attributes of ipsative scales. While the validity coefficients were low due to low reliability levels, the reliabilities of the ipsative and normative scales were generally similar, and the extent of variation due to socially desirable responses appeared to be lower for the ipsative scales. The primary point illustrated was generation of negative scale intercorrelations resulting from the ipsative scoring system. We can thus conclude again that, given their extensive practical and psychometric limitations, ipsative scales should be developed with caution and careful justification.

Summary

This chapter has described selected techniques appropriate for scaling items and measuring the affective characteristics of people. Also presented was a comparison of ipsative and normative scales. We turn now to the important topic of examining the validity of affective instruments.

Notes

1. Note that you should have some judges review the positive and negative aspects of the item stems. It could be that a stem you feel is positive could be perceived as negative by the respondent. This would lower the internal consistency reliability of any scale containing this item.

2. Note that previously we have used the term "scale" to represent a cluster of items on a particular instrument. For the semantic-differential technique, we will be consistent with Osgood et al. (1957) and use the term "scale" to represent a single "item."

3. Some researchers do include a few scales from the potency or activity dimensions to see where these scales load in a factor analysis of the total set of scales. In this situation, the

potency and activity scales function as marker scales to facilitate interpretation of the factor structure.

4. Some researchers avoid running the empirical factor analysis and rely solely on judgmental groupings of scales. This can be very risky, since the final groupings of scales should always be empirically determined. See the discussion in Chapter 4 regarding the relationship of content and construct validity.

5. Recall that to generate a correlation matrix the covariances between the variables are normalized (divided by the square root of the product of their separate variances) to get the correlation. That is,

$$r = \frac{COV_{xy}}{\sqrt{VAR_x VAR_y}}$$

6. Since the sum of all scale scores on an ipsative instrument add to the same constant, a common practice has been to delete one of the scales prior to using the scale scores as predictors in multiple regression, in order to reduce the multicollinearity problem.

Additional Readings

Scaling

Airasian, P.W., Madaus, G.F., and Woods, E.M. (1975). Scaling attitude items: A comparison of scalogram analysis and ordering theory. *Educational and Psychological Measurement*, 35, 809–819.

Andrich, D. (1978). Application of a psychometric rating model to ordered categories which are scored with successive integers. *Applied Psychological Measurement*, 2, 581–594.

Andrich, D. (1978). Scaling attitude items constructed and scored in the Likert tradition. *Educational and Psychological Measurement*, 38, 665–680.

Andrich, D. (1988). The application of an unfolding model of the PIRT type to the measurement of attitude. *Applied Psychological Measurement*, 12, 33–51.

Baker, F.B. (1992). Equating tests under the graded response model. *Applied Psychological Measurement*, 16, 87–96.

Bejar, I.I. (1977). An application of the continuous response level model to personality measurement. *Applied Psychological Measurement*, 1, 509–521.

Cicchetti, D.V., Showalter, D., and Tyrer, P.J. (1985). The effect of number of rating scale categories on levels of interrater reliability: A Monte Carlo investigation. *Applied Psychological Measurement*, 9(2), 31–36.

Cliff, N., Collins, L.M., Zatkin, J., Gallipeau, D., and McCormick, D.J. (1988). An ordinal scaling method for questionnaire and other ordinal data. *Applied Psychological Measurement*, 12, 83–97.

Comrey, A.J., and Montag, I. (1982). Comparison of factor analytic results with two-choice and seven-choice personality item formats. *Applied Psychological Measurement*, 6, 285–289.

Dawes, R.M. (1977). Suppose we measured height with rating scales instead of rulers. *Applied Psychological Measurement*, 1, 267–273.

DeCotiis, T.A. (1978). A critique and suggested revision of behaviorally anchored rating scales developmental procedures. *Educational and Psychological Measurement*, 38, 681–690.

Dodd, B.G. (1990). The effect of item selection procedure and stepsize on computerized adaptive attitude measurement using the rating scale model. *Applied Psychological Measurement*, 14, 355–366.

Edwards, A.L., and Ashworth, C.D. (1977). A replication study of item selection for the Bem sex role inventory. *Applied Psychological Measurement*, 1, 501–507.

French-Lazovik, G., and Gibson, C.L. (1984). Effects of verbally labeled anchor points on the distributional parameters of rating measures. *Applied Psychological Measurement*, 8(1), 49–57.

Ivancevich, J.M. (1977). A multitrait-multirater analysis of a behaviorally anchored rating scale for sales personnel. *Applied Psychological Measurement*, 1, 523–531.

King, D.W., King, L.A., and Klockars, A.J. (1983). Bipolar adjective rating scales for self-description: Reliability and validity data. *Educational and Psychological Measurement*, 43, 879–886.

King, L.A., King, D.W., and Lockars, A.J. (1983). Dichotomous and multipoint scales using bipolar adjectives. *Applied Psychological Measurement*, 7, (2), 173–180.

Klockavs, A.J., King, D.W., and King, L.A. (1981). The dimensionality of bipolar scales in self-description. *Applied Psychological Measurement*, 5, 219–221.

Kroonenberg, P.M. (1985). Three-mode principal components analysis of semantic differential data: The case of a triple personality. *Applied Psychological Measurement*, 9(1), 83–94.

Maranell, G.M. (Ed.) (1974). *Scaling: A sourcebook for behavioral scientists.* Chicago: Aldine.

McCormich, C.C., and Kavanaugh, J.A. (1981). Scaling interpersonal checklist items to a circular model. *Applied Psychological Measurement*, 5, 421–447.

Rost, J. (1990). Rasch models in latent classes: An integration of two approaches to item analysis. *Applied Psychological Measurement*, 14, 271–282.

Schwartz, S.A. (1978). A comprehensive system for item analysis in psychological scale construction. *Journal of Educational Measurement*, 15, 117–123.

Wright, C.R., Michael, W.B., and Brown, G.F. (1983). The Ram Scale: Development and validation of the revised scale in Likert format. *Educational and Psychological Measurement*, 43, 1089–1102.

Response Sets

Adkins, D.C., and Ballif, B.L. (1972). A new approach to response sets in analysis of a test of motivation to achieve. *Educational and Psychological Measurement*, 32, 559–577.

Couch, A., and Keniston, K. (1960). Yeasayers and naysayers: Agreeing response set as a personality variable. *Journal of Abnormal and Social Psychology*, 60, 151–174.

Edwards, A. (1958). *The social desirability variable in personality assessment and research*. New York: Hold, Rinehart and Winston.

Gordon, L.V. (1971). Are there two extremeness response sets? *Educational and Psychological Measurement*, 31, 867–873.

Hattie, J. (1983). The tendency to omit items: Another deviant response characteristic. *Educational and Psychological Measurement*, 43, 1041–1045.

Phifer, S.J., and Plake, B.S. (1983). The factorial validity of the bias in attitude survey scale. *Educational and Psychological Measurement*, 43, 887–891.

Schriescheim, C.A. (1981a). The effect of grouping on randomizing items on leniency response bias. *Educational and Psychological Measurement*, 41, 401–411.

Schriescheim, C.A. (1981b). Leniency effects on convergent and non-discriminant validity for grouped questionnaire items: A further investigation. *Educational and Psychological Measurement*, 41, 1093–1099.

Thissen, D., et al. (1983). An item response theory for personality and attitude scales: Item analysis using restricted factor analysis. *Applied Psychological Measurement*, 7, 211–226.

VanHeerden, J., and Hoogstraten, J. (1979). Response tendency in a questionnaire without questions. *Applied Psychological Measurement*, 13, 117–121.

Normative and Ipsative Scale Properties

Bartlett, C.J., Quay, L.C., and Wrightsman, L.S. (1960). A comparison of two methods of attitude measurement: Likert-type and forced-choice. *Educational and Psychological Measurement*, 20(4), 699–704.

Cattell, R.B. (1966). The meaning and strategic use of factor analysis. In R.B. Cattell (Ed.), *Handbook of multivariate experimental psychology*. Chicago: Rand-McNally.

Edwards, A.L., Abbott, R.D., and Klockars, A.J. (1972). A factor analysis of the EPPS and PRF personality inventories. *Educational and Psychological Measurement*, 32, 23–29.

Guilford, J.P. (1952). When not to factor analyze. *Psychological Bulletin*, 49, 26–37.

Heilbrun, A.B., Jr. (1963). Evidence regarding the equivalence of ipsative and normative personality scales. *Journal of Consulting Psychology*, 27, 152–156.

Horn, J.L., and Cattell, R.B. (1965). Vehicles, ipsatization, and the multiple-method measurement of motivation. *Canadian Journal of Psychology*, 19, 265–279.

Horst, P., and Wright, C.E. (1959). The comparative reliability of two techniques of personality appraisal. *Journal of Clinical Psychology*, 15, 388–391.

Sharon, A.T. (1970). Eliminating bias from student ratings of college instructors. *Journal of Applied Psychology*, 54, 278–281.

Tamir, P., and Lunetta, V.N. (1977). Comparison of ipsative and normative procedures in the study of cognitive preferences. *Journal of Educational Research*, 71, 86–93.

Wright, C.E. (1961). A factor dimension comparison of normative and ipsative measurements. *Educational and Psychological Measurement*, 21, 433–444.

Zavala, A. (1965). Development of the forced-choice rating scale technique. *Psychological Bulletin*, 63, 117–124.

4 THE VALIDITY OF AFFECTIVE INSTRUMENTS

The investigation of the validity of an affective instrument addresses the general question: "Does the instrument measure what it is supposed to measure?" Contrary to the thinking of some researchers, a test is not certified once and for all as "valid." Rather, the investigation of validity is an ongoing process. The process continually addresses the appropriateness of the inferences to be made from scores obtained from the instrument (see Cronbach, 1971). That is, validity focuses on the interpretations one wishes to make for a test score in a particular situation. As stated in the *Standards for Educational and Psychological Tests*:

> Validity is the most important consideration in test evaluation. The concept refers to the appropriateness, meaningfulness, and usefulness of the specific inferences made from test scores. Test validation is the process of accumulating evidence to support such inferences. A variety of inferences may be made from scores produced by a given test, and there are many ways of accumulating evidence to support any particular inference. Validity, however, is a unitary concept. Although evidence may be accumulated in many ways, validity always refers to the degree to which that evidence supports the inferences that are made from the scores. The inferences regarding specific uses of a test are validated, not the test itself. (American Psychological Association, 1985, p. 9)

Validity Evidence

Arguments for validity are based upon two types of evidence: judgmental and empirical. The judgmental evidence is generally gathered prior to the actual administration of the items to the target group and consists mainly of methods for examining the adequacy of the operational definition of the affective characteristics in light of its conceptual definition. The empirical evidence is argued after the instrument has been administered to the target respondents so that relationships among items within the instrument, as well as relationships to instruments measuring similar of different constructs, can be examined with respect to the theory underlying the variables measured. In this chapter we will describe the three commonly identified types of validity: content, construct, and criterion-related. Techniques for gathering appropriate judgmental and empirical evidence for each type of validity will also be described and illustrated. Since this text addresses affective characteristics, emphasis will be placed upon content and construct validity.

Content Validity

Definition

Content validation should receive the highest priority during the process of instrument development. Unfortunately, some developers rush through the process with little appreciation for its enormous importance, only to find that their instrument "does not work" (lack of construct validity or internal consistency reliability) when the response data are obtained. The importance of content validity can be seen when its definition is considered in light of the conceptual and operational definitions of the affective characteristics presented in Chapters 1 and 2.

According to Cronbach (1971), content validity is assessed by answers to the question: *To what extent do the items on the test (instrument) adequately sample from the intended universe of content?* We know from Chapter 1 that underlying any affective characteristic is a theoretical rationale and conceptual definition that describes the universe of possible items or content areas to be included in the instrument. Given the conceptual definitions, the developer adopts development procedures that generate the operational definitions described in Chapter 2. The responses obtained from administration of the instrument then reflect these operational definitions and are used to make inferences back to the conceptual definitions underlying the affective characteristics. Thus, unless the instrument developer carefully addresses the process of content validation, interpretation of the resulting data will most likely be meaningless (i.e., lack validity).

Evidence

The evidence of content validity is primarily *judgmental* in nature and is mostly gathered prior to the actual administration of the instrument. Two primary areas become the focus of the evidence of content validity: the conceptual and the operational definitions of the affective characteristics.

Conceptual Definitions. The theoretical basis for the conceptual definitions is developed through a comprehensive review of appropriate literature. Instrument developers must specify and summarize their literature base in the technical manual. This is essential, since the evidence of content validity revolves around judgments regarding the universe of content from which the instrument developers have sampled in developing the instrument.

It is recommended that a panel be established consisting of about five content experts with professional expertise in the area of the affective characteristic under consideration. Appropriate experts could be university professors and/or graduate students from the education or psychology areas. It is essential that the experts be thoroughly grounded in the literature representing the affective characteristic.

The panel of experts should be provided a bibliography and summary of the literature used as a definition of the universe of content. Individually or as a group, the experts can then review the materials and comment on the adequacy of the conceptual definition of the affective characteristic as it relates to the proposed use of the instrument. Simple rating sheets could be developed for this task so that the experts could rate and comment on such areas as comprehensiveness of theory and adequacy of sampling from the content universe. Following this review of the theoretical base, the operational definitions can be addressed.

Operational Definitions. The operational definitions discussed in Chapter 2 are the vehicles by which the developer samples from the universe of content specified by the conceptual definition. It is essential that the operational definitions be reviewed by these same five content experts and their assessment reported in the Technical Manual as evidence that the sampling of items adequately reflects the intended universe of content. Inadequate sampling will necessarily lead to invalid inferences regarding test score interpretations. Put simply, correspondence between the operational and conceptual definitions is essential for content validity.

It is proposed that the judgmental data be obtained in two ways. First, the panel of five experts can be given the operational definitions, such as those contained in Tables 2–1 and 2–2 in Chapter 2. Through group or individual discussion and possibly ratings, the correspondence between the conceptual and operational definitions should be ascertained.

A second judgmental rating exercise can be carried out to examine the extent to which the items truly reflect the content categories specified in developing the operational definitions. This judgmental evidence is best collected from a larger group of content experts. It is suggested that from 15–20 experts who are somewhat knowledgeable in the area of the affective characteristic be used. These experts will not be judging the comprehensiveness of the literature review, so they will not have to have the same high level of credentials as the prior set of experts. Typically, a dedicated group of graduate students or teachers would be ideal judges.

Table 4–1 contains a sample rating form to be used in this exercise. The form begins with instructions regarding the rating task and then lists the definitions of the categories such as those illustrated from Table 2–2. The judges are then asked to (1) assign each item to the category it best fits; and (2) to indicate how strongly (comfortable) they feel about their assignment of the item to the category.

Table 4–2 contains a hypothetical display of data obtained for items 15 and 1 from the *Gable-Roberts Attitude Toward Teacher Scale* (see Table 4–6). For each item, the frequency and percentage of assignment to each category are listed. A criterion level of 90% agreement is recommended for an item to remain in a particular category without revision. After the high-percentage category is identified, the mean "comfort" rating is calculated for *only the items assigned to that category*.

The final step consists of listing the item stems in the order of their ranked "comfort" ratings, as illustrated in Table 4–3. This information summarizes the best items within each category as judged by the content experts. On the basis of the information gathered through the rating procedure, items can be rewritten or added.

Thus far we have described content validation as a judgmental process. It should be noted that some fairly complex empirical procedures are also available. In general, such procedures consist of an analysis of the content expert's sorting of the items into any number of mutually inclusive content categories. These judgmental data are then analyzed to ascertain if there

THE VALIDITY OF AFFECTIVE INSTRUMENTS

Table 4–1. Sample Content-Validity Rating Form

Instructions. The statements that follow are being considered for inclu
(*identify name of the survey*) survey. Please assist us in reviewing the c
the statements by providing two ratings for each statement. The conceptual
definitions of the categories these statements are supposed to reflect as well as
the rating instructions are listed below.

Categories	Conceptual Definition
I. Name of category	Definition
II. Name of category	Definition
III. Name of category	Definition
IV. Name of category	Definition

RATING TASKS
A. Please indicate the category that each statement best fits by circling the
   appropriate numeral. (Statements not fitting any category should be placed
   in Category V.)
B. Please indicate how strongly you feel about your placement of the
   statement into the category by circling the appropriate number as follows:
   3   no question about it
   2   strongly
   1   not very sure

Statements	Categories	Rating
1. (list statements here)	I II III IV V	1 2 3
2.	I II III IV V	1 2 3
3.	I II III IV V	1 2 3
(Continue for all items)		

Table 4–2. Hypothetical Content Validity Ratings for Two Statements

Statement		I	II	III	IV	V
15 Presents the subject so that it	F	1	18	1		
can be understood.	%	5	90	5		
	Mean[a]		2.90			
1 Motivates students to learn.	F		19	1		
	%		95	5		
	Mean		2.78			
(continue for all items)						

[a]Note that the mean rating is calculated for category with the highest percentage only.

Table 4–3. Ranked Mean Ratings for Category II

Statement	Ranked Mean Rating
15 Presents the subject so that it can be understood.	2.90
1 Motivates students to learn.	2.78
(continue for other items)	

are underlying meaningful content categories that reflect the judges' ordering of items. The analysis technique, called *latent partition analysis* (Wiley, 1967), creates a joint-proportion matrix where each entry indexes the proportion of sorters who placed a given pair of items in the same manifest category. This matrix, which is similar to a correlation matrix, is then analyzed to see if there exist latent categories that explain variation in the proportions. (The latent categories can be roughly thought of as "factors" derived from factoring a correlation matrix.) The latent categories are named on the basis of their item content, and the results are used to further refine the content of the items. The feature of such an analysis is that the resulting instrument can be administered to a target group so that a factor analysis of actual response data can be carried out. The beauty of this approach is that the "judgmentally" derived content categories of the content experts can then be compared to the "empirically" derived constructs of the respondents. Since the goal of construct validity, to be presented in a later section, is to provide finer interpretations of the scores on the instrument, it is often the case that the interpretation of the constructs derived through the factor analysis is greatly facilitated by studying how the content experts sorted the items. Readers are referred to two studies which illustrate how the content and construct validity information contributes to the overall validation process, namely, Gable and Pruzek (1972) and Coletta and Gable (1975).

This section has emphasized the importance of establishing the correspondence between the conceptual and operational definitions associated with the affective instrument. Techniques were described for gathering information to defend the argument that the items developed adequately sample from the intended universe of content being measured by the instrument. It was noted that the content-validity argument is mostly based upon judgmental data. Given that arguments for content validity were convincing and that appropriate revisions in the instrument have been made, the basis of the argument now switches from judgmental to empirical data during construct validation.

Construct Validity

Definition

Construct validation addresses the question: *To what extent do certain explanatory concepts (constructs) explain covariation in the responses to the items on the instrument?* Whereas the content-validity argument focused on experts' judgments regarding the adequacy with which the test items reflected specified categories in the content universe, the construct validity argument focuses directly on response-data variation among items to ascertain evidence that the proposed content categories actually reflect constructs. These constructs (or concepts) have been previously specified through the conceptual and operational definitions of the affective characteristic (see Chapters 1 and 2). The argument that the instrument actually measures the construct is only successful when relationships among the items (operation definitions) comprising the instrument, as well as relationships with specified variables from other known instruments, exist in a manner judged to be consistent with the conceptual and operational definitions. Thus, construct validation is *an ongoing process* of testing hypotheses regarding response-data relationships for the items (or scales) of the developing instrument and other, known, instruments. The sections that follow will describe the empirical evidence relevant for arguing the case for construct validity.

Evidence

Evidence of construct validity is gathered by administering the instrument to a *representative sample of respondents for which the instrument was designed.* Empirical analyses of these data are then carried out in the midst of theoretically based logical arguments regarding the existence of meaningful constructs. Six analysis techniques will be described and illustrated —namely, correlations with other variables, factor analysis, the multitrait-multimethod analysis (including confirmatory-factor analysis), causal modeling, Rasch latent trait analysis, and the known-groups procedure.

Correlation

The most commonly employed statistical technique for examining construct validity is correlation (r). Unfortunately, many researchers fail to uncover the richness of this strategy because their analysis strategy is not grounded in the theory underlying the variables. Some researchers continually list correlations between their target instrument and another instrument with no statement regarding the meaning of the correlation. For example, a researcher may state that instrument A correlates .20 with instrument B with no explanation of whether this magnitude of relationship is supportive of construct validity on the basis of the theory underlying the two variables. Many graduate-student Ph.D. proposals and theses merely contain lists of correlations with other measures with no arguments supportive of construct validity.

Simply put, all arguments for construct validity must be based upon theories underlying the variables in question. This amplifies the importance of clear conceptual definitions generated during the process of instrument development (see Chapter 1). It is from these conceptual definitions and their theoretical base that hypotheses are generated regarding the traits measured by the instrument and those from other known instruments. Clearly, the hypotheses need to be stated in advance of gathering the data so that the resulting data can be seen to support or fail to support the proposed relationship (see Carmines and Zeller, 1979; Cronbach and Meehl, 1955). An example from the area of work values will illustrate this point.

Chapter 1 included a brief description of Super's *Work Values Inventory* (1970). While that instrument was in the prepublication stage, Gable (1970) revised and added selected items to the 15 *WVI* scales and studied the construct validity of the revised *WVI* using a sample of 503 grade-11 students from three school districts. The literature on work values was first reviewed to develop a good understanding of the work values concept and also to identify a list of what Cronbach (1971) has called the other "known indicators." These known indicators represent other well-known instruments assessing constructs theoretically related to work values. The *Edwards Personal Preference Schedule* (Edwards, 1959), the *Kuder Preference Record* (Kuder, 1951), *Survey of Interpersonal Values* (Gordon, 1960), and the *Study of Values* (Allport, Vernon, and Lindzey, 1960) were identified. Normative versions of selected scales from the *EPPS* and *SOV* and the complete *KUD* and *SIV* measures were employed. In addition, Super's stated relationship of work values with aptitude, achievement, social class, and sex were examined. Aptitude was measured by *Differential Aptitude Test* (Psychological Corporation, 1982) scores, achievement by the prior year's grades in the content areas. Finally, social class was categorized using the Warner, Meeker, and Eells (1949) 7-point scale based on head-of-household occupation (1 = highest, 7 = lowest); and sex was coded male = 1 and female = 0.

Table 4–4 illustrates the use of correlations to examine construct validity for one of the 15 *WVI* scales labeled "Altruism." Super (1970) had defined Altruism as an orientation toward helping people. Teachers and Peace Corps volunteers would most likely have high Altruism scores. Prior to gathering the actual data, hypotheses were generated on the basis of the theory underlying Altruism and selected scales from the other known measures and variables (e.g., achievement). Table 4–4 contains a listing of the measures/constructs used for analysis of the Altruism scale. Each construct label is followed by a +, 0, or – sign to indicate the direction of the hypothesized relationship suggested by the appropriate theories underlying the variables. Also included are the obtained correlations for the 503 grade-11 students. Given the large sample size, emphasis was not placed upon statistical significance. Rather, the focus became the direction and magnitude of the relationships in light of theoretical expectations.

It is quite clear that the Altruism scale correlated as predicted with several other known measures and variables. For example, people with a high score on the *WVI* Altruism scale tended to exhibit personality profiles with high Affiliation ($r = .47$) and Nurturance ($r = .56$) on the *EPPS*, and high interest in Social Service activities ($r = .53$) as measured by the *Kuder*. Further, they emphasized the interpersonal value of Benevolence ($r = .62$) on the *SIV*, exhibited a general value orientation with high emphasis in the Social ($r = .49$) area on the *SOV*, and tended to be female ($r = -.37$). Also, as hypothesized by Super, levels of Altruism tended not to be related to aptitude and achievement measures or with social class. Thus, evidence was present to support the argument for construct validity of the *WVI* Altruism scale. Considering again the question addressed in a construct-validity analysis, we can now make finer distinctions regarding the interpretation of Altruism as a construct resulting from responses to the *WVI* items. That is, counselors have more evidence for their understanding and interpretation of Altruism, since they know that people with high Altruism scores share certain personality preferences (*EPPS*), interests (*Kuder*), and values (*SIV* and *SOV*) as documented in Table 4–4 and described above.

While these data represent only one sample, they enter into the ongoing process of construct validity to provide additional information for interpretation of the *WVI* Altruism scores. It is the cumulative evidence from several construct-validity studies using different samples of individuals and constructs that allows a researcher to state with some confidence the extent to which certain explanatory concepts (constructs) explain covariation in the responses to the items on an instrument.

Table 4-4. An Illustration of Examining Construct Validity Using Correlations

Instrument	Scale	Direction of Hypothesized Relationship with WVI-Altruism	Correlation[a]
Edwards	Achievement	0	
Personal	Affiliation	+	.47
Preference	Autonomy	0	
Schedule	Change	0	.28
	Dominance	0	
	Nurturance	+	.56
Kuder	Outdoor	0	
Preference	Mechanical	0	
Record	Computational	0	
	Scientific	0	
	Persuasive	0	
	Artistic	0	
	Literary	0	
	Social Service	+	.53
	Clerical	0	
Survey of	Conformity	0	
Interpersonal	Recognition	0	
Values	Independence	0	
	Benevolence	+	.62
	Leadership	0	
Study of Values	Theoretical	0	
	Economic	0	
	Aesthetic	0	
	Social	+	.49
	Political	0	
Differential	Verbal Reasoning	0	
Aptitude	Numerical Reasoning	0	
Test	Abstract Reasoning	0	
	Mechanical Reasoning	0	
	Space Relations	0	
Achievement	English	0	.11
	Math	0	
	Science	0	
	Social Studies	0	
Social Class		0	
Sex[b]		−	−.37

[a]Only correlations greater than .10 have been included: decimals have been omitted.
[b]Sex was coded male = 1 and female = 0.

Factor Analysis

Earlier in this chapter we noted that construct validity addresses the question: "To what extent do certain explanatory concepts (constructs) explain covariation in the responses to the test items?" So far we have discussed two empirical techniques for examining construct validity, each based upon generating correlations between selected variables. For the first technique, we simply correlated the two variables and examined their hypothesized relationship with respect to the theory underlying each variable. In the second technique, we displayed the correlations in a multitrait-multimethod matrix so that we could estimate the amount of trait and method variance present in the correlation coefficients. We will now continue the empirical analysis and turn to the relationships among the items on the instrument to ascertain if there exist constructs that help us explain the covariation among the items. If meaningful covariation among items exists, the clustering of items to form scales on the instrument will be supported. Consider the set of *Gable-Roberts Attitude Toward Teacher Scale* (GRATTS) items displayed in Table 4–5. The original attitude instrument contained 22 items. If a researcher asked what this instrument really measures, one would have to list and describe the 22 items one at a time. For the communication of the intent of the instrument, as well as the reporting of data to users, this would be a very cumbersome and inefficient manner for describing the concepts measured by the instrument. Researchers would ask: "Don't these items reflect a few different aspects of attitude toward teacher?" Obviously, the answer is "yes," and the instrument developer needs to address this question during the process of instrument development. We should note, though, that the factor analysis only assists in identifying clusters of variables (e.g., items) that share variation. Once the factors are named, it is quite appropriate, and some would say essential, to further examine the relationships between the derived factors and other variables. As Nunnally (1978) suggests, the factor analysis serves as a prelude to more extensive examinations of the existence of meaningful constructs.

Exploratory and Confirmatory Analyses. Factor analysis is a method of identifying or verifying, within a given set of items, subsets of those items which are clustered together by shared variation to form constructs or factors. In a purely exploratory analysis, one simply enters the items into the analysis and describes the resulting factors, independent of any preconceived theory of interrelations.

In the case of instrument development, however, factor analysis is used to examine the relationships between the judgmentally developed content

Table 4–5. Gable-Roberts Attitude Toward Teacher Scale Items[a]

The teacher in this course:
1. motivates students to learn.
2. likes his (her) job.
3. is fair in dealing with students.
4. is willing to help students individually.
5. is successful in getting his (her) point across.
6. is interested in students.
7. lacks enthusiasm.
8. tries to cover too much material in too short a time.
9. assigns too much homework.
10. does not make learning fun.
11. is generally cheerful and pleasant.
12. disciplines too strictly.
13. is not interesting to listen to in class.
14. has a sense of humor.
15. presents the subject so that it can be understood.
16. is too structured.
17. is too busy to spend extra time with students.
18. fails to stimulate interest in the subject matter.
19. is not interested in his (her) work.
20. does not evaluate student work fairly.
21. likes students.
22. tests too frequently.

[a]Underlined items are negative item stems and should be reverse scored.

categories and the empirically derived constructs. As such, we are actually testing hypotheses regarding the interrelationships among the items. These derived constructs are examined in light of theoretical predictions that follow from the literature review and of operational definitions of the targeted categories specified during the content validity process. Thus we can, in one sense, consider any factor analysis executed for the purpose of supporting construct validity to be of a confirmatory nature. Methodological differences among various types of factor analysis, however, provide other bases for determining whether the analysis is described as exploratory or confirmatory.

One of the major methodological differences is in the amount of information which is initially specified by the researcher, rather than generated by the analysis. In true confirmatory-factor analysis (CFA), such as that developed for the LISREL computer program (Jöreskog and Sörbom, 1984), the researcher postulates a model which the data are expected to fit. This model describes the number of factors to be derived and which variables are related to each factor. The results of the analysis indicate how well the empirical data actually fit the postulated model. In exploratory factor analysis (EFA), such as principal-component analysis and common-factor analysis, the number of factors and the relationship of items to factors is generally determined by the analysis rather than by the instrument developer's theoretical predictions. Once these factors are derived, the developer must determine whether they are sufficiently similar to the judgementally developed content categories to support the construct validity of the instrument.

Since it has been established that the test developer has formulated hypotheses regarding the number of factors and the items associated with each prior to the factor analysis, either EFA or CFA may be employed and the results interpreted according to these hypotheses. Thus, either type of analysis may be confirmatory in interpretation, if not necessarily so in methodology. For comparisons of exploratory and confirmatory factor analysis results in the study of an affective instrument, see Michael, Bachelor, Bachelor, & Michael (1988) and Welsh, Bachelor, Wright, and Michael (1990).

There are several areas, however, in which CFA provides information superior to that resulting from EFA. These areas include: (1) the ability to yield unique factorial solutions, (2) the definition of a testable model, (3) assessments of the extent to which a hypothesized model fits the data, (4) specific data on individual model parameters to aid in improvement of the model, and (5) the ability to adequately test factorial invariance across groups (Marsh, 1987).

In spite of the advantages of CFA, the choice between the two types of factor analysis often boils down to the researcher's access to and familiarity with the computer programs required to run the various types of analyses. EFA can be run using the widely available SPSSx and SAS computer programs, as well as several others, both on mainframe computers and on PCs. The relative ease with which the data can be processed and interpreted using these programs makes this an attractive option. CFA, on the other hand, is run most often using the LISREL VII (or VI) software, which is not as widely available, is more difficult to run, and is somewhat more difficult to interpret. In order to provide the reader with a choice of methodologies, we will describe the use of principal-component analysis using SPSSx and the maximum likelihood method of confirmatory-factor analysis using LISREL VII. The reader will then be free to choose the method best suited to his or her situation or to use a combination of methods.

Since factor analysis is a complex, but essential technique in instrument development, whichever method is chosen, we will spend considerable time discussing its purpose and general strategy—and will illustrate its use in instrument development. Prior to running either analysis, certain decisions have to be made; then the output has to be clearly understood and properly interpreted within the context of examining the existence of hypothesized constructs. (Interested readers are referred to Tabachnick and Fidell's excellent 1983 book on multivariate statistics for more advanced reading on EFA and to Byrne's (1989) work for CFA.)

Previous instructional experience, as well as reviews of test manuals and journal articles, indicate that the technique of factor analysis is often employed but not always well understood. For this reason considerable emphasis will be placed on factor analysis as a technique for examining construct validity.

Purpose and Strategy. The purpose of factor analysis is to *examine empirically the interrelationships among the items and to identify or verify clusters of items that share sufficient variation to justify their existence as a factor or construct to be measured by the instrument.* That is, the factor analysis technique examines the item-level intercorrelation matrix. Using some complex mathematical procedures beyond the scope of this book, the procedure "decomposes" the correlation matrix into a set of roots (eigen values) and vectors (eigen vectors). These roots and vectors are then appropriately scaled (multiplied together) to generate a matrix, usually called a factor *loading matrix.* Whereas the correlation matrix has the same number of rows and columns as items contained in the instrument, the loading matrix contains the same number of rows as there are items and the same number of columns as there are factors derived in the solution. A similar matrix is produced by different mathematical methods in CFA. The entries in the matrix represent the relationship (usually correlations for EFA and regression weights for CFA) between each item and the derived factor.[1] The EFA instrument developer lists the items defining each factor and ascertains if the empirically identified items that are clustered together share common conceptual meaning with respect to the content of the items. If the items clearly share some conceptual meaning, this concept is described and referred to as a construct measured by the instrument. In CFA, the instrument developer has specified which items will load on each factor according to preliminary research. The results of this analysis indicate how well the empirical data actually conform to these specifications, that is, whether the items actually form the theorized constructs. If either method is successful, it would be unnecessary to inform the researcher that the instrument measures 20 or 22 different things. Rather, the three or four constructs measured by the instrument could be discussed. Thus, factor analysis is a data-reduction technique in that the 20 or 22 items could be described as measuring three or four constructs. The aim of factor analysis, then, is to seek parsimony in the description of the instrument (i.e., to employ a minimum amount of information to describe the maximum amount of variation shared among the variables).

Relationships of Constructs to Content Categories. Readers should carefully note that the constructs which empirically are either identified by the EFA or supported by the CFA, based on the analysis of actual response data, are meant to correspond to the judgmentally specified item clusters or categories examined during the content-validity stage of instrument development. Simply put, the derived constructs of the EFA should ideally reflect the judgmental categories from which the conceptual and operational definitions of the affective characteristic were developed (see Chapters 1 and 2). In the case of CFA, the model representing these constructs should fit the data adequately. For either type of factor analysis, when this is not the case, the instrument's construct validity is in question. For the EFA, two types of problems could occur. First, it could be that the factor analysis did not generate any conceptually meaningful factors. Second, it could happen that meaningful factors were derived but they did not correspond to the judgmental categories. In the first situation, the developer has a very serious problem, since the analysis of actual responses to the items describes what the instrument really measures. Given no clear factors, the developer must reassess the conceptual and operational definitions as well as the process of content validity and, after revisions, gather new response data for a new factor analysis. In the second situation, the developer apparently has an instrument that measures some meaningful constructs. While this is certainly a better situation, the lack of correspondence of the constructs to the judgmental categories needs to be examined. For the CFA, unsatisfactory results would include non-significant factor loadings and low Goodness-of-Fit values, indicating a poor fit of the data to the model representing the hypothesized factor structure. This could be caused by either of the problems mentioned above, the lack of any clusters or clusters which do not match the theoretical framework. In either case, the response of the instrument developer would be the same as to the EFA results. Again, the ideal situation is a clear correspondence between the content and construct validity studies. Falling short of this goal is a signal for problems in the future use of the instrument.

SPSS^x Exploratory Factor Analysis

Initial Decisions. One of the early decisions pertains to the number of respondents needed in relation to the number of variables (items) to be factored. Recommendations regarding the N:p ratio (i.e., number of observations for each variable (N) versus the number of variables (p)) tend to vary based on what text is consulted. For example, Nunnally (1978) suggests a N:p of 10:1, whereas Cattell (1978) uses 6:1, and Everitt (1975) suggests 5:1. Arrindell and van der Ende (1985) have reviewed this topic and provided data to support their argument that high N:p ratios such as 10:1 are not necessary to produce stable factor solutions. It appears that many researchers fail to understand that the issue is really one of *representative* variation for each variable in the sample in relation to variation expected in the population. It is true that N:p ratios less than 10:1 can yield stable factors when various N:p ratios are compared. But the substantive issue to the researcher should be the conceptual meaningfulness of the factor solution in the context of construct validity. Ratios of 10:1 usually result in the representative variation needed to derive conceptually meaningful factors, if they truly exist. It is quite dangerous to recommend that ratios less than 10:1 can be used, because ill-conceived samples of respondents could result in erroneous conclusions about factor structure (i.e., the constructs exist and we failed to describe them adequately). Thus, while Arrindell and van der Ende (1985) may be empirically correct, we will continue to agree with Nunnally (1978) that N:p ratios of 10:1 are highly recommended. At times it is necessary to protect ourselves from potential disasters. Prior to running the SPSS^x program, the researcher has to decide what entries to insert in the diagonal of the correlation matrix, the criterion for the number of roots to be selected, and the method for rotating the derived factors. The researcher has a choice of *what values to insert in the diagonal of the correlation matrix prior to the factoring.* The particular choice made reflects how the researcher wishes to deal with the variances of the items. That is, the total variance (V_T) of an item theoretically consists of common (V_C) and unique (V_U) variance, such that $V_T = V_C + V_U$. Common variance is that portion of the total variance that is shared with the other items; unique variance is that portion that is uncorrelated or not shared with the other variables. The values selected for the diagonal of R (i.e., the correlation matrix) are estimates of the amount of variance shared by the particular item and all the other items (i.e., an initial communality estimate). We should appreciate that the choice of these diagonal values consumed many years of research by psychometricians. Essentially, the decision boils down to two choices, each implies a different application of the mathematical model. The first choice is to leave the 1's in the diagonal of the correlation matrix and carry out a *principal–component analysis*.[2] Operationally, the 1's represent the amount of variance for each variable which has been entered into the factor analysis.[3] The use of 1's in the diagonal means that all of the variance (i.e., common and unique) for each variable has been entered into the analysis and that no distinction is made between common and unique variance in that they are operationally merged together. The second approach consists of inserting squared multiple correlations (SMCs) into the diagonal of the correlation matrix prior to the factoring procedure. These SMCs represent an estimate of how much of the variance of each item is shared with the set of remaining items (i.e., common variance). The SMCs are known to be good initial estimates of the common portion of variance in each item. Thus the procedure attempts to distinguish between common and unique variance and is called a *common-factor analysis*. Some researchers favor this approach since they feel that much of the error variance (noise) in the analysis has been removed. Operationally, the resulting factor structure from the principal component and common-factor analyses will most often be quite similar. Developers should run both and compare the results.

The second decision pertains to the criterion for the *number of factors to be extracted from the solution*. Two commonly followed practices are possible. The first criterion employs a procedure developed by Guttman (1953) and popularized by Kaiser (1958) and is known as "Kaiser's criterion." When 1's have been inserted in the diagonal for a principal-component analysis, all factors with eigenvalues (roots) greater than or equal to 1.0 (i.e., the unity criterion) are retained (Rummell, 1970). The rationale for this criterion is that we know that the contribution of each item to the total variance in the solution is 1 (i.e., its value in the diagonal of R). Also, we will later illustrate how summing the squares of the factor loadings (correlations) associated with each factor tells us how much variance the factor accounts for in the solution. Thus, the unity criterion specifies that only factors accounting for as much variance as a single item should be retained (Comrey, 1978). A second criterion is employed when SMCs have been inserted into the diagonal of R (i.e., common-factor analysis). In this situation, factors associated with roots greater than or equal to zero are extracted in the solution. Comrey notes that a common-factor analysis with a zero-root criterion will lead to more factors retained than a principal-component analysis employing the unity criterion. In practice, instrument developers should try both procedures and ascertain which yields a more meaningful solution in relation to the content categories examined in the content validity phase.

The final decision pertains to the *choice of rotation procedures*. (Rotation of the factor matrix will become clearer when the illustration is presented in a later section.) To understand the need for rotation of the factor matrix, we must realize that the underlying factor structure that provides the parsimonious description of the correlation matrix exists in a geometric space. That is, the clusters of items can be geometrically presented (i.e., each item is a point in a geometric space), but we must find a solution (i.e., a reference system) that allows us to view the clusters in a clear and meaningful manner. The factors in the initial factor matrix are actually axis systems (x and y axes), in the geometric sense, and can be rotated to obtain a clearer picture of where the clusters of items (i.e., points in space) are in the geometric space. The closer we can get a cluster of items to a particular axis, the more the cluster will contribute to the naming of the factor. To understand this point, imagine yourself standing in the corner of a room. The three-dimensional room actually has an x, y, and z axis. Pretend there is a cluster of about 10 pingpong balls (items) hanging from the ceiling forming the shape of a large ellipse. To name the cluster you need to assign it in the simplest two-dimensional case to the right wall (y axis) or the floor (x axis). Since the ellipse is not really near the wall or floor, you envision rotating the room so that the ellipse gets closer to the wall and farther away from the floor. Note that you kept the wall and floor at right angles. In another situation, you might have two ellipses, neither of which are really near the wall or floor. The optimal way to get the floor and wall nearer to the two ellipses may be to allow the wall and floor to have less than a right angle (i.e., an oblique angle).

When we rotate a factor matrix in an attempt to locate clusters of items nearer to an axis and keep the axes at right angles, we have performed an *orthogonal rotation* called a *varimax rotation* (Kaiser, 1958). This procedure keeps the axes (factors) independent or not related. An *oblique rotation* allows the axes to collapse so that the derived factors are not independent but correlated to some extent. It is recommended that instrument developers run both varimax and oblique rotations to see which results in a more meaningful solution. The principal of rotating the factor matrix will become clearer when actual data are used to illustrate the technique in the next section.

A final comment regarding varimax and oblique rotations is in order. Some researchers have become confused after running a varimax rotation—they operationally state that their derived factors are now uncorrelated. It is the axis system that remains uncorrelated. When, in order to name a factor, one selects those items correlating above, say, .40 with the factor, the resulting scale scores formed by summing responses to the selected

items are not orthogonal, but usually have moderate correlatio
the derived factors are orthogonal, but the scale scores used to o
the factors are not orthogonal.

Another point of confusion to many researchers is the use of the *factor scores*. In most cases, developers select items that load highly on t factor and sum individuals' responses to the items to generate "scores on the factor." It is an error to report these scores as factor scores; these scores should always be referred to as scale scores or "scores on the items defining the factor." True factor scores are formed by combining information from the factor-loading matrix with other matrices we are not discussing to yield a new matrix with the same number of rows as individuals and columns as factors. The factor-score matrix is like the original raw-data matrix, which had the same number of rows as individuals and columns as items, except that the columns no longer reflect the number of items, because a data reduction technique (factor analysis) has been carried out. Thus, each person has a new score on each factor, and these data could be entered into a new analysis, such as regression, where the factor scores would be predictors. We will not be addressing this procedure further in this volume. Simply put, when you sum across items defining a factor, do not call the result a factor score; it is a *scale score*. See an article by Glass and Maguire (1966) entitled "Abuses of factor scores" for a technical discussion of this point.

Computer Output: Exploratory Factor Analysis

The 22-item *Gable-Roberts Attitude Toward Teacher Scale* partially presented in Table 2–2 will be used to illustrate how exploratory factor analysis (EFA) can be used to examine construct validity. Since the analysis of computer output is often complex, actual computer output from the SPSS[x] package will be discussed. While the mainframe version of SPSS[x] was used for this example, the program lines and output for the PC version are nearly identical. (It should be noted, however, that EFA can be agonizingly slow to run on many PC's when there are more than 20 or so items to be factored.) Table 4–5 contains the 22 attitude items, which were rated on a 5-point Likert scale (strongly agree, 5; agree, 4; uncertain, 3; disagree, 2; strongly disagree, 1). The underlined item numbers indicate negative item stems which were reverse scored (i.e., 5 = 1; 4 = 2; 2 = 4; 1 = 5) prior to the analysis so that high scores would reflect positive attitudes. The scale was administered to 695 grade-11 students who rated six social studies teachers. Table 4–6 contains the EFA output.[4] For instructional purposes

Table 4–6. SPSS^x Principal Components Analysis followed by Varimax and Oblique Rotations

---

4	RECODE	V7 TO V10 V12 V13 V16 TO V20 V22 (5 = 1) (4 = 2) (3 = 3) (2 = 4) (1 = 5)
5	VAR LABELS	V1 MOTIVATES STUDENTS TO LEARN/
6		V2 LIKES JOB/
7		V3 IS FAIR IN DEALING WITH STUDENTS/
8		V4 IS WILLING TO HELP STUDENTS INDIVID./
9		V5 IS SUCCESSFUL IN GETTING POINT ACROSS
10		V6 IS INTERESTED IN STUDENTS/
11		V7 LACKS ENTHUSIASM/
12		V8 TRIES TO COVER TOO MUCH IN A SHORT TIME/
13		V9 ASSIGNS TOO MUCH HOMEWORK/
14		V10 DOES NOT MAKE LEARNING FUN/
15		V11 IS GENERALLY CHEERFUL AND PLEASANT/
16		V12 DISCIPLINES TOO STRICTLY/
17		V13 IS NOT INTERESTING TO LISTEN TO/
18		V14 HAS A SENSE OF HUMOR/
19		V15 PRESENTS SUBJECT ... CAN BE UNDERSTOOD/
20		V16 IS TOO STRUCTURED/
21		V17 IS TOO BUSY TO SPEND TIME WITH STUDENTS/
22		V18 FAILS TO STIMULATE INTEREST IN SUBJECT/
23		V19 IS NOT INTERESTED IN HIS (HER) WORK /
24		V20 DOES NOT EVALUATE STUDENT WORK FAIRLY/
25		V21 LIKES STUDENTS/
26		V22 TESTS TOO FREQUENTLY/
27	FACTOR	VARIABLES = V1 TO V22/
28		PRINT = DEFAULT UNIVARIATE CORRELATION/
29		ROTATION = VARIMAX/
30		ROTATION = **OBLIMIN**/
31		PLOT = EIGEN/

---FACTOR ANALYSIS---

ANALYSIS NUMBER 1 LISTWISE DELETION OF CASES WITH MISSING VALUES

	MEAN	STD DEV	LABEL
V1	3.55396	1.13481	MOTIVATES STUDENTS TO LEARN
V2	4.03165	1.01807	LIKES JOB
V3	3.88633	1.11708	IS FAIR IN DEALING WITH STUDENTS
V4	3.92518	1.00008	IS WILLING TO HELP STUDENTS INDIVID.
V5	3.78417	1.10254	IS SUCCESSFUL IN GETTING POINT ACROSS
V6	3.91079	1.02734	IS INTERESTED IN STUDENTS
V7	4.01439	1.10008	LACKS ENTHUSIASM
V8	3.51223	1.28595	TRIES TO COVER TOO MUCH IN A SHORT TIME
V9	4.13237	1.18213	ASSIGNS TOO MUCH HOMEWORK
V10	3.59856	1.27320	DOES NOT MAKE LEARNING FUN
V11	3.80432	1.17820	IS GENERALLY CHEERFUL AND PLEASANT
V12	4.04604	1.06322	DISCIPLINES TOO STRICTLY

Table 4–6.   (Cont.)

---FACTOR ANALYSIS---

	MEAN	STD DEV	LABEL
V13	3.68777	1.26994	IS NOT INTERESTING TO LISTEN TO
V14	3.98273	1.05592	HAS A SENSE OF HUMOR
V15	3.71511	1.12836	PRESENTS SUBJECT . . . CAN BE UNDERSTOOD
V16	3.81151	1.13136	IS TOO STRUCTURED
V17	3.82734	1.09181	IS TOO BUSY TO SPEND TIME WITH STUDENTS
V18	3.67914	1.16471	FAILS TO STIMULATE INTEREST IN SUBJECT
V19	4.05180	1.08841	IS NOT INTERESTED IN HIS (HER) WORK
V20	3.76835	1.12202	DOES NOT EVALUATE STUDENT WORK FAIRLY
V21	3.96978	1.08192	LIKES STUDENTS
V22	4.10072	1.14695	TESTS TOO FREQUENTLY

NUMBER OF CASES = 695

CORRELATION MATRIX:

	V1	V2	V3	V4	V5	V6	V7
V1	1.00000						
V2	.33402	1.00000					
V3	.50214	.40861	1.00000				
V4	.46952	.44955	.57279	1.00000			
V5	.52872	.38479	.53226	.49629	1.00000		
V6	.46144	.45734	.56871	.65405	.48547	1.00000	
V7	.46915	.41902	.45863	.47772	.44094	.55320	1.00000
V8	.28318	.18241	.45787	.33012	.37688	.41638	.33295
V9	.31583	.30781	.50571	.41060	.32156	.49738	.39632
V10	.52812	.21992	.49267	.41659	.47093	.45178	.45576
V11	.44114	.42562	.52281	.47793	.47014	.53792	.44687
V12	.37771	.32479	.50546	.48838	.36741	.55914	.45525
V13	.42115	.19378	.41678	.32762	.43857	.39720	.38897
V14	.40001	.31952	.43810	.43814	.42504	.47942	.41329
V15	.51616	.27253	.48298	.44205	.59217	.48893	.43398
V16	.27561	.22161	.37523	.36448	.26653	.42809	.32635
V17	.40876	.30179	.46945	.53845	.34845	.48725	.39917
V18	.48898	.22610	.43153	.36903	.42513	.44690	.40509
V19	.31155	.48356	.41253	.41658	.35154	.50413	.45909
V20	.42911	.27764	.51468	.43140	.39632	.48331	.41129
V21	.41737	.43519	.56704	.53592	.43422	.66131	.45194
V22	.33126	.28232	.44193	.39098	.33627	.49067	.36087

	V8	V9	V10	V11	V12	V13	V14
V8	1.00000						
V9	.51173	1.00000					
V10	.45668	.45756	1.00000				
V11	.36583	.43141	.53446	1.00000			
V12	.42746	.53397	.42987	.46386	1.00000		

Table 4–6.   (Cont.)

---FACTOR ANALYSIS---

V8	V9	V10	V11	V12	V13	V14
V13	.41483	.36351	.53906	.45025	.44713	1.00000	
V14	.36626	.35738	.46107	.58218	.49613	.46018	1.00000
V15	.38771	.36644	.54013	.50536	.42412	.50196	.54250
V16	.40023	.45933	.32952	.32901	.42648	.35913	.35550
V17	.34839	.39173	.40927	.40159	.52323	.39962	.36487
V18	.40428	.38881	.54072	.44244	.41222	.48745	.41493
V19	.31251	.34855	.31761	.41580	.42503	.35990	.41828
V20	.37596	.41533	.43510	.41255	.47156	.37288	.38337
V21	.36534	.43463	.43052	.52663	.50351	.39164	.55072
V22	.45247	.50027	.34151	.38354	.52673	.37281	.44165

	V15	V16	V17	V18	V19	V20	V21
V15	1.00000						
V16	.33149	1.00000					
V17	.35652	.36790	1.00000				
V18	.54763	.33239	.42775	1.00000			
V19	.36284	.30165	.45982	.41096	1.00000		
V20	.40646	.39803	.44015	.44032	.42989	1.00000	
V21	.46034	.35791	.44813	.39251	.50792	.48326	1.00000
V22	.34175	.44661	.40053	.31438	.40212	.41788	.50409

	V22
V22	1.00000

EXTRACTION 1 FOR ANALYSIS 1, PRINCIPAL-COMPONENTS ANALYSIS (PC)
INITIAL STATISTICS:

VARIABLE	COMMUNALITY	FACTOR	EIGENVALUE	PCT OF VAR	CUM PCT
V1	1.00000	1	9.98085	45.4	45.4
V2	1.00000	2	1.29887	5.9	51.3
V3	1.00000	3	1.24819	5.7	56.9
V4	1.00000	4	.81549	3.7	60.7
V5	1.00000	5	.77930	3.5	64.2
V6	1.00000	6	.69598	3.2	67.4
V7	1.00000	7	.63075	2.9	70.2
V8	1.00000	8	.62395	2.8	73.1
V9	1.00000	9	.59229	2.7	75.8
V10	1.00000	10	.57035	2.6	78.3
V11	1.00000	11	.53713	2.4	80.8
V12	1.00000	12	.50536	2.3	83.1
V13	1.00000	13	.47680	2.2	85.3
V14	1.00000	14	.45936	2.1	87.3
V15	1.00000	15	.40372	1.8	89.2
V16	1.00000	16	.38981	1.8	90.9

Table 4–6.　(Cont.)

--FACTOR ANALYSIS---

VARIABLE	COMMUNALITY	FACTOR	EIGENVALUE	PCT OF VAR	CUM PCT
V17	1.00000	17	.37747	1.7	92.7
V18	1.00000	18	.35257	1.6	94.3
V19	1.00000	19	.34239	1.6	95.8
V20	1.00000	20	.33943	1.5	97.4
V21	1.00000	21	.32478	1.5	98.8
V22	1.00000	22	.25517	1.2	100.0

```
9.981 +   •
      |
      |
      |
      |
      |
      |
      |
      |
      |
  E   |
  I   |
  G   |
  E   |
  N   |
      |
  V   |
  A   |
  L   |
  U   |
  E   |
  S   |
      |
      |
      |
      |
      |
      |
      |
      |
1.248 +       •   •
      |
 .696 +           •   •   •
 .459 +                       •   •   •   •   •   •   •
 .255 +                                           •   •   •   •   •   •   •   •
 .000 + - + - + - + - + - + - + - + - + - + - + - + - + - + - + - + - + - + - + - + - +
          1   2   3   4   5   6   7   8   9  10  11  12  13  14  15  16  17  18  19  20  21  22
```
PC EXTRACTED 3 FACTORS.

Table 4–6.   (Cont.)

17 JUN 85 FACTOR ANALYSIS AND RELIABILITY
17:39:17 UNIVERSITY OF CONNECTICUT IBM 3081 D MVS SP1.3.0

---FACTOR ANALYSIS---

FACTOR MATRIX:

	FACTOR 1	FACTOR 2	FACTOR 3
V1	.65850	−.26557	−.28389
V2	.52925	.44234	−.41757
V3	.75433	.04952	−.04468
V4	.71484	.22385	−.20053
V5	.67081	−.22324	−.30677
V6	.78465	.23363	−.07728
V7	.67409	.06972	−.18765
V8	.60234	−.12786	.43060
V9	.65537	.11829	.39193
V10	.69684	−.41038	.02750
V11	.71883	−.05751	−.15316
V12	.71880	.14940	.23426
V13	.64168	−.37598	.11884
V14	.68652	−.08070	−.04561
V15	.70055	−.37676	−.15436
V16	.56396	.10633	.43609
V17	.65554	.13770	.06640
V18	.65951	−.35909	.00791
V19	.63322	.30407	−.12795
V20	.66511	.03363	.10088
V21	.74020	.23141	−.08499
V22	.63872	.22423	.35940

FINAL STATISTICS:

VARIABLE	COMMUNALITY	FACTOR	EIGENVALUE	PCT OF VAR	CUM PCT
V1	.58474	1	9.98085	45.4	45.4
V2	.65013	2	1.29887	5.9	51.3
V3	.57346	3	1.24819	5.7	56.9
V4	.60132				
V5	.59393				
V6	.67624				
V7	.49447				
V8	.56457				
V9	.59711				
V10	.65475				
V11	.54348				
V12	.59387				
V13	.56723				
V14	.47990				

Table 4-6.   (Cont.)

---FACTOR ANALYSIS---

VARIABLE COMMUNALITY FACTOR EIGENVALUE PCT OF VAR CUM PCT

V15	.65655
V16	.51954
V17	.45310
V18	.56396
V19	.50980
V20	.45368
V21	.60866
V22	.58741

VARIMAX ROTATION 1 FOR EXTRACTION 1 IN ANALYSIS 1—KAISER
NORMALIZATION.
   VARIMAX CONVERGED IN   7 ITERATIONS.
ROTATED FACTOR MATRIX:

	FACTOR 1	FACTOR 2	FACTOR 3
V1	.66664	.36561	.08168
V2	.08077	.80159	.03265
V3	.42838	.48970	.38749
V4	.30834	.65785	.27107
V5	.64720	.41113	.07763
V6	.31412	.63882	.41167
V7	.39809	.53178	.23065
V8	.36011	.03972	.65827
V9	.21374	.24371	.70145
V10	.72699	.13262	.32962
V11	.51392	.46029	.25981
V12	.26537	.38326	.61365
V13	.64603	.07370	.38006
V14	.48682	.37020	.32537
V15	.74631	.25211	.18974
V16	.15728	.16011	.68496
V17	.27548	.42853	.43997
V18	.66998	.15332	.30262
V19	.18090	.62208	.30016
V20	.35243	.35114	.45407
V21	.29077	.61588	.38053
V22	.13063	.31715	.68539

FACTOR-TRANSFORMATION MATRIX:

	FACTOR 1	FACTOR 2	FACTOR 3
FACTOR 1	.60399	.57699	.54980
FACTOR 2	−.76164	.62104	.18495
FACTOR 3	−.23473	−.53046	.81457

Table 4–6.   (Cont.)

---FACTOR ANALYSIS--

OBLIMIN ROTATION 2 FOR EXTRACTION 1 IN ANALYSIS 1— KAISER
NORMALIZATION.
   OBLIMIN CONVERGED IN 14 ITERATIONS.
PATTERN MATRIX:

	FACTOR 1	FACTOR 2	FACTOR 3
V1	.18694	−.74275	−.15721
V2	.84449	.03665	−.06275
V3	.32759	−.33635	.27312
V4	.57079	−.19614	.15875
V5	.24317	−.71271	−.15985
V6	.51869	−.16407	.32562
V7	.41545	−.33931	.09288
V8	−.20071	−.24171	.65933
V9	.05565	−.01529	.73990
V10	−.13731	−.77983	.13915
V11	.29739	−.48523	.09596
V12	.21139	−.08350	.60551
V13	−.18858	−.67379	.23129
V14	.19315	−.44626	.19119
V15	.01696	−.82687	−.04455
V16	−.01561	.03642	.74675
V17	.29447	−.14101	.39165
V18	−.09234	−.71410	.12397
V19	.56287	−.03533	.23872
V20	.18452	−.24426	.39022
V21	.50704	−.14815	.29849
V22	.16351	.09437	.74139

STRUCTURE MATRIX:

	FACTOR 1	FACTOR 2	FACTOR 3
V1	.47133	−.74054	.33968
V2	.80249	−.32187	.25131
V3	.59293	−.64474	.59449
V4	.72531	−.55296	.49676
V5	.51249	−.73524	.34224
V6	.72443	−.59156	.62472
V7	.61070	−.58613	.45078
V8	.17362	−.52328	.71730
V9	.35623	−.46240	.77067
V10	.28194	−.79493	.52855
V11	.56198	−.67869	.49009
V12	.49052	−.52682	.73688
V13	.21771	−.71740	.54001
V14	.47731	−.64525	.52179
V15	.38531	−.80943	.43281

Table 4–6.   (Cont.)

--FACTOR ANALYSIS---

FACTOR 1	FACTOR 2	FACTOR 3	
V16	.26355	-.38133	.71983
V17	.51563	-.50140	.58870
V18	.29019	-.74155	.49379
V19	.67404	-.43397	.48206
V20	.45331	-.55250	.60243
V21	.69459	-.55475	.58391
V22	.41349	-.40394	.75253

FACTOR CORRELATION MATRIX:

	FACTOR 1	FACTOR 2	FACTOR 3
FACTOR 1	1.00000		
FACTOR 2	-.46684	1.00000	
FACTOR 3	.39660	-.56917	1.00000

we will proceed through the output and illustrate how the EFA information can be used to examine construct validity.

Item Stems.   On page 114 the output presents the item stems and the SPSS^x procedure lines needed to run the principal-component analysis followed by varimax and oblique rotations. Note that negative item stems have been reverse scored by the recode statement.

Means and Standard Deviations.   The item means (after reverse scoring of negative item stems) and standard deviations on page 114 seem typical for such attitude items, and sufficient variability in responses appears to be present. If the means were near either extreme on the response scale and the standard deviations were low, the resulting correlations between items would tend to be low and hinder a meaningful factor analysis.

Interitem Correlation.   The interitem correlations (pages 115–116) indicate that several items share moderate amounts of variation, but one cannot identify clusters of items that appear to relate to each other while not relating to other items not in the cluster. Clearly, such an eyeball approach (inneroccular procedure) to factor analysis would be difficult, especially with a large number of items.

Eigenvalues and the Variance Accounted For.   We turn next to page 116, which lists the eigenvalues and the percent of variance accounted for by each derived factor in the solution. The eigenvalues or lambdas (λ) represent the roots referred to earlier. Employing the unity criterion results in three factors being extracted. The size of the root is directly related to the importance of the derived factor, because the sum of the roots will equal the total amount of variance entered into the factor analysis. This amount of variance is actually the sum of the diagonal entries in the correlation matrix that was factored. In this example, the principal-component analysis uses 1's in the diagonal of the original correlation matrix. These 1's represent the amount of variance for each item that is entered into the analysis. Thus, the sum of the diagonal entries in the correlation matrix, R (i.e., the trace of R), equals 22 (the number of items) and represents the total variance in the solution. (In a common-factor analysis squared multiple correlations are inserted in the diagonal of R so that the trace of R is less than the number of items.) Since the sum of the roots equals the sum of the diagonal entries in R, the amount of variance accounted for by each factor *prior to rotation* is obtained by dividing the root by the trace of R. Thus, in our example, $9.98 \div 22 = .454$, indicating that 45.4% of the variance has been accounted for by Factor I *prior to rotation*. Also, note that the output indicates that the three-factor solution has accounted for 56.9% of the total variance.

Number of Factors.   The number of factors derived by the solution is operationally defined as the number of factors associated with eigenvalues or roots greater than 1 (three factors in this case). While the default option in most computer programs will use the unity root criterion, researchers can also specify the number of factors to be extracted. It is recommended that initially the unity criterion be employed, because forcing the number of factors is sometimes a debatable procedure. After examining the initial factor solution, some researchers attempt to extract a specified number of factors. The procedure is defended as an attempt to force a solution hypothesized by the developer; other researchers feel this may tend to artificially create the intended factor structure.

A second option available for determining the number of factors is called the *scree test*. This procedure, suggested by Cattell (1966), involves plotting the latent roots (y axis) against the factor number (x axis) so that the shape of the resulting curve can be examined. The point (factor number) at which the curve stops decreasing and straightens out is taken to indicate the maximum number of factors to be extracted in the solution. Cattell suggests that factors beyond this point represent "factorial litter" or *scree* ("scree" is the term applied to the small rocky debris found at the bottom of a rocky slope). While the scree test and Kaiser criterion will yield quite similar results, researchers may wish to examine both criteria. Page 117 of the output illustrates the scree test for our attitude items. Note that the scree test and the unity criterion both suggest a three-factor solution.

Initial Communality. To the left of the eigenvalue display (page 116) appears a listing of estimated communalities (EST COMMUNALITY) all of which have values of 1. Communalities represent the amount of variance in each item accounted for by the solution. The values on page 116 represent the communality estimates *prior* to the analysis, and thus represent the diagonal entries in R or the total amount of variance entered into the solution for each variable. Since we are using a principal-component analysis, all of the values are 1.

Unrotated Factor Matrix. The next matrix (FACTOR MATRIX, page 118) represents the derived factor-loading matrix prior to rotation. This matrix has the same number of rows as items and columns as the number of derived factors. The entries represent correlations between each item and the derived factor, so we can attempt to name the factors by looking at items with the highest correlations. If we do this, we see that the matrix is not generally interesting or useful, since, by design, the first factor (principal component) contains most of the variance (i.e., 45.4%). Since the entries in the matrix are correlations, we could generate the sum of the squared entries in Factor I and thus see that the value would equal the first eigenvalue, 9.98.

Final Communalities. Since this unrotated matrix tells us little about the content of the factors, we proceed in the output to pages 118–119, which contain a listing (COMMUNALITY) of the final communalities resulting from the solution. These values are calculated as the sum of the squared correlations in each row of the factor matrix on pages 118–119 the varimax rotated matrix on page 119. For example, .5847 or 58.5% of the variance in item 1 was accounted for by the factor solution.

Varimax Rotation. We now turn to a focal point in the analysis, the *varimax rotated factor matrix* (ROTATED FACTOR MATRIX), usually labeled F, on page 119. Prior to discussing the entries in the F matrix, we need to note what the rotation process accomplishes. Recall that the unrotated factor matrix on page 118 contained many high entries in Factor I and that the other factors contained few large entries. Since we name a

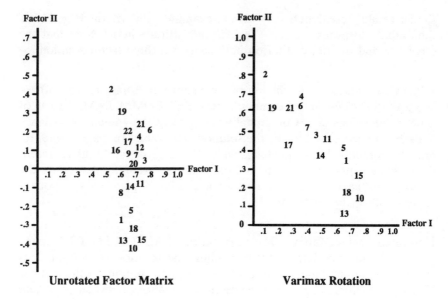

Figure 4–1.   Unrotated and varimax rotated factor matrix plots.

factor by describing the item content for those items correlating highly with the factor, it is evident that the unrotated matrix would always lead to one overall factor determined by most of the items and some other generally uninterpretable factors. Thus, we rotate the factors in a geometric sense to try and uncover a clearer factor structure. To understand the rotation concept, note that two factors at a time can be plotted in a geometric space as is illustrated in Figure 4–1. Items loading .40 or above on either Factor I or Factor II have been plotted for the unrotated and rotated matrices. In a varimax rotation, the axis system remains at right angles (90°), which implies that the factors are orthogonal or independent. The correlations listed under Factors I and II in the factor matrix are then the coordinates to be plotted. For example, in the varimax rotated matrix, item 1 has coordinates of .67 "over" and .37 "up," with axes I and II, respectively. When we observe the factor structure exhibited in the unrotated and rotated matrices, it is obvious why the unrotated matrix is of little value to the instrument developers, as all of the items cluster near Factor I. When the correlations are plotted for the varimax rotated matrix, it is clear that items 10, 13, 18, and 15 will contribute most to the name of Factor I, and items 2, 19, 21, 4, and 6 will contribute most to the naming of Factor

II. Based upon the plot in Figure 4–1, it is not yet clear where items 1, 5, 14, 11, 7, and 3 will be assigned until the loadings and item content are considered further. The actual naming of the factors will be discussed in a later section.

It should be made very clear that the rotation process has distributed the total amount of variance accounted for by the three-factor solution across the factors. That is, Factor I no longer accounts for 45.4% of the variance. Instead, the variance accounted for by each factor is now 20.3%, 18.9%, and 17.7%, respectively, which still sums to the total variance accounted for by the three-factor solution (i.e., 56.9%). Again, these values can be generated by summing the squares of the entries (correlations) in each column of the varimax-rotated matrix and dividing each sum by 22, the total amount of variance in the solution. Most computer programs do not report the amount of variance accounted for by each factor *after rotation*. As a result, many researchers reporting the results of a factor analysis erroneously report the percentages associated with the factors prior to rotation. It is not really necessary to calculate the proper percentages by hand using the procedure described above, since the variance accounted for will be reflected in the reported alpha internal-consistency reliabilities to be discussed in the next chapter (i.e., factors accounting for higher amounts of variance will have higher alpha reliabilities).

Transformation Matrix. The next matrix (p. 119) is used during the rotation process (TRANSFORMATION MATRIX) and can be ignored by the instrument developer.

Oblique Rotation. The next section of the output contains the results of an *oblique rotation* of the unrotated factor matrix. Prior to discussing the results, we need to present the rationale for conducting oblique rather than orthogonal (varimax) rotations. In a varimax rotation, the axis system is maintained at 90°. The axis system is simply rotated in all possible directions so that the *x* (Factor I) and *y* (Factor II) axes each get close to a distinct cluster of items. In this way, the entries listed under Factor I in the factor-loading matrix will have high loadings on Factor I and low loadings on Factor II; for Factor II the reverse will be true. Refer again to Figure 4–1 containing the plot for Factors I and II resulting from the varimax rotation. Notice that, if we envisioned an ellipse around the cluster of primary items defining each factor, we would see that the ellipses are not located directly next to either axis system. That is, the ideal axis system for describing the relationship between Factors I and II appears to be one with less than a 90° angle. In other words, while the axis system representing

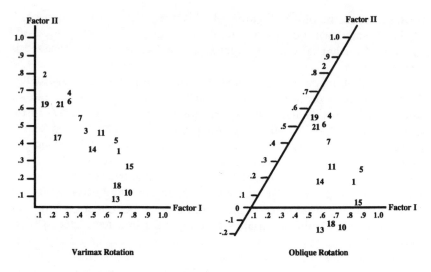

Figure 4–2.   Varimax and oblique rotation plots.

the factors is orthogonal, the clusters of items actually used to define the factor are not orthogonal. Since this will be the case in most applications in education or psychology, it is beneficial to also examine a factor solution that allows the axis system to be less than 90°, the oblique rotation. In this rotation the axis system can collapse to less than 90° so that each axis becomes closer to the cluster of items defining the factor. Figure 4–2 repeats the varimax-rotated plot and includes the plot of a corresponding oblique rotation for the attitude toward teacher data.[5] Inspection of the plot indicates that it is now clearer that items 1 and 5, and possibly 11 and 14, belong to Factor I. The final decision would depend on the content of the items.

While the entries in a factor matrix created by an oblique rotation are regression weights, they can be treated similarly to the correlations in the varimax matrix for purposes of identifying the factor structure. One restriction is that it is no longer appropriate to calculate sums of squares of the row or column entries, since the entries are not correlations. If, for some reason, you wanted to calculate the percent of variance accounted for by the oblique factors after rotation, you would have to refer back to the varimax rotation, identify the comparable factor, calculate the column sums of squares in the and then varimax matrix, and divide by the total sum of the roots (or the number of items for principal component). The variance accounted for after rotation will be the same for each factor for the oblique and varimax solutions.

Returning to page 120 in the output, we see that the oblique rotation results in a PATTERN MATRIX containing regression weights. Selecting those items that load .40 or greater on the factors indicates that the three factors are defined by almost the same items as the varimax rotation. In most applications, the same primary items will define the factors while the items with loadings, say below .50 on one or both factors, may get moved around in the oblique rotation. But, we do observe a difference between the varimax and oblique rotations regarding Factors I and II (see computer output pages 119 and 120). The items with the highest loadings indicate that Factors I and II have been switched in order from the varimax to the oblique rotation. This is a typical finding for the oblique rotation. The "real" order is defined by the variance accounted for after rotation as calculated earlier for the varimax rotation. It is recommended that the labels for the oblique rotation simply be switched to agree with the varimax order.

Factor Correlations. The final matrix of interest contains *correlations between the derived factors* and is labeled the FACTOR CORRELATION MATRIX. No such matrix is generated for the varimax rotation, because the off-diagonal entries are always zero. The factor correlations indicate the extent to which the derived factors or axes are related.[6]

For example, Factors I and II for the GRATTS data are correlated .47. (In the next section on Factor Interpretation, we will note that the—.47 in the output becomes .47 when all of the signs for the loadings in Factor II are reversed during interpretation.) This indicates that the constructs underlying the factor are not independent constructs. In the next chapter on reliability, we will see that factors correlated .30 to .40 or higher could be combined to generate a larger number of items defining the overall construct. Assuming that this collapsing makes conceptual sense in light of the item content, higher alpha reliabilities would result.

One wonders why people tend to run varimax rotations when the oblique rotation tells us if the factors are related while giving us a varimax equivalent if the factor correlations are near zero. The reason for the popularity of the varimax rotation is that it first appeared in 1958 when Kaiser reported its use; reliable oblique rotation programs were not readily available in most canned computer programs until the 1970s. There is no problem with running both rotations and comparing the results, but one should always run at least the oblique to see if the factors are correlated.

Table 4–7. Attitude Toward Teacher Factor-Loading Matrix Varimax Rotation[a] (*N* = 695)

Item	Factor 1	Factor II	Factor III
1	67	37	
2		80	
3	43	49	39
4	31	66	27
5	65	41	
6	31	64	41
7	40	53	23
8	36		66
9	21	24	70
10	73	13	33
11	51	46	26
12	27	38	61
13	65		38
14	49	37	33
15	75	25	19
16	16	16	69
17	28	43	44
18	67	15	30
19	18	62	30
20	35	35	45
21	29	62	38
22	13	32	69

[a]For ease of interpretation only entries above .10 have been included and decimals have been omitted.

Factor Interpretation.   Now that we have reviewed the computer output, we are ready to examine the factor structure that summarizes the information in the correlation matrix. For the varimax rotation; we interpret the VARIMAX ROTATED FACTOR MATRIX, and for the oblique rotation, the FACTOR PATTERN matrix. The first step is to display the varimax and oblique loading matrices. For ease of interpretation, enter only those loadings above .10, as illustrated in Tables 4–7 and 4–8. For either matrix (or both matrixes), underline the computer output loadings above .40 to identify the items that contribute most to naming the factor. If an item has a loading above .40 on more than one factor, temporarily assign the item to both factors. Later, a review of the item content defining each factor can assist in assigning the item to one factor.[7]

Table 4–8. Attitude Toward Teacher Factor Pattern Matrix Oblique Rotation[a] (*N* = 695)

Item	Factor I	Factor II	Factor III
1	74	19	−16
2		84	
3	34	33	27
4	20	57	16
5	71	24	−16
6	16	52	33
7	34	41	
8	24	−20	66
9			74
10	78	−14	14
11	49	30	
12		21	60
13	67	−19	23
14	45	19	19
15	83		
16			75
17	14	29	39
18	71		12
19		56	24
20	24	18	39
21	15	51	30
22		16	74

[a]For ease of interpretation only entries above .10 have been included and decimals have been omitted. Note that the factor order for the oblique rotation was changed to be consistent with the varimax solution and that Factor I was reflected (i.e., signs were reversed).

To avoid confusion in interpreting the factors, it is recommended that the response format be set up so that high scores are associated with positive attitudes, positive item stems, and positive loadings in the factor matrix. For example, for a Likert 5-point agreement scale, code a 5 for "strongly agree" to an item such as "This teacher motivates students to learn." You can then examine the signs of the loadings in the factor matrix to see if the positive item stem was associated with a positive loading. If it is not, you need to ascertain why the positive stem has a negative loading. It may or may not be a problem. If all of the positive item stems defining the factor (loadings above .40) have negative loadings, you can simply *reflect the factor* (reverse all of the + − signs). This merely locates the factor in a different quadrant geometrically; it does not change the magnitude of the relationships among items or factors. Reflecting a factor in the oblique FACTOR PATTERN matrix also necessitates reversing all of the signs in the factor's row and column in the FACTOR CORRELA-TION matrix. Because you have now located the factor in a different quadrant, the direction of the relationships of the factor with other factors has also been changed. In most cases, reflecting all appropriate factors will result in all positive relationships in the FACTOR CORRELATION matrix. If within a particular factor you find a few negative loadings (i.e., a bipolar factor), look at the item stems to see if the content is stated in a negative direction (e.g., This teacher does *not* make learning fun). If you reverse scored all of the negative item stems prior to the factor analysis, you now have a problem. That is, your reverse scoring based upon judgment did not agree with the direction of the item as perceived by the respondent. A review of the item stem is in order. If you did not reverse score the negative item stems, the negative loading merely reflects the negative relationship you have created and it can simply be ignored (i.e., changed to positive).

After identifying the items that load .40 or greater on the factors, create tables for the varimax and oblique rotations listing the item numbers, item stems, and ranked loadings for each factor as illustrated in Tables 4–9 and 4–10. For the oblique rotation you will also need to create a table of factor correlations as illustrated in Table 4–11. You are now ready to interpret the factors. The items with the highest loadings share the most variance with the factor you have derived. Your job is to ascertain just what concepts define the factor. Review the item content to identify the underlying theme shared by the items. Respondents tended to rate these items in a consistent manner on the basis of some conceptual framework; and this consistency is what created the intercorrelations among the items and contributed to the development of the factor. What were the respondents perceiving when they read the items?

Content and Construct Validity. The prior work in content validity will assist in this review process. Consider the operational definitions created for the affective characteristic as illustrated in Tables 2–1 and 2–2. Recall that the *judgmental* categories you built into the instrument were targeted to be constructs measured by the instrument. That is, you and the content experts specified the universe of content to be measured. Now the items have been rated by the intended users of the instrument and their perceptions (ratings) have been used to develop the empirical relationships among the items. These empirical relationships are used to answer the construct validity question: "To what extent do certain explanatory concepts (constructs)

Table 4–9. Principal-Component Analysis with Varimax Rotation: Attitude Toward Teacher Items[a] (N = 695)

	Item Number	Stem	Loading
Factor I			
Presentation of subject	15	Presents the subject so that it can be understood.	.75
	10	Does not make learning fun.	.73
	18	Fails to stimulate interest in the subject matter.	.67
	1	Motivates students to learn.	.67
	13	Is not interesting to listen to in class.	.65
	5	Is successful in getting his (her) point across.	.65
	11	Is generally cheerful and pleasant.	.51
	14	Has a sense of humor.	.49
Factor II			
Interest in job and students	2	Likes his (her) job.	.80
	4	Is willing to help students individually.	.66
	6	Is interested in students.	.64
	19	Is not interested in his (her) work.	.62
	21	Likes students.	.62
	7	Lacks enthusiasm.	.53
	3	Is fair in dealing with students.	.49
Factor III			
Teaching techniques	9	Assigns too much homework.	.70
	22	Tests too frequently.	.69
	16	Is too structured.	.69
	8	Tries to cover too much material in too short a time.	.66
	12	Disciplines too strictly.	.61
	20	Does not evaluate student work fairly.	.45
	17	Is too busy too spend extra time with students.	.44

[a]Underlined item numbers reflect negative stems, which were reverse scored.

Table 4–10. Principal-Component Analysis with Oblique Rotation: Attitude Toward Teacher Items[a] (N = 695)

	Item Number	Stem	Loading
Factor I			
Presentation of subject	15	Presents the subject so that it can be understood.	.83
	10	Does not make learning fun.	.78
	1	Motivates students to learn.	.74
	18	Fails to stimulate interest in subject matter.	.71
	5	Is successful in getting his (her) point across.	.71
	13	Is not interesting to listen to in class.	.67
	11	Is generally cheerful and pleasant.	.49
	14	Has a sense of humor.	.45
Factor II			
Interest in job and students	2	Likes his (her) job.	.84
	4	Is willing to help students individually.	.57
	19	Is not interested in his (her) work.	.56
	6	Is interested in students.	.52
	21	Likes students.	.51
	7	Lacks enthusiasm.	.41
Factor III			
Teaching techniques	16	Is too structured.	.75
	22	Tests too frequently.	.74
	9	Assigns too much homework.	.74
	8	Tries to cover too much material in too short a time.	.66
	12	Disciplines too strictly.	.60

[a]Underlined item numbers reflect negative stems, which were reverse scored.

Table 4–11. Attitude Toward Teacher Factor Intercorrelation Matrix Oblique Rotation (N = 696)

	Factor I	Factor II	Factor III
Factor I	1.00	.47	.40
Factor II		1.00	.57
Factor III			1.00

explain covariation in the responses to the test items?" That is, the derived factors are creations derived on the basis of covariation among the items. Your task is to justify how these derived factors actually represent concepts or constructs.

As we discussed earlier, correspondence between the judgmental categories and derived factors is essential and must be examined, since the factor structure represents what the instrument really measures. In many cases, minor discrepancies between the judgmental categories and empirical factors will contribute to a finer interpretation of the derived factors.[8] If the discrepancies are major, though, you have a problem to be solved through the three R's: rethink, rewrite, and readminister.

Describing the Factor. Careful consideration of the item content should have facilitated naming the factors. Readers are encouraged to review the item content in Tables 4–9 or 4–10 to see how the following factor names were generated: Factor I, Presentation of Subject; Factor II, Interest in Job and Students; Factor III, Teaching Techniques. Now that you have named the factor, you are ready to write up the factor description. Three components are crucial for a proper factor description. First, state the name you have given to the factor. Second, justify the name by merging some actual item content into your description. Third, describe the perceptions or attributes of a person scoring highly on the factor. For Factor I in Table 4–9, the description could be:

Factor I was called Presentation of Subject, because items defining the factor described the delivery of the lecture, as well as the impact of the delivery on students. Teachers rated highly on the factor would be perceived by students as giving clear, interesting lectures which provided stimulation and motivation for learning.

If an oblique rotation were used, the final step would be to describe the intercorrelations among the factors displayed in Table 4–11. Note that for these data the factors are correlated above .40, so the possibility of collapsing the factors can be considered. As we noted earlier, the decision to collapse any of the factors is based upon the level of reliability of the uncollapsed factors and the conceptual meaningfulness of such collapsing. If the factors are reliable and clearly meaningful, collapsing is optional. If the alpha reliability (see Chapter 5) of the factors is low and collapsing makes conceptual sense, you may try to collapse them to obtain a factor with a larger number of items and thus a higher alpha reliability.

Scale-Level Factor Analysis.   In the previous section, the use of an item-level factor analysis was illustrated for examining construct validity. It is also possible to conduct a factor analysis at the scale level. That is, responses are summed across items defining the respective scales. The scale-level intercorelation matrix is then submitted to a factor analysis to examine the existence of more global underlying factors. This type of information can add greatly to the interpretation of the instrument, especially when the instrument attempts to assess several somewhat-related constructs.

Studies using the *Tennessee Self-Concept Scale* (Fitts, 1965) illustrate such scale-level factor analyses. The TSS is a 100-item instrument with 90 items contributing to a 3 × 5 self-concept classification scheme. The three levels of the first dimension represent the individual's internal frame of reference; the five levels of the second dimension represent an external frame of reference. A potential psychometric problem with the instrument is that the scoring procedure employs a 3 × 5 grid, which results in each item contributing to both a row (internal) and column (external) dimension of self-concept. This situation can lead to spuriously high correlations due to the item-scale overlap. In addition to these eight scale scores, four other scale scores are generated through various combinations of the items, resulting in a total of 12 scale scores.

The construct validity of the 12 scales was examined by Rentz and White (1967) and Gable, LaSalle, and Cook (1973). In each study the scale-level intercorrelation matrix was factored and two relatively independent dimensions of self-concept, similar to self-esteem and conflict-integration, accounted for the scale interrationships. Thus, the scale-level factor analysis contributed information that would lead to finer interpretations of the TSS scores.

Factoring Several Instruments.   The construct validity of an instrument can also be examined through a scale-level factor analysis that also includes scales from other carefully selected instruments or variables. The intent of the analysis is to ascertain if the scales load on factors in a manner consistent with theoretical expectations.

This technique can be illustrated by considering the instruments and variables described earlier in the chapter regarding the use of correlations to examine construct validity. Complete sets of data for 503 high-school juniors were obtained for the target instrument, the *Work Values Inventory* (WVI), as well as selected scales from the following instruments: the *Edwards Personal Preference Schedule* (EPPS), the *Kuder Preference Record* (KUD), the *Survey of Interpersonal Values* (SIV), the *Study of Values*

(SOV), and the *Differential Aptitude Test* (DAT).[9] In addition, data were obtained for school grades, social class, and sex (Gable, 1970). Fourteen of the *WVI* scales were intercorrelated with the other 36 scales, resulting in a 50 × 50 intercorrelation matrix. The purpose of the analysis was to provide a clearer interpretation of the factor structure of the *WVI* by seeing if the targeted scales from the other measures would load on factors with the *WVI* scales, as predicted on the basis of a literature review.

Table 4–12 contains the loading matrix resulting from the image analysis (i.e., a type of factor analysis) and varimax rotation. The factor structure was found to be supportive of the construct validity of the *WVI* for several reasons. For example, Factor I was defined by a cluster of *WVI* scales reflecting a high emphasis on the work values of Economic Returns, Security, Supervisory Relations, Associates, Achievement, and Prestige. While it is clearly the *WVI* scales that define the overall factor, small but reasonable loadings do appear for scales from other instruments in predicted directions. Note that loadings above .20 were found in predicted directions for *EPPS* Achievement and Affiliation; *SIV* Recognition, Independence (–), and Benevolence (–); and *SOV* Economic. Also consider Factor III, which was defined by high emphasis on *WVI* Altruism; *EPPS* Affiliation and Nurturance; *KUD* Social Service; *SIV* Benevolence; *SOV* Social; and sex (females higher emphasis). Further, low emphasis was found for *KUD* Mechanical, Computational, and scientific; *SOV* Theoretical, Economic, and Political; and *DAT* Mechanical Reasoning. Note that the predicted lack of relationship between *WVI* work values and student achievement or aptitude was supported in that Factor IV was defined solely by the *DAT* scales and Factor V by student achievement and *DAT* scores.

Obviously, the crucial aspect of such an analysis is the selection of instruments based upon the literature review, since the factor analysis is confirmatory in nature. Another key aspect is that obtaining complete sets of data across several instruments takes testing time and good rapport with schools and students. Unmotivated respondents and missing data will thoroughly ruin the analysis. If the data can be collected, the contribution to examining construct validity will be worth the effort.

In summary, this section has described and illustrated the use of as EFA to examine construct validity. It was emphasized that the empirically derived constructs should correspond with the judgmentally derived content categories developed during the content-validity phase of developing the istrument. Discrepancies between the derived constructs and content categories could be quite serious and indicate need for further developmental work.

Table 4–12. An Illustration of a Scale-Level Factor Analysis[a]

Scales	I	II	III	IV	V	VI	VII	VIII	IX	X	XI	XII
WVI												
Economic Returns	65		-23									
Security	68											
Supervisory Relations	65											
Surroundings	64											
Associates	58	29					23					
Altruism		44	67				22					
Achievement	54	41					20					
Esthetics		68				28						
Creativity		67										
Intellectual Stimulation						-21						
Prestige	59	30								22		
Management	37	37								48		
Variety	20	57									23	
Independence		54						43				
Achievement	23	27					31			38		30
Affiliation	20		41				71	59				
EPPS												
Autonomy		21										
Change		26					40			61		
Dominance		20					26					
Nurturance			49				70					
Outdoor			-23					59		59		
Mechanical			-56			25			30			
Computational			-38			-41						
Scientific			-39			-48			31			
Persuasive									-48			

Test	Scale	1	2	3	4	5	6	7
KUD	Artistic							
	Literary							
	Social Service	24	72					
	Clerical							43
SIV	Conformity	32	21					
	Recognition	-23	26			56		
	Independence	-20	68				60	
	Benevolence		27				69	63
	Leadership		27					69
SOV	Theoretical		-43			-34		
	Economic	27	-46			-20		
	Aesthetic		72					
	Social							29
	Political		-44			61		
DAT	Verbal Reasoning			60	45			
	Numerical Reasoning			62	35			
	Abstract Reasoning			72	20			
	Mechanical Reasoning			52		-34		
	Space Relations			71				
ACII	English			28	74			
	Math			23	67			
	Science			14	77			
	Social Studies				78			
	Social Class							
	Sex		-59	-37			-57	

a For ease of interpretation, all entries were multiplied by 100, columns 3 and 6 were reflected, only loadings above 20 were included, and underlined entries were used to name the factors. Sex code: females = 0, males = 1.

Table 4–13. Twenty Illustrative Items from a Leadership-Behavior Feedback Instrument

1. Gives negative feedback when necessary.
2. Gives immediate and ongoing feedback when appropriate.
3. Develops specific plans for performance improvement.
4. Gives positive feedback when deserved.
5. Provides honest appraisal of career potential.
6. Establishes a partnership with the client.
7. Understands the client's view of the situation.
8. Knows what kinds of decisions the client is, and is not, prepared to make.
9. Talks to the client in everyday language rather than jargon.
10. Keeps the client informed of progress and changes along the way.
11. Is sensitive to client personnel.
12. Is valuable in helping to prepare presentations for clients.
13. Is available at any time when necessary.
14. Encourages the use of teamwork.
15. Varies leadership style and amount of involvement based on needs.
16. Takes into account the project team's needs before making delivery commitments to clients.
17. Insures that meetings are held often enough.
18. Insures that meetings are effective.
19. Gives detailed instructions when needed.
20. Gives appropriate orientation to people in new assignments.

Confirmatory Factor Analysis

Initial Decisions.   For CFA, the decisions to be made prior to computer analysis are concerned both with content and with methodology. Unlike EFA, where the number of factors is usually determined by the results of the analysis, for CFA the decision is made *a priori*. Based on a review of the relevant literature and the judgmental categories identified during the content-validity stage of instrument development, the developer has to decide how many factors are needed to represent the constructs measured and which items relate to each factor. For the LISREL CFA, the program input includes a description of the factor-loading matrix (Lambda X), indicating how many columns or factors that matrix has and which items load on each factor. In LISREL terminology, the factors represent latent (unobservable) traits or variables, and the individual items represent observed variables. The CFA analysis requires that two additional matrices be analyzed. The first matrix (Phi) contains the relationships among the factors, expressed either in variances and covariances or in correlations. This matrix will have the same number of rows and columns as there are factors. The second additional matrix (Theta Delta) contains the proportion of the variance in each item which cannot be accounted for by the factor solution, or the unique variance in each item. This is a diagonal matrix with one entry for each of the items.

There are a few methodological decisions necessary for this analysis. The first decision involves the selection of an estimation procedure. Although the LISREL program offers several choices of methods of estimation, by far the most frequently used is that of Maximum Likelihood. Because the estimates produced by this method are very robust, this will normally be the optimal method for CFA for affective measures, assuming the data are in the form of rating scales or another type of continuous response. (If your data do not fit this description, the LISREL manual appropriate for the version you are using contains the information on alternate methods.) A second decision involves the form in which your data will be analyzed. In LISREL, although raw data may be input using the PRELIS program, the analysis is actually based on relational data, using either the correlation or the covariance matrix. While many of the analyses performed using this program require the covariance matrix, it is generally, although not universally, agreed that the correlation matrix should be analyzed for a single group CFA.

One other decision concerns the somewhat technical matter of model identification, which has to do with the relationship between the amount of information which is known and the amount which is sought. While a thorough discussion of this subject is beyond the scope of this book (see Kenny, 1979), suffice it to say that if the model is not identified, it is impossible to provide unique estimates for all of the parameters in question. Luckily, identification is usually not a problem when running CFA, as long as the researcher uses one of two strategies. The most commonly used of these strategies is the "marker variable" method of setting the loading of one observed variable for each factor to 1. For CFA, however, marker variables are often not used because of the loss of information on one item from each factor. Instead, the second strategy is used, in which the factor variance/covariance matrix is turned into a correlation matrix by specifying 1's in the diagonal. While the solutions arrived at using the two methods are the same, except for the unit of measurement assigned to the parameter estimates, the factor correlation method allows us to obtain information on all observed variables, rather than all but one in each factor.

Computer Output: Confirmatory Factor Analysis

As with the PCA illustration, we will discuss actual computer output, this time from the LISREL VII program. A 20-item subset from a longer instrument will be used to illustrate CFA (Table 4–13). The original instrument was designed to measure the satisfaction of employees with the leadership behaviors of their superiors. The items were rated on a 5-point Likert Scale (Highly Satisfied, 5; Satisfied, 4; Neither Satisfied nor Dissatisfied, 3; Dissatisfied, 2; Highly Dissatisfied, 1). All of the items have positive stems, so no reverse scoring was required. The scale was administered to 569 employees who rated 84 managers. The PRELIS program was used to generate the correlation matrix from the raw data. Table 4–14 contains the LISREL output which we will examine section by section, referring to page numbers, and, whenever possible, line numbers.

Total Sample Size and Missing Values.   (Below line 2933) This PRELIS output clarifies the *listwise* deletion of data by first indicating the total number of cases with complete data sets, and then listing the number of cases eliminated for each possible number of missing values. For this data set, most of the cases eliminated had very little missing data. If we had a very small data set we might want to consider the use of *pairwise* deletion, although this technique has sometimes been known to cause terminal errors in the LISREL program (Byrne, 1989).

Univariate Summary Statistics.   The means and standard deviations for the 20 items seem reasonable for this type of data. And although there is a consistent negative skew, indicating more positive responses than negative, there is sufficient variation in the responses for meaningful factor analysis.

Lisrel Control Lines.   The Lisrel input lines are printed on the output twice in slightly different formats. The first format is exactly the way in which it was entered and ensures that the researcher will have a copy of the input to assist in any subsequent analyses. The second listing contains a computer-generated description of the format of the correlation matrix as well as labels for each of the items. Since no item labels were input, these are also computer-generated. Looking at the first set of control lines (lines 2934–2943), the DA line (2937) indicates that there are 20 items (NI = 20), a sample of 569 (NOBS = 569), and that the correlation matrix is to be analyzed (MA = KM). The MO line (2938) indicates again the 20 items (NX = 20), as well as three factors (NK = 3). The third element on this line

Table 4-14. LISREL Computer Output

```
2930   0   PRELIS
2931   0   /VARIABLES = S1 TO S5 S6 TO S11 S12 TO S20 (CO)
2932   0   /MATRIX = OUT (*)
2933   0   /TYPE = CORRELATION
DISTRIBUTION OF MISSING VALUES
TOTAL SAMPLE SIZE = 569
NUMBER OF MISSING VALUES    0   1   2   3   4   5   6   7   8   9  10  11  12  13  14  15  16  17  18  19  20
NUMBER OF CASES  569  46  11   3   5   2   3   2   1   0   0   1   1   1   0   0   0   0   0   0   1
LISTWISE DELETION
TOTAL EFFECTIVE SAMPLE SIZE = 569
UNIVARIATE SUMMARY STATISTICS FOR CONTINUOUS VARIABLES
```

VARIABLE	MEAN	ST. DEV.	SKEWNESS	KURTOSIS	MINIMUM	FREQ.	MAXIMUM	FREQ.
S1	3.455	0.999	−0.338	−0.522	1.000	14	5.000	77
S2	3.383	1.134	−0.290	−0.832	1.000	28	5.000	97
S3	3.165	1.104	−0.094	−0.693	1.000	39	5.000	69
S4	3.789	1.035	−0.630	−0.256	1.000	13	5.000	159
S5	3.513	1.058	−0.316	−0.447	1.000	22	5.000	114
S6	3.830	0.965	−0.575	−0.274	1.000	6	5.000	152
S7	3.921	0.953	−0.724	−0.001	1.000	6	5.000	171
S8	3.909	0.932	−0.682	−0.017	1.000	5	5.000	162
S9	4.086	0.922	−0.861	0.315	1.000	6	5.000	223
S10	3.935	0.856	−0.584	0.061	1.000	3	5.000	152
S11	3.793	0.955	−0.575	−0.125	1.000	8	5.000	138
S12	3.821	1.061	−0.817	0.055	1.000	19	5.000	164
S13	4.030	0.937	−0.936	0.687	1.000	10	5.000	200
S14	3.766	0.936	−0.527	−0.035	1.000	9	5.000	129
S15	3.520	1.050	−0.310	−0.569	1.000	17	5.000	110
S16	3.320	1.099	−0.371	−0.579	1.000	37	5.000	73
S17	3.487	0.970	−0.381	−0.413	1.000	12	5.000	74
S18	3.446	1.064	−0.401	−0.449	1.000	26	5.000	90
S19	3.661	0.969	−0.687	0.216	1.000	17	5.000	99
S20	3.677	0.968	−0.378	−0.413	1.000	8	5.000	121

Table 4–14. (Cont.)

```
2934  0   LISREL
2935  0   /CFA—LEADERSHIP SATISFACTION
2936  0   /MATRIX = IN (*)
2937  0   /DA  NI = 20  NO = 569  MA = KM
2938  0   /MO  NX = 20  NK = 3  PH = ST
2939  0   /LK
2940  0   /'STAFFDEV'  'CLIENT'  'TEAMWORK'
2941  0   /PA  LX
2942  0   /5(1 0 0)  6(0 1 0)  9(0 0 1)
2943  0   /OU  TV  MI  TO
```

THE FOLLOWING LISREL CONTROL LINES HAVE BEEN READ:

```
CFA—LEADERSHIP SATISFACTION
DA NI = 20 NO = 569 MA = KM
KM FI = LSDDDTA FO
(5E14.6)
LA
S1    S2    S3    S4    S5    S6    S7    S8
S9    S10   S11   S12   S13   S14   S15   S16
S17   S18   S19   S20
MO NX = 20  NK = 3  PH = ST
LK
STAFFDEV  CLIENT  TEAMWORK
PA  LX
5(1 0 0)  6(0 1 0)  9(0 0 1)
OU  TV  MI  TO
CFA—LEADERSHIP SATISFACTION
```

NUMBER OF INPUT VARIABLES 20
NUMBER OF Y—VARIABLES 0
NUMBER OF X—VARIABLES 20
NUMBER OF ETA—VARIABLES 0
NUMBER OF KSI—VARIABLES 3
NUMBER OF OBSERVATIONS 569

CFA—LEADERSHIP SATISFACTION
CORRELATION MATRIX TO BE ANALYZED

	S1	S2	S3	S4	S5	S6
S1	1.000					
S2	0.618	1.000				
S3	0.529	0.629	1.000			
S4	0.442	0.631	0.536	1.000		
S5	0.485	0.520	0.598	0.514	1.000	
S6	0.214	0.314	0.309	0.338	0.262	1.000
S7	0.147	0.248	0.255	0.297	0.225	0.574
S8	0.194	0.220	0.242	0.252	0.215	0.512
S9	0.124	0.162	0.216	0.252	0.195	0.450
S10	0.203	0.220	0.285	0.253	0.212	0.406
S11	0.169	0.254	0.258	0.316	0.224	0.476
S12	0.232	0.287	0.381	0.299	0.306	0.311
S13	0.185	0.299	0.310	0.273	0.224	0.220
S14	0.202	0.308	0.325	0.407	0.303	0.330
S15	0.277	0.421	0.383	0.412	0.293	0.309
S16	0.188	0.297	0.313	0.289	0.257	0.342
S17	0.318	0.462	0.421	0.367	0.305	0.279
S18	0.262	0.372	0.366	0.337	0.279	0.330
S19	0.298	0.399	0.358	0.355	0.326	0.286
S20	0.296	0.408	0.398	0.357	0.317	0.265

Table 4–14. (Cont.)

CORRELATION MATRIX TO BE ANALYZED

	S7	S8	S9	S10	S11	S12
S7	1.000					
S8	0.706	1.000				
S9	0.517	0.489	1.000			
S10	0.432	0.357	0.415	1.000		
S11	0.507	0.475	0.378	0.464	1.000	
S12	0.308	0.252	0.250	0.299	0.227	1.000
S13	0.182	0.104	0.144	0.259	0.184	0.480
S14	0.317	0.268	0.295	0.299	0.365	0.314
S15	0.298	0.268	0.265	0.294	0.357	0.444
S16	0.280	0.244	0.266	0.308	0.379	0.381
S17	0.211	0.178	0.168	0.263	0.244	0.412
S18	0.320	0.302	0.291	0.289	0.343	0.442
S19	0.301	0.235	0.244	0.289	0.268	0.461
S20	0.266	0.225	0.163	0.293	0.272	0.291

CORRELATION MATRIX TO BE ANALYZED

	S13	S14	S15	S16	S17	S18
S13	1.000					
S14	0.345	1.000				
S15	0.394	0.527	1.000			
S16	0.295	0.388	0.464	1.000		
S17	0.348	0.393	0.406	0.397	1.000	
S18	0.312	0.375	0.467	0.435	0.547	1.000
S19	0.382	0.368	0.426	0.353	0.496	0.557
S20	0.315	0.388	0.431	0.387	0.406	0.364

CORRELATION MATRIX TO BE ANALYZED

	S19	S20
S19	1.000	
S20	0.433	1.000

CFA—LEADERSHIP SATISFACTION
PARAMETER SPECIFICATIONS

LAMBDA X

	STAFFDEV	CLIENT	TEAMWORK
S1	1	0	0
S2	2	0	0
S3	3	0	0
S4	4	0	0
S5	5	0	0
S6	0	6	0
S7	0	7	0
S8	0	8	0
S9	0	9	0
S10	0	10	0
S11	0	11	0
S12	0	0	12
S13	0	0	13
S14	0	0	14
S15	0	0	15
S16	0	0	16
S17	0	0	17
S18	0	0	18
S19	0	0	19
S20	0	0	20

Table 4-14. (Cont.)

	STAFFDEV	CLIENT	TEAMWORK			
PHI						
STAFFDEV	0					
CLIENT	21	0				
TEAMWORK	22	23	0			
THETA DELTA	S1	S2	S3	S4	S5	S6
	24	25	26	27	28	29
THETA DELTA	S7	S8	S9	S10	S11	S12
	30	31	32	33	34	35
THETA DELTA	S13	S14	S15	S16	S17	S18
	36	37	38	39	40	41
THETA DELTA	S19	S20				
	42	43				

CFA—LEADERSHIP SATISFACTION
LISREL ESTIMATES (MAXIMUM LIKELIHOOD)
LAMBDA X

	STAFFDEV	CLIENT	TEAMWORK
S1	0.680	0.000	0.000
S2	0.829	0.000	0.000
S3	0.781	0.000	0.000
S4	0.729	0.000	0.000
S5	0.689	0.000	0.000
S6	0.000	0.704	0.000
S7	0.000	0.830	0.000
S8	0.000	0.768	0.000
S9	0.000	0.632	0.000
S10	0.000	0.569	0.000
S11	0.000	0.650	0.000
S12	0.000	0.000	0.626
S13	0.000	0.000	0.538
S14	0.000	0.000	0.611
S15	0.000	0.000	0.699
S16	0.000	0.000	0.603
S17	0.000	0.000	0.675
S18	0.000	0.000	0.701
S19	0.000	0.000	0.689
S20	0.000	0.000	0.598

Table 4-14. (Cont.)

PHI	STAFFDEV	CLIENT	TEAMWORK
STAFFDEV	1.000		
CLIENT	0.437	1.000	
TEAMWORK	0.687	0.578	1.000

THETA DELTA

S1	S2	S3	S4	S5	S6
0.538	0.313	0.389	0.469	0.525	0.505

THETA DELTA

S7	S8	S9	S10	S11	S12
0.312	0.411	0.600	0.677	0.578	0.609

THETA DELTA

S13	S14	S15	S16	S17	S18
0.710	0.627	0.512	0.636	0.544	0.509

THETA DELTA

S19	S20
0.526	0.642

SQUARED MULTIPLE CORRELATIONS FOR X—VARIABLES

S1	S2	S3	S4	S5	S6
0.462	0.687	0.611	0.531	0.475	0.495

SQUARED MULTIPLE CORRELATIONS FOR X—VARIABLES

S7	S8	S9	S10	S11	S12
0.688	0.589	0.400	0.323	0.422	0.391

SQUARED MULTIPLE CORRELATIONS FOR X—VARIABLES

S13	S14	S15	S16	S17	S18
0.290	0.373	0.488	0.364	0.456	0.491

SQUARED MULTIPLE CORRELATIONS FOR X—VARIABLES

S19	S20
0.474	0.358

TOTAL COEFFICIENT OF DETERMINATION FOR X—VARIABLES IS 0.995

CHI-SQARE WITH 167 DEGREES OF FREEDOM = 488.86 (P = .000)
                GOODNESS OF FIT INDEX = 0.918
       ADJUSTED GOODNESS OF FIT INDEX = 0.897
          ROOT MEAN SQUARE RESIDUAL = 0.050

CFA—LEADERSHIP SATISFACTION
SUMMARY STATISTICS FOR FITTED RESIDUALS
SMALLEST FITTED RESIDUAL = -0.135
  MEDIAN FITTED RESIDUAL = 0.000
 LARGEST FITTED RESIDUAL = 0.153
STEMLEAF PLOT

```
-12 | 51
-10 | 20
 -8 | 4330
 -6 | 9619877655421
 -4 | 85554332229200
 -2 | 9774432199998755444330
 -0 | 998665444311000099887776332000000000000000000000
  0 | 133444455567777880000112334677899
  2 | 01112334567890234456
  4 | 01356680056689999
  6 | 235899124478
  8 | 0221445779
 10 | 01804
 12 | 6
 14 | 33
```

Table 4-14. (Cont.)

SUMMARY STATISTICS FOR STANDARDIZED RESIDUALS
SMALLEST STANDARDIZED RESIDUAL = -4.373
 MEDIAN STANDARDIZED RESIDUAL = 0.000
 LARGEST STANDARDIZED RESIDUAL = 7.782
STEMLEAF PLOT

```
-4 | 43222
-3 | 554110
-2 | 999877666555543332110 0
-1 | 99776555544333111110
-0 | 99998887776665555555544443333222211000000000000000000000000
 0 | 1111122222223333333333344566666677888888
 1 | 0000011111222224455556 78899
 2 | 011113333355667789
 3 | 00223469
 4 | 0011568
 5 | 6
 6 |
 7 | 8
```

LARGEST NEGATIVE STANDARDIZED RESIDUALS

RESIDUAL FOR	S4 AND	S1 = -3.095
RESIDUAL FOR	S5 AND	S2 = -4.341
RESIDUAL FOR	S7 AND	S1 = -3.422
RESIDUAL FOR	S10 AND	S7 = -2.778
RESIDUAL FOR	S10 AND	S8 = -4.373
RESIDUAL FOR	S11 AND	S7 = -2.590
RESIDUAL FOR	S12 AND	S2 = -2.651
RESIDUAL FOR	S13 AND	S8 = -4.203
RESIDUAL FOR	S14 AND	S1 = -2.709
RESIDUAL FOR	S14 AND	S12 = -2.897
RESIDUAL FOR	S16 AND	S1 = -3.055

RESIDUAL FOR S17 AND S7 = -4.156
RESIDUAL FOR S17 AND S8 = -4.211
RESIDUAL FOR S17 AND S15 = -3.452
RESIDUAL FOR S18 AND S13 = -2.906
RESIDUAL FOR S19 AND S15 = -2.961
RESIDUAL FOR S19 AND S16 = -2.881
RESIDUAL FOR S20 AND S12 = -3.471
RESIDUAL FOR S20 AND S18 = -2.595

LARGEST POSITIVE STANDARDIZED RESIDUALS

RESIDUAL FOR S2 AND S1 = 4.465
RESIDUAL FOR S5 AND S3 = 4.044
RESIDUAL FOR S6 AND S4 = 3.636
RESIDUAL FOR S8 AND S7 = 7.782
RESIDUAL FOR S10 AND S3 = 2.729
RESIDUAL FOR S11 AND S4 = 3.332
RESIDUAL FOR S11 AND S10 = 4.000
RESIDUAL FOR S12 AND S10 = 2.730
RESIDUAL FOR S13 AND S12 = 5.639
RESIDUAL FOR S14 AND S4 = 3.449
RESIDUAL FOR S14 AND S10 = 2.864
RESIDUAL FOR S14 AND S11 = 4.116
RESIDUAL FOR S15 AND S11 = 3.046
RESIDUAL FOR S15 AND S14 = 4.815
RESIDUAL FOR S16 AND S6 = 3.024
RESIDUAL FOR S16 AND S10 = 3.184
RESIDUAL FOR S16 AND S11 = 4.594
RESIDUAL FOR S17 AND S2 = 3.171
RESIDUAL FOR S18 AND S17 = 3.913
RESIDUAL FOR S19 AND S18 = 4.051
RESIDUAL FOR S20 AND S3 = 2.719
RESIDUAL FOR S20 AND S10 = 2.784

Table 4–14. (Cont.)

CFA—LEADERSHIP SATISFACTION
T-VALUES

LAMBDA X

	STAFFDEV	CLIENT	TEAMWORK
S1	17.489	0.000	0.000
S2	23.062	0.000	0.000
S3	21.164	0.000	0.000
S4	19.203	0.000	0.000
S5	17.813	0.000	0.000
S6	0.000	18.222	0.000
S7	0.000	22.963	0.000
S8	0.000	20.531	0.000
S9	0.000	15.852	0.000
S10	0.000	13.917	0.000
S11	0.000	16.423	0.000
S12	0.000	0.000	15.732
S13	0.000	0.000	13.098
S14	0.000	0.000	15.259
S15	0.000	0.000	18.156
S16	0.000	0.000	15.028
S17	0.000	0.000	17.346
S18	0.000	0.000	18.240
S19	0.000	0.000	17.808
S20	0.000	0.000	14.871

PHI

	STAFFDEV	CLIENT	TEAMWORK
STAFFDEV	0.000		
CLIENT	10.807	0.000	
TEAMWORK	23.687	16.649	0.000

THETA DELTA

S1	S2	S3	S4	S5	S6
14.854	11.697	13.161	14.202	14.745	14.411

THETA DELTA

S7	S8	S9	S10	S11	S12
11.328	13.246	15.209	15.677	15.043	15.396

THETA DELTA

S13	S14	S15	S16	S17	S18
15.930	15.507	14.687	15.558	14.953	14.658

THETA DELTA

S19	S20
14.806	15.592

Table 4–14. (Cont.)

CF—LEADERSHIP SATISFACTION
MODIFICATION INDICES AND ESTIMATED CHANGE
MODIFICATION INDICES FOR LAMBDA X

	STAFFDEV	CLIENT	TEAMWORK
S1	0.000	5.420	10.767
S2	0.000	2.794	0.025
S3	0.000	0.645	2.628
S4	0.000	9.538	4.707
S5	0.000	0.031	0.821
S6	10.167	0.000	6.993
S7	7.342	0.000	9.468
S8	3.937	0.000	14.280
S9	0.696	0.000	0.021
S10	5.533	0.000	16.098
S11	3.354	0.000	10.224
S12	1.190	0.665	0.000
S13	0.324	5.544	0.000
S14	0.035	7.253	0.000
S15	0.204	0.041	0.000
S16	3.618	4.261	0.000
S17	5.472	12.220	0.000
S18	3.466	1.274	0.000
S19	0.018	0.820	0.000
S20	8.618	0.007	0.000

ESTIMATED CHANGE FOR LAMBDA X

	STAFFDEV	CLIENT	TEAMWORK
S1	0.000	-0.095	-0.181
S2	0.000	-0.060	-0.008
S3	0.000	0.030	0.083
S4	0.000	0.121	0.115
S5	0.000	0.007	-0.050
S6	0.128	0.000	0.121
S7	-0.098	0.000	-0.129
S8	-0.075	0.000	-0.164
S9	-0.035	0.000	-0.007
S10	0.104	0.000	0.202
S11	0.076	0.000	0.152
S12	-0.062	0.040	0.000
S13	-0.034	-0.121	0.000
S14	-0.011	0.132	0.000
S15	0.025	0.009	0.000
S16	-0.110	0.102	0.000
S17	0.129	-0.164	0.000
S18	-0.101	0.052	0.000
S19	-0.007	-0.042	0.000
S20	0.171	-0.004	0.000

NO NON-ZERO MODIFICATION INDICES FOR PHI
NO NON-ZERO MODIFICATION INDICES FOR THETA DELTA
MAXIMUM MODIFICATION INDEX IS 16.10 FOR ELEMENT (10, 3) OF LAMBDA X

(PH = ST) refers to the Phi matrix, which contains relationships among the factors. By making Phi equal to ST, these values become standardized, turning Phi into a correlation matrix for the three factors. It was not necessary to describe the other two matrices in this line, as the factor-loading matrix and the item-uniqueness matrix are used in their default forms and are therefore automatically included. The next two lines (2939–2940) give the names of the factors. Unlike EFA, the instrument developer already knows which items form each factor, and so can name the factors before this analysis is run. The next two lines (2941–2942) indicate which items load on which of the three factors. According to these lines, the first five items, S1 through S5, will load on the first factor, Staffdev; the next six items, S6 through S11, will load on the second factor, Client; and the final 9 items, S12 through S20, will load on the third factor, Teamwork. The final line (2943) indicates the optional output requested, in this case, T values (TV), modification indices (MI), and an 80-column line width (TO).

The remainder of the lines on page 142 repeat the LISREL input lines with the inclusion of a computer-generated description of the format of the correlation matrix and computer-generated labels for the 20 observed variables. The six lines at the top of page 143 serve as a check on the number of parameters included in the analyses. The lines with zeros are of no concern to us. They are necessary only when the program is used to perform more complex structural-equation analyses. The number of input, x, and ksi variables, however, as well as the number of observations, should match the input program lines (ksi = factor).

Correlation Matrix   While the proximity of the items in each scale makes it almost possible to detect some clusters from this matrix, there are far too many pairs to do this systematically. However, it is clear from this output that there is a great deal of inter-item relationship within this data set.

Parameter Specifications. (page 145)   This section serves as a further check on the program input to make sure you have correctly indicated which parameters you wish the program to estimate. In this case, the Lambda X or factor loading matrix on page 145 shows the 20 observed variables loading on the factors as described above. The zeros indicate that each observed variable is specified to load on only one factor.

The Phi matrix, immediately following the Lambda-X matrix, indicates that the researcher wants the program to estimate all three correlations among the three factors, bringing the number of parameters to be estimated up to 23. The 0's in the diagonal indicate that these parameters are not to be estimated, in this case because they were each given a value of 1.

The Theta Delta matrix, in the middle of page 146, has one cell for each of the observed variables. Each of these cells represents that proportion of the variance in each item which cannot be accounted for by the factor solution. In all, there are 43 parameters to be computed.

Lisrel Estimates.   This section, which begins on page 147, is the heart of the output. It contains the results of the maximum-likelihood analysis, including the contents of the three relevant matrices, the squared-multiple correlation for each item, and the coefficient of determination for the entire instrument, as well as four different measures of how well the proposed model fits the empirical data.

The Lambda-X matrix contains the factor loadings for each of the items. Since the factors have been allowed to be correlated, this matrix is analogous (although not equal) to the pattern matrix generated by the Principal-Components Analysis with oblique rotation which was described earlier. The loadings, which are regression weights, appear to be reasonably high. Table 4–15 shows how these data would be displayed in papers and journal articles.

The Phi matrix (page 148), which is similar to the factor-correlation matrix in EFA, shows strong correlations among the three factors, especially between the Staff-Development and Teamwork factors (.69). While these relationships are strong enough to allow factors to be combined, it is unlikely that the developer would choose to do so in this case, as there are only three factors, and each one has sufficient items for acceptable reliability estimates. The factor correlations are displayed in Table 4–16.

The next set of parameter estimates on page 148 of the output is for the Theta-Delta matrix. The values in Theta Delta represent the proportion of error variance in each of the items, that part of the total item variance which is not explained by the factor solution. For example, looking at item S1, 54% of its variance *cannot* be accounted for by the factor solution. This information is useful in identifying particular items which fit less well into the factor solution. While there are no hard and fast guidelines as to what values are acceptable, obviously smaller values indicate a greater amount of shared variance and a stronger relation to the factor. In this example, as a group, the values are moderate but acceptable. It is interesting to note that most of the higher values are related to items in the Teamwork factor (S12 to S20), indicating more error associated with that cluster of items than with the other two. The proportion of measurement error for item S13 (.71) is sufficiently high that the item should be

Table 4–15. Maximum-Likelihood Factor Loadings

Item Number	Stem	Staff Development	Client	Treatment
		Loadings		
1.	Gives negative feedback when necessary	.68		
2.	Gives immediate and ongoing feedback when appropriate	.83		
3.	Develops specific plans for performance improvement	.78		
4.	Gives positive feedback when deserved	.73		
5.	Provides honest appraisal of career potential	.69		
6.	Establishes a partnership with the client		.70	
7.	Understands the client's view of the situation		.83	
8.	Knows what kinds of decisions the client is, and is not, prepared to make		.77	
9.	Talks to the client in everyday language rather than jargon		.63	
10.	Keeps the client informed of progress and changes along the way		.57	
11.	Is sensitive to client personnel		.65	
12.	Is valuable in helping to prepare presentations for clients			.63
13.	Is available at any time when necessary			.54
14.	Encourages the use of teamwork			.61
15.	Varies leadership style and amount of involvement based on needs			.70
16.	Takes into account the project team's needs before making delivery commitments to clients			.60
17.	Insures that meetings are held often enough			.68
18.	Insures that meetings are effective			.70
19.	Gives detailed instructions when needed			.69
20.	Gives appropriate orientation to people in new assignments			.60

Note: All T values > 13.10

Table 4–16. Factor Intercorrelations

	Staff Development	Client	Teamwork
Staff Development	1.00	.44	.69
Client		1.00	.58
Teamwork			1.00

examined carefully to make sure that it is clearly written and eliciting the desired information.

The *squared multiple correlations* (SCMs) for each item are found in the middle of page 148 of the output. These are estimates of the lower bounds of reliabilities for the individual items. They represent the proportion of variance in each item, which is accounted for by the three factors, much like communalities in PCA. For each item, the sum of the value in Theta Delta and the SMC is 1. Therefore, the same items which appeared to have suspiciously high values in Theta Delta have low values in this table.

The *Coefficient of Determination*, found on page 149 immediately following the SCMs, is a generalized estimate of the reliability of the instrument as a whole. It is a measure of how well the total set of 20 items measures all three constructs (Jöreskog & Sörbom, 1989). While the instrument developer is usually far more concerned with the reliabilities of the separate factors than with total instrument reliability, this value still provides useful information. Because it is dependent upon how well the data actually fit the hypothesized model, it serves as an additional measure of model fit, although its generally high values make it more useful in spotting cases of very poor fit than in supplying additional information on better-fitting models. For this measure, values range from 0 to 1.0, with higher values indicting better model fit. The value estimated for our data, .995, while indicating good model fit, is not unusually high.

The next four statistics really answer the question of whether or not the empirical data confirm the existence of the hypothesized constructs. The *Chi-Square*, two *Goodness-of-Fit* values, and the *Root-Mean-Square Residual (RMR)*, all found in the middle of page 149, are indications of how well the actual data fit the proposed model. If the items do not cluster as predicted, the data do not fit the model. This results in a Chi-Square value which is very large as compared to the degrees of freedom, and in Goodness-of-Fit values well below the maximum of 1. In addition, a poorly fitting model will usually, but not always, result in an unacceptably large Root-Mean-Square Residual.

While Chi-Square can be used as a test statistic, with non-significance indicating good fit, this is not appropriate when the correlation matrix is analyzed. An alternative method is to use the ratio of the Chi-Square value to its degrees of freedom. Even if the covariance matrix is analyzed, the tendency for Chi-Square to be significant for large sample sizes often makes this method preferable.

If the items load strongly and cleanly on the indicated factors and the factor solution accounts for most of the variation in the item scores, the ratio of the Chi-Square value to its associated degrees of freedom will be somewhere between 1:1 and 5:1, with the smaller ratio indicating better fit. Not all researchers agree that a 5:1 ratio is acceptable. Upper bounds of acceptability range from 2:1 (Carmines and McIver, 1981) to 5:1 (Wheaton, Muthen, Alwin, and Summers, 1977), depending upon the author. In addition, the two Goodness-of-Fit indices will be close to 1 and the Root-Mean-Square Residual will be less than .05.

For these data the Chi-Square is just under 3 times the degrees of freedom (488.86/167 = 2.93), a ratio which is generally considered to indicate good fit of the data to the model. The other three values also indicate a reasonable fit between the model and the data. However, it still may be useful to examine more detailed information on the individual items in order to determine whether any of them are especially weak in terms of contributing to the quality of the factor solution.

The basic LISREL output includes several different indications of how well individual items are performing in terms of the factor solution. We have already discussed the factor loadings themselves, the error values in the Theta-Delta matrix, and the squared-multiple correlations. The output also includes summary statistics for the fitted residuals, beginning on the bottom of page 149. These values are the differences between the cells in the input-correlation matrix and those in the matrix estimated by the program. This latter matrix is generated by the empirical data and the factor-analytical model input by the researcher. If the model as postulated fits the data well, the residuals will be small. The larger the residuals, the worse job the model has done of describing the data.

The problem with these residual values is that the importance of their magnitude depends on the metric of the variables. So the output also includes summary statistics for standardized residuals, which we will use. Since these values can be interpreted in much the same way as Z-scores, they provide us with more easily understandable data. Any standardized residuals with values greater than 2.56 could indicate problems with the model and should be considered. For these standardized residuals, page 150 of the output first lists the summary statistics: largest negative value; median; and largest positive value. Next is a stemleaf plot of the actual standardized residuals with the whole numbers to the left of the slashed line, and the decimals, rounded to one place, to the right. For example, the first entry represents a rounded, standardized residual value of 4.4. Looking at this plot, the instrument developer can see that most of the standardized residuals had values close to zero. In fact, over 20 of the pairs had residuals of 0.0 or none at all.

Following the plot is a listing of all pairs of items with standardized residuals greater than 2.56. Although it seems at first glance that this data set has resulted in a large number of suspect standardized residuals, when one takes into account the number of cells in the correlation matrix, it does not seem so extreme. Of the nearly 200 cells reconstructed, 41 resulted in standardized residuals greater than 2.56. Inspection of this list reveals that items S7 and S8 produced the greatest single value, while item S10 appears more than any other. Certainly, this information should be used in evaluating the contribution of those items to the construct validity of the instrument.

In addition to the basic output, other information on individual items is available by request. For this analysis, both T-values and Modification Indices were requested on the OU line (line 2943, page 142). The *T-values*, parameter estimates divided by their standard errors, indicate whether or not the estimated parameters are significantly different from 0. T-values less than 2 are questionable. For this type of analysis, the factor loadings are the primary parameters to scrutinize in this way. If the factor loading for any item resulted in a T-value of less than 2, it would indicate that the item does not really load on the factor at all. This result would force the instrument developer to consider either dropping that item, or, if theoretically plausible, assigning it to another factor. If several items resulted in very low T-values, the construct validity of the instrument would be in question. Inspection of the T-values for the factor loadings for this instrument, found on page 152 of the output, as well as the other parameters, shows them all to be well above the critical value of 2.

Modification Indices were also requested on the OU line. Shown on page 154, these values represent the minimum amount Chi-Square would decrease if you allowed a parameter which has been declared equal to 0 to take on a value (freed a fixed parameter). For CFA, again it is the factor-loading matrix that is of interest, as it is the only matrix with fixed elements equal to zero. These elements represent the factor loadings of items on factors other than the one the instrument developer has postulated. For example, it was specified that item S1 would load on Staff Development and nowhere else. This meant that for row one of the Lambda-X matrix, the value of the cell in the first column, representing the loading of the item on the Staff-Development factor, would be estimated. The values of the other two cells in the row, however, representing loadings on the Client and Teamwork factors, would be set to zero. The program supplies modification indices for all parameters which have been set to zero. Each of these indices indicates the reduction in the value of Chi-Square if that parameter alone were allowed to take on a value. Thus, according to the modification indices generated by this analysis, if item S1 were allowed to load on the Teamwork factor as well as on the Staff-Development factor, the Chi-Square value would decrease by at least 10.77. (Remember that a lower value of Chi-Square indicates a better-fitting model.)

In the search for a better-fitting model, the modification indices are an excellent indication of problems with individual items. However, there are three important points to remember when considering changes to the model based on these values. The first is that they are only valid for one parameter. If you change more than one, the change in Chi-Square will not be the sum of the modification indices. In fact, the amount of that change cannot be predicted. The second, critical point is that you should never free a parameter based solely on the modification index. This should only be done if it makes conceptual sense (Jöreskog and Sörbom, 1989). Closely related to this point is the caution that once you begin changing your model based on statistical rather than conceptual information, you change the whole flavor of the analysis. In fact, the analysis becomes more exploratory than confirmatory in nature (Byrne, 1989).

On page 155, immediately following the modification indices are the estimated changes in the Lambda-X matrix if elements were freed. Again, these changes are based on the freeing of one element at a time rather than freeing several as a group. Following this, the element with the highest index is listed. For these data, it is the cell in the tenth row and third column of the factor-loading matrix. This element represents the loading of item S10, which has been assigned to the Client factor, on the Teamwork factor. It is interesting to note that this item also appeared in more of the "largest standardized residual" pairs than any other item. Inspection of the item, "Keeps the client informed of progress and changes along the way," indicates that it clearly belongs in its original grouping. Perhaps the reason it also loads on the Teamwork factor is that it is similar to those items by virtue of the fact that they all deal with involvement of others. However, it would not make sense conceptually to allow this item to load on both factors. This reasoning would hold even if the modification index were large enough to make a significant difference in the value of Chi-Square, which this one is not.

Table 4–17. Summary of Goodness-of-Fit and Selected Diagnostic Measures

Chi-Square	488.86 (d.f. = 167)
Chi-Square/Degrees of Freedom	2.93
Goodness-of-Fit Index	.92
Adjusted-Goodness-of-Fit Index	.90
Root-Mean-Square Residual	.05
Coefficient of Determination	.995
Largest Standardized Residual (Items 7 8)	7.78
Largest Modification Index (Item 10)	16.10

Conclusions/Guidelines. In order to reach a conclusion concerning the construct validity of the instrument, all of the above output must be taken into consideration. As with EFA, there are no hard and fast cutoff points to determine statistical probability. Although theoretically the Chi-Square value is a hypothesis test. The test is not valid when the correlation matrix is analyzed. That is why the ratio of Chi-Square to degrees of freedom is used (Jöreskog and Sörbom, 1989). Table 4–17 contains a summary of the goodness-of-fit values and other relevant output usually included in journal articles.

In evaluating the results of the analysis, the Chi-Square to degrees of freedom ratio is probably the most important single value. As discussed above, if this ratio is larger than 5:1, the model is seriously flawed. If the ratio is less than 2:1, break out the champagne! Ratios between 2:1 and 5:1 are in the gray area of model fit, becoming more suspect as they approach five. So the Chi-Square value in Table 4–17 represents a fit of the model to the data which is less than perfect, but generally thought of as acceptable.

Goodness-of-Fit Index and Adjusted Goodness-of Fit Index values of .90 and above are usually considered to indicate reasonable model fit (Mulaik, James, Van Alstine, Bennett, Lind and Stilwell, 1989). The difference between the two values is that the adjusted index takes into account the degrees of freedom. Since the two values for our data are .90 and .92, the interpretation of these results as indicating a less than perfect but acceptable model is strengthened. The Root-Mean-Square Residual of .05 also adds credibility to our assessment of model fit, as this is the lowest acceptable value (Byrne, 1989).

The last two items in Table 4–17 describe the extent to which individual items are responsible for lack of fit and identify those items which are most suspect. The standardized residual for items S7 and S8 is fairly large, with a value of 7.78. Close inspection of the wording of these items is indicated. The modification index of 16.10 for item S10 also indicates inspection of the item, as described above, but does not indicate a change in the model unless this change is consistent with the theoretical under-pinnings of the instrument.

Putting all of this information together, the instrument developer can say with some certainty that the hypothesized model fits the data margin-ally well, indicating support for the construct validity of the instrument.

It is possible to further strengthen the evidence for construct validity by comparing the Chi-Square value and associated degrees of freedom of the hypothesized model with those of competing models. One such competing model would be developed if, on inspection of the modification indices and other information, the researcher chose to alter the model in an at-tempt to improve its fit. The specifications of the alternative model would be entered in the same way as those for the hypothesized model, and the results of the two analyses would be compared by a method developed by Bentler and Bonett (1980). In this method the Chi-Square value and asso-ciated degrees of freedom of the new model are subtracted from those of the old. If the difference in the Chi-Square values are significant, given the difference in degrees of freedom, it can be said that the new model is significantly better than the old one. So, if the developer decided to free item S10 to load on Teamwork, as well as on Staff Development, based on the modification indices, the degrees of freedom for the model would decrease by 1, from 167 to 166. In addition, the Chi-Square value would decrease by at least 16.10, to 472.76. If you subtract the Chi-Square value and the degrees of freedom of the new solution from the old one, you get a Chi-Square value of 16.10, which is significant with 1 degree of freedom. This indicates that the new solution is significantly better than the original one, statistically. (Again, it is important to remember that the model should be changed on this basis only if it makes sense theoretically.)

The same technique would be used for other types of model compari-sons as well. If there existed strong conflicting theories. as to the factor structure of the instrument, the instrument developer would rerun the analysis based on these other theories and compare the results to deter-mine the best-fitting model. Even without conflicting theories, it is possible to strengthen the evidence for a reasonable model by comparing the hy-pothesized model to a null model, one in which each item forms its own factor, implying no underlying constructs. A significant Chi-Square value, given the associated degrees of freedom, resulting from subtracting the values of the hypothesized model from those of the null model, would reinforce the construct validity of the instrument.

For further examples of confirmatory factor analyses, see also Bachelor (1989), Ulosevich, Michael and Bachelor (1991), and Welsh, Bachelor, Wright, and Michael (1990).

Multitrait-Multimethod Matrix

The multitrait-multimethod (MTMM) matrix technique has become an increasingly popular way for examining construct validity. Originally introduced in 1959 by Campbell and Fiske, the technique is essentially a systematic way of analyzing correlation coefficients. The use of computers to analyze large data sets gathered from multiple instruments and the emergence of new software have contributed to increased use of the techniques as is evidenced by the increased number of journal articles reporting results using this analysis strategy. The technique appears difficult to understand at first as it appears to become a semantic game. Actually, the technique is quite clear and indeed powerful for examining construct validity under certain conditions. We will first describe the rationale for the technique, along with its associated vocabulary. Following this, the analysis strategy will be described, and some exemplary studies found in the literature will be discussed.

Rationale. Campbell and Fiske (1959) employ the terms *convergent* and *discriminant* validity. To understand these terms, consider a new instrument that you are trying to validate. On the basis of the theory underlying the instrument, you can predict whether scores on the new instrument should relate to scores on the *known* instrument (convergent validity). For example, in the previous section we predicted that the new *Work Values Inventory* (WVI) Altruism scale should correlate positively with the *Survey of Interpersonal Values* (SIV) Benevolence scale (convergent validity), but should not correlate with the *SIV* Conformity scale (discriminant validity). That is, depending on the situation, construct validity can be supported by either high or low correlations.

Campbell and Fiske (1959) also describe the score on an instrument as a trait-method unit. That is, the trait being measured (e.g., Altruism) is assessed by a particular method (e.g., self-report rating scale). The resulting score received on the Altruism scale then reflects variation due to the trait "Altruism" and variation due to the self-report measurement. When we generate correlations between different scales (traits), using different measurement methods (e.g., self-report and teacher rating), we observe systematic variation (correlation) in the scores, which is due to the trait being measured and the measurement technique.

Table 4–18.   Sample Multitrait-Multimethod Matrix for Three Traits and Two Methods

	Traits	Method 1			Method 2		
		A_1	B_1	C_1	A_2	B_2	C_2
Method 1 (Self Report)	A_1 (Peer Relations)	(R)					
	B_1 (Physical Abilities)	HM	(R)				
	C_1 (School)			(R)			
Method 2 (Peer Rating)	A_2 (Peer Relations)	V_A			(R)		
	B_2 (Physical Abilities)		V_B		HH	(R)	
	C_2 (School)	HH		V_C	HM		(R)

The goal of the MTMM technique is to estimate the relative contributions of the trait and method variance to the respective correlation coefficient. To achieve these goals, we need *more than one trait measured by more than one method.* For example, Campbell and Fiske (1959) illustrate the technique using the traits of Courtesy, Honesty, Poise, and School Drive assessed by two different methods: peer ratings and self-report. (Readers should note that the Altruism, Benevolence, and Conformity example presented earlier illustrated the concepts of convergent and discriminant validity but does not really fit the MTMM framework, because only one method, self-report, was employed.)

Analysis Strategy.   Table 4–18 contains a MTMM shell which will be used to illustrate the strategy for estimating the relative contributions of trait and method variance, along with convergent and discriminant validity. For this example, self-concept traits A, B, and C (e.g., peer relations, physical abilities, and school) are measured by methods 1 and 2 (e.g., self-report and peer rating), resulting in six variables. The intercorrelations among these six variables are then generated, along with the reliabilities of each variable. These reliabilities can be either internal consistency or stability estimates. The data are then displayed as in Table 4–18 so that the diagonal entries in parentheses are *reliability diagonals.* To introduce some new vocabulary, we note that the reliabilities are calculated for the same trait and method so the reliability diagonal contains *monotrait-monomethod* (MM) values. The entries in the solid triangles represent intercorrelations among different traits using the same method, so they are referred to as *heterotrait-monomethod* (HM) values. Further, the correlations between the same trait using different methods yield entries in the *validity diagonals*. (These entries are, in fact, similar to the correlations we discussed in the earlier section entitled "Correlation"). Finally, we have correlations between different traits using different methods. These values are found in the two dashed-line triangles and are referred to as *heterotrait-heteromethod* (HH) values. Now that readers are thoroughly confused with semantic labels, we will proceed cautiously to analyze how the MTMM display assists in separating trait and method variance.

First, the entries in the reliability diagonals should indicate that a sufficient amount of reliable variance (say at least .75) is present in each measure. *Second*, the entries in the validity diagonal indicate convergent validity, since they represent the correlation of the same trait using two different methods. These entries should be significantly high and consistent with theoretical expectations so that it is worthwhile to probe further to determine how much of the relationship was due to the trait versus the methods employed. *Third*, each respective validity-diagonal value (i.e., V_A) should be higher than the correlations in the adjacent HH triangle (dashed-line triangle). That is, the A_1A_2 correlation should exceed the A_1B_2 and A_1C_2 correlations, since the B_2 and C_2 variables have neither trait nor method in common with A_1. When the A_1A_2 for V_A correlation is higher than the A_1B_2 and A_1C_2 values, we can say that the magnitude of the A_1A_2 validity coefficient is largely due to shared-trait variance and not to variation shared between methods 1 and 2. As noted by Campbell and Fiske (1959), this rule may be common sense but is often violated in the literature. *Fourth*, the correlation of a variable should be higher when a different method is used to measure the same trait than when the same method is used to measure different traits. Looking at the validity diagonal entry V_A and the HM solid-triangle entries A_1B_1, A_1C_1, and B_1C_1, this means that V_A, which reflects the same trait (A) and different methods (1 and 2), should have a higher value than correlations generated from any combination of variables, which reflect different traits but the same method (i.e., A_1B_1, A_1C_1, and B_1C_1). If this were not the case, we would know that much of the magnitude of V_A (A_1A_2) resulted from common variation due to method and not trait. A *fifth* guideline suggested by Campbell and Fiske (1959) is that the same pattern of relationship be exhibited in each of the HM and HH triangles.

While this analytical strategy may appear confusing at first, readers are encouraged to study the vocabulary carefully so that they understand how the estimates of trait- and method-variance contributions are determined. If one is seriously developing a new instrument, the study of convergent and discriminant validity to estimate trait and method variance is quite important as one seeks to determine the fine interpretations of the constructs underlying a score on the instrument. To thoroughly understand the MTMM technique, readers are encouraged first to carefully read Campbell and Fiske's (1959) article. Following this, some of the studies listed at the end of the chapter can be reviewed.

CFA Illustration.   The growing use of confirmatory factor analysis has led to the development of analysis techniques combining CFA with MTMM analysis. While some work was done in this area in the 70s and early 80s (Kenny, 1976; Rezmovic and Rezmovic, 1981), most of what has been done has taken place in the last few years, as more researchers have become familiar with the relevant computer software. In a study by Vance, MacCallum, Coovert, and Hedge (1988), 256 jet-engine mechanics in the U.S. Air Force were rated on three job tasks (traits): 1) completion of forms; 2) installation of starters; 3) installation of lockwires. There were five different types of ratings used, including three forms of a written proficiency-rating scale with Likert-type choices ranging from 1 (never meets acceptable level of proficiency) to 5 (always exceeds acceptable level of proficiency). The three forms of this scale were administered to: 1) supervisors; 2) peers; and 3) the mechanics themselves. The fourth and fifth types of ratings were the two parts of the *Walk Through Performance Test* (WTPT): 1) the performance of a timed task; and 2) the description of the procedure necessary to perform another task.

The method of analysis developed by Widaman (1985) for using CFA to evaluate convergent and discriminant validity was selected, and the LISREL VI confirmatory-factor analysis program was used. It was hypothesized that the best-fitting model for these data would include a factor for each of the three traits and a factor for each of the four methods (the two parts of the WTPT were combined into one factor, although the scores were kept separate). Each data point in the factor-loading matrix represented the score for a combination of a trait and a method, so there were 15 rows in this matrix (3 tasks × 5 methods). Each of these scores was specified to load on both the task and the method factor which was appropriate to it. For example, the self-rating score for filling out forms was set to load on both the Forms and the Self-factors. It was further hypothesized that the three trait factors would be correlated, since someone who did well on one of the tasks would probably do well on the others, whereas the method factors would not be correlated.

The hypothesized model resulted in a very reasonable fit to the empirical data, with a Chi-Square value of 93.45 for 72 degrees of freedom (X^2/DF = 1.3). This model was then compared to two nested models to examine questions of convergent and divergent validity. (A nested model is a model whose free parameters are subsets of the original model.) The two alternative models were identical to the hypothesized model except for one specific difference in each.

The comparisons were carried out by subtracting the Chi-Square value and the degrees of freedom of the hypothesized model from corresponding values of each alternative model. When these differences are calculated on nested models, the difference in Chi-Square is distributed as Chi-Square with degrees of freedom equal to the difference in degrees of freedom between the two models. Thus, if the difference in Chi-Square is significant, it can be stated that the hypothesized model fits the data significantly better than the alternative being considered.

To examine the convergent validity of the task factors, an alternative model containing only the four method factors was used. When the fit of this model was compared to that of the hypothesized model, the Chi-Square value of the difference, taking into account the degrees of freedom of the difference, was significant, indicating that the model including the task factors had a significantly better fit to the empirical data than did the model without these factors. Convergent validity is supported here by demonstrating that the model which allows the scores to cluster on each of the traits fits the data better than one which does not allow for this clustering.

The discriminent validity of the task factors was examined using an alternative model with one general factor encompassing all three tasks. All scores were forced to load on this factor, as well as on one of the method factors. Again, when the Chi-Square values and degrees of freedom were compared, the difference was significant, indicating a better fit for the hypothesized model. This illustrates that the fit of the model is significantly improved when the scores are allowed to separate (discriminate) among the three tasks, rather than being combined.

The researchers also compared a model with no method factors to the hypothesized model to determine the presence of method variance. The results of this analysis indicated a significant amount of method variance.

Causal Modeling

Path Analysis.   Path analysis is a causal-modeling technique that employs a series of regression analyses to examine relationships among variables *theoretically related* to the target variable under investigation. The importance of a theoretical base for all variables included in this type of analysis can not be overstated. With respect to construct validity, the technique provides more information than that obtained from simple correlations, since several variables are examined. In addition, the series of conducted regression analyses leads to causal statements between the set of independent variables used in the regression procedures and the dependent (i.e., target) variable.

To illustrate this technique a study reported in the *School Situation Survey* (*SSS*) manual (Helms and Gable, 1989) will be described. The *SSS* contains 34 items responded to on a 5-point Likert frequency scale (i.e., "never to always"). Four Sources of Stress (Teacher Interactions, Academic Stress, Peer Interactions, and Academic Self-Concept) and three Manifestations of Stress (Emotional, Behavioral, and Physiological) are measured. Three path analyses were used to obtain finer construct interpretations of the three Manifestations of Stress constructs. In addition to the four Sources of Stress, additional variables were included in the path model on the basis of the literature and previous analyses of *SSS* pilot data. These variables included gender, grade level, grade-level structure, cognitive ability (i.e., achievement), and perceived family stress.

In the context of an examination of construct validity, it is important to again note that the variables included were primarily supported through the literature. For example, gender differences were reported in the literature by Douglas and Rice (1979), who found that females obtained significantly higher scores than did males on the *General Anxiety Scale for Children* and obtained somewhat higher scores, though not significantly, on the *Test Anxiety Scale for Children*. High scores on these measures are suggestive of high stress levels. In a study of children's perceptions of their teachers' feelings toward them, Davidson and Lang (1960) reported that females, more than males, felt that their teachers liked them. Pannu (1974) investigated seven anxiety-inducing elementary-school situations and found that, generally, females obtained higher anxiety scores than males and consistently scored higher on four specific situations: taking tests, peer rejection, threat of being rejected by a teacher, and being sent to the principal's office without knowing why. Males, on the other hand, consistently had higher anxiety scores regarding parents' demand to see report cards.

In the research on the *SSS*, three grade levels (5, 7, and 9) from two types of grade-level structures were used to represent the wide variation in middle school configurations. For example, the fifth-grade students were selected from a kindergarten through fifth-grade (K–5) school configuration,

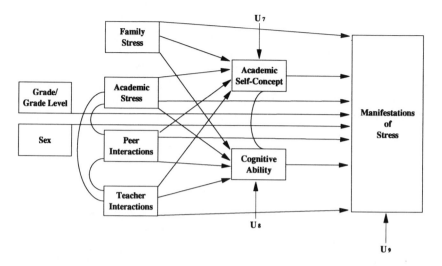

Figure 4–3.   Proposed model of child stress.

and also from a fifth-grade through eighth-grade (5–8) school configuration, so that different social hierarchies, which could place different demands on students, could be studied in the context on Elkind's (1981) notion of power. The question of interest to researchers in this context was: Would a trend for differences in perceived stress levels become apparent between students from the "lower" and "higher" grade-level structures?

Cognitive ability was measured by Total Reading and Total Math scores from the respective school systems' standardized achievement tests. Since the four schools used two different measures, all data were converted to normal-curve-equivalent (NCE) scores, in an attempt to represent achievement indicators that would be as comparable as possible. Finally, a perceived family stress indicator was included. Garmezy (1983), Hetherington (1979), and Hoffman (1979) discussed the impact of divorce, maternal employment, and paternal unemployment as indicators of potential family stress. Data were gathered on these variables, so that a composite indicator of family stress could be generated where high scores reflected higher perceived stress levels.

The causal-modeling technique of path analysis was used to test theoretical models of child stress. The generic model from which each of the three manifestations models was derived is presented in Figure 4–3. The resulting Manifestations models used the respective scores on the Manifestations of Stress scales as the outcome variables. The antecedent variables noted earlier appear to the left of the box labeled Manifestations of Stress. The U in the figures refers to variance unique to the scales.

A series of separate regression analyses, one for each outcome variable, was generated to determine the path coefficients. The F values of the beta weights were tested at the .05 level, so that the relationship between the antecedent and the respective outcome variable, as indicated by the path, could be examined. The paths that were not significant were deleted, and the resulting revised models were tested against their corresponding full or saturated models by the F test for incremental validity (Land 1969; Pedhazur, 1982). The magnitude of the relationships for each of the manifestation variables was of sufficient size to suggest that the set of antecedent variables would contribute to examining the construct validity of the *SSS*, since they provided a major contribution to explaining the outcome variables. In each case, the family stress and grade and grade-level structure variables were not statistically significant.

Significant relationships were found between sex (male = 1, female = 0) and each of the three manifestation variables. This evidence indicated that males experienced greater behavioral responses to stress, while females experienced more emotional and physiological responses to stress. The relationship between academic self-concept and cognitive ability was consistent with the existing literature regarding self-concept and achievement, which reports that students of the lower achievement levels experience poor self-concept.

For illustration purposes, the trimmed model for Behavioral Manifestations is presented in Figure 4–4. The model indicates that students who experience stress as a result of interactions with their teachers may react by acting out in class or being rude to their teachers (Note the line from Teacher Interactions to Behavioral Manifestations and the coefficient of .497; acting out and being rude are example items from the Behavioral Manifestation scale.). On the other hand, females and students experiencing stress caused by academic performance tended to indicate fewer behavioral symptoms. These variables, however, had a strong mediating relationship with Academic Self-Concept (Note that higher Academic Self-Concept scores reflect lower self-concept.), suggesting that children who experience either stressor and have a poor self-concept will likely exhibit behavioral symptoms. Behavioral Manifestations of stress were not found to be directly caused by Peer Interactions. However, Academic Self-Concept appeared to mediate, suggesting that the way a student reacts to stress caused by interactions with classmates is contingent upon the student's academic self-concept. In other words, if self-concept is low and stressful relationships with peers encountered, students may react behaviorally by being rude or engaging in verbal attacks.

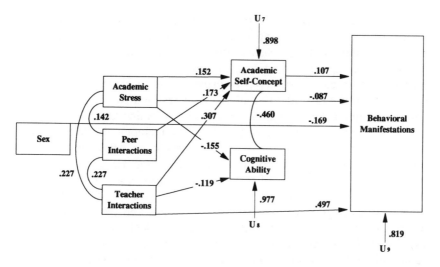

Figure 4–4. Seven-variable trimmed model for explaining behavioral manifestations of stress.

Readers interested in examining the use of path-analytic techniques for a corporate world self-efficacy study by Bandura should review Wood and Bandura's (1989) paper entitled "Social Cognitive Theory of Organizational Management." This reference can be found at the end of Chapter 1.

Structural Equation Modeling. Another method of gathering evidence relating to construct validity is structural equation modeling. Structural equation modeling (SEM) is similar to path analysis in that it examines both correlational and causal relationships among variables. Although it is more difficult to run and to interpret than path analysis, SEM is often preferred because it is better suited to deal with observed variables which represent constructs, and because it involves fewer assumptions about the attributes of the data. Like path analysis, SEM can be very useful in determining the construct validity of an instrument, by providing information on both the relationships between the observed variables and the constructs they represent and the relationships among the measured constructs themselves. If the analysis shows these relationships to be consistent with the existing body of literature and the theoretical rationale of the developer, support for construct validity of the instrument is enhanced. The following example will illustrate the use of this method.

As part of a study of middle-school students which examined the relationships among family background, adolescent bonding, and involvement with controlled substances, Slocumb (1989) developed a 37-item instrument designed to measure three types of adolescent bonding. In addition to the customary methods of establishing the construct validity of the instrument, the structural-equation modeling technique which was used to test the research hypotheses also served to provide further evidence in this area.

A sample of 495 students was asked to respond to a 4-part questionnaire, containing items dealing with socioeconomic status (SES), family integrity, adolescent bonding, and adolescent development. While the other sections of the questionnaire had previously been validated on similar populations, Part II, dealing primarily with bonding, was developed by the researcher for the purpose of this study, and thus required the collection of reliability and validity data. This section contained 37 items comprising three scales designed to measure family, school and peer bonding. The development of this section and subsequent collection of reliability and validity data to support it were carried out prior to, as well as during, the actual administration of the instrument, in accordance with the methods suggested in other sections of this book.

The major research hypothesis stated that SES, family integrity, and bonding would all have direct effects on the development (controlled substance attitudes and behaviors, and other mildly delinquent behaviors) of the students. In addition, it was hypothesized that SES and family integrity would be correlated and would influence bonding.

The final LISREL VI solution to the model, shown in diagrammatic form in Figure 4–5, is very similar to the hypothesized model. Each of the constructs is represented by an oval. These include SES, bonding, family integrity, and development. Each of the observed variables used to measure these constructs is represented by a small rectangle. The relationships between the observed variables and the constructs are shown by arrows leading from the constructs to the variables. The values with these arrows represent the strength of the relationships in both standardized (in parentheses) and unstandardized forms. The arrows pointing into the observed variables from the outside represent the unique variation in each. Arrows from one construct to another represent the relationships among the constructs, with single-pointed arrows indicating causality and double-pointed arrows indicating correlation. The values along those arrows indicate the strength of the relationships between the constructs, again in both standardized and unstandardized form.

The instrument developed to measure bonding is represented by the oval in the center. According to this model, this general construct of bonding is measured by the three scales of the instrument: family, school, and peer bonding. The diagram describes a relationship in which SES and

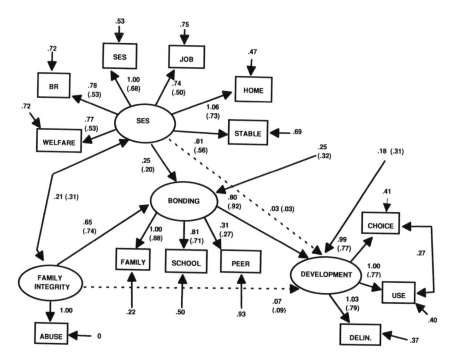

Figure 4–5. LISREL VI solution to the model of adolescent development (reprinted with permission)

family integrity are correlated with each other but do not have a causal relationship. Both of these variables, in turn, have causative influences on the amount of bonding practiced by the adolescent. And bonding, in turn, has a direct effect on the development of the adolescent in terms of choices made concerning controlled substances, actual use of these substances, and incidence of other mildly delinquent behaviors. The slashed lines from SES and family integrity to development indicate that the two family variables have no significant direct effects on development, only indirect effects mediated by bonding.

In terms of the bonding variable, this pattern of causality is identical to the hypothesized model, which was based on a thorough review of the relevant literature. The fact that the relationships of SES, family integrity, and development to bonding are shown to be exactly as hypothesized reinforces the contention that the three bonding scales are measuring what they were intended to measure. Together with the strong relationships between the scales and the construct, especially the family and school-bonding scales, these findings add support for the construct validity of the instrument. Clearly, this type of analysis can provide additional support for construct validity when the resulting model is similar to that hypothesized. However, when the hypothesized model is not substantiated by the analysis, it is often difficult to determine where the problems lie. If the instrument in question was developed properly and has produced reasonable evidence of construct validity using other methods, it is not likely that the instrument itself is the main source of the misfit of the model. In this study, if the bonding construct had not been shown to influence development as hypothesized, it would not necessarily be assumed that the instrument was at fault. Other possible sources of misfit in the model would be examined as well, including the theory on which the model was based.

Rasch Latent Trait Analysis

The previous sections have described the use of several different procedures to examine what can be called "variable definition" in the context of construct validity. This examination will now be extended to employ the Rasch latent trait procedure (Rasch, 1966).

While latent trait techniques have been used extensively in developing cognitive achievement tests (see, for example, Wright & Stone, 1979), their use in developing affective instruments is more recent (see Wright and Masters, 1982). The benefits of the Rasch techniques for obtaining empirical support for both content and construct validity make the procedure an essential part of the instrument development process. When, for example, classical techniques result in incomplete score interpretations, the operational definition of the variable provided by the Rasch model may result in finer construct interpretations that lead to more complete descriptions of high- and low-scoring respondents. This is not to say that the classical factor-analytic and latent trait techniques address the same research question and that the factor analysis failed in finding appropriate answers. In fact, the models do address different questions and provide different information to the instrument developer.[10] The results of the factor analysis depend on sample variability, as correlations among items are examined to address the question:

Are there clusters of items that share sufficient variation to justify their existence as a factor or construct?

On the other hand, the latent trait analysis deals with the "difficulty" of people agreeing with each item, in the context of fitting actual response proportions to probabilities of selecting each response option as specified by the model. Questions addressed by the analysis are as follows:

To what extent are the items well defined along the affective continuum?; *Where are people located on the affective continuum?*; and, based on the observed response patterns in relation to the latent trait model, *How well do the items and people fit the model?*

The purpose of this section is to illustrate how the factor analysis and latent trait procedures can contribute valuable information to the instrument development process.

Gable, Ludlow, and Wolf (1990) compared the utility of the information yielded by the classical factor analysis and latent trait psychometric models to examine the psychometric qualities of the *School Situation Survey* (SSS) (Helms and Gable, 1989), a 34-item attitude instrument that assesses seven variables—four Sources and three Manifestations of school-related stress for grades 3–12 students. A description of the development of the *SSS*, which used classical procedures to examine content and construct validity and alpha reliability, was presented. The additional information obtained by using a Rasch model for rating-scale data was then described. Emphasis was placed upon the adequacy of variable definition and upon an analysis of item and person goodness-of-fit statistics. We note that these analyses and findings have direct application to the development of instruments for assessing feedback to managers, corporate values, and employee satisfaction in the corporate world.

The classical techniques employed to develop the *SSS* included (a) the specification and review of items for defining the targeted variables, as well as support for content validity, (b) Likert's summated rating technique, utilizing the "criterion of internal consistency," (c) correlational (e.g., path analysis) and principal-component results that supported the existence of empirically derived clusters of items that were conceptually meaningful and corresponded to the content domains targeted by the developers, and (d) in light of Nunnally's domain sampling model, a review of the reliability indices that lent further support to the adequacy of item sampling. But as we will illustrate in the next section, these classical procedures did not clearly isolate a problem with the construct validity of one targeted variable.

Data from the *SSS* for 1958 grade 6–8 students were analyzed under the assumption that the data fit a Rasch rating scale model (Andrich, 1978a;

Wright and Masters, 1982); the computer program employed was Scale (Masters, Wright and Ludlow, 1981). Two examples were presented to illustrate practical instrument-development aspects of latent trait analysis:

1. the lack of adequate variable (i.e., construct) definition, and
2. the use of item- and person-fit statistics to reveal item content ambiguity.

Inadequate Definition of a Variable.   Analyses of the data indicated that most of the SSS variables fit a Rasch rating scale model. Student responses were found to be distributed across the Likert response continuum. Further, the item difficulties were spread across much of the continua for the separate variables. It was thus possible to describe high- and low-scoring people on a respective variable, in a manner consistent with the originally hypothesized variable. This is a crucial aspect of the validity issue in the instrument-development process.

However, the Rasch latent trait technique did uncover a problem with one of the SSS Source of Stress variables: Academic Stress. Figure 4–6 presents the variable map for students completing the three items: 21, "I worry about not doing will in school"; 28, "I am afraid of getting poor grades"; and 34, "I worry about taking tests." Displayed are the positions of the 1829 students and three items on the Academic-Stress variable. Of particular importance are the positions of the three items on the continuum that facilitates the definition of the variable. The three-item difficulty estimates (i.e., positioned at being able to respond "always" to the items) were clustered near the center of the continuum, with item calibration values of .06 and −.05 logits.

While the response-frequency data indicated that the ratings were distributed across most of the score range, the item difficulties suggested that there was a weakness in variable definition. The lack of differentiation among items is a construct-validity issue, as it results in little information about the Academic-Stress construct. That is, because the items are not spread out to define a variable, it is difficult to interpret what it means to differentiate between high- and low-scoring students. While the classical techniques employing alpha-reliability and factor-analytic procedures provide support for Nunnally's domain sampling model and initial supportive information for the ongoing examination of construct-validity interpretations, the latent trait model identified the restricted nature of the item definition of the targeted variable. It is clear that a few new items that assess different locations on the underlying continuum need to be developed.

MAP SHOWING POSITIONS OF PEOPLE AND ITEMS ON THE VARIABLE

SCORE (FREQ)	PERSON POSITION	ERROR	PEOPLE (N=1829)	ITEMS (L=3)	ITEM VALUE (SE) MISFIT
11(128)	2.16	0.97	xxxxxxxxxxxxxxxxxxxxxxxxxxxxxxxxxxxxxxxxxxxxxxxx		
10(192)	1.48	0.72	xxxxxxxxxxxxxxxxxxxxxxxxxxxxxxxxxxxxxxxxxxxxxxxx		
9(186)	1.04	0.62	xxxxxxxxxxxxxxxxxxxxxxxxxxxxxxxxxxxxxxxxxxxxxxxx		
8(232)	0.69	0.58	xxxxxxxxxxxxxxxxxxxxxxxxxxxxxxxxxxxxxxxxxxxxxxxx		
7(206)	0.36	0.56	xxxxxxxxxxxxxxxxxxxxxxxxxxxxxxxxxxxxxxxxxxxxxxxx		
				28	0.06(0.0)-2
6(262)	0.05	0.56	xxxxxxxxxxxxxxxxxxxxxxxxxxxxxxxxxxxxxxxxxxxxxxxx	21 34	-0.05(0.0)-2 3
5(194)	-0.28	0.58	xxxxxxxxxxxxxxxxxxxxxxxxxxxxxxxxxxxxxxxxxxxxxxxx		
4(184)	-0.62	0.60	xxxxxxxxxxxxxxxxxxxxxxxxxxxxxxxxxxxxxxxxxxxxxxxx		
3(126)	-1.02	0.65	xxxxxxxxxxxxxxxxxxxxxxxxxxxxxxxxxxxxxxxxxxxxxxxx		
2(78)	-1.51	0.75	xxxxxxxxxxxxxxxxxxxxxxxxxxxxxxxxxxx		
1(34)	-2.26	1.02	xxxxxxxxxxxxxxx		

Figure 4–6. Variable map for the Academic•Stress scale.

In contrast, the item difficulties of the six items (N = 1958) on the Behavioral-Manifestation-of-Stress scale in Figure 4–7 indicate a higher degree of differentiation of the variable for the following items: (a) 29, "I try to get attention by action silly in class"; (b) 27, "I talk back to my teacher"; (c) 4, "I get into fights"; (d) 25, "I yell at my classmates"; (e) 20, "I pick on other students"; and (f) 9, "I talk in class when I should be quiet." Since these items are spread out in their calibrations, there is a more adequate definition of this variable. Hence, a more complete score interpretation is possible for both low- and high-scoring people. At the upper end of the continuum, the hardest terms to agree with (i.e., Items 29, 27, 4, and 25) define an "aggressive behavioral act depicted by 'talking in class.' " Thus, for the Behavioral scale, the continuum is reasonable and consistent with the original conception of the variable.

Item Fit. Item and person fit can now be addressed to obtain further insight into the variables being measured. The item-fit-statistic information for the N = 1598 students responding to the six Behavioral-scale items was examined. It was found that items 27 and 29, with calibration values of .45 and .47, were the most difficult for students to respond to at "always." With positive t-values exceeding 3.00, these two items were identified as not fitting the measurement model. This was because low-scoring students who were not expected to respond "always," were, in fact, giving such a response. These were students who, in general, felt that they exhibited relatively few of the behaviors targeted by the remaining four items on the scale, but unexpectedly said that they "always" exhibited the behaviors identified in items 27 and 29.

At this point, it is not clear whether it is the content of the items or the characteristics of the students that has resulted in these unexpected response patterns. In order to clarify this situation, the response frequencies were examined. Relatively few students said that they never talk in class (Item 9), yet relatively few also said that they always try to get attention by acting silly in class (Item 29) or always talk back to teachers (Item 27). A consideration of the structure of Item 29 suggests that competing behaviors may be involved. A student may tend to feel that he or she "always" wants "attention" but may, nonetheless, not tend to "act silly."

Person Fit. Regarding person fit, we now turn to an examination of the response patterns for those students with large positive-fit statistics (i.e., t > 2.00). We find that numerous students scored higher than expected (i.e., responding "always") on Items 27 and 29. To illustrate this finding, we selected a few of the students who exhibited unexpected response patterns.

MAP SHOWING POSITIONS OF PEOPLE AND ITEMS ON THE VARIABLE

SCORE (FREQ)	PERSON POSITION	ERROR	PEOPLE (N=1958)	ITEMS (L=6)	ITEM VALUE (SE) MISFIT
23 (0)	2.92	0.95			
22(0)	2.28	0.68			
21(0)	1.90	0.56			
20(4)	1.62	0.50	xx		
19(2)	1.38	0.47	x		
18(10)	1.17	0.44	xxxx		
17(8)	0.98	0.43	xxx		
16(18)	0.80	0.42	xxxxxxxx		
15(22)	0.63	0.42	xxxxxxxxxx	29	0.47(0.0) 8
14(30)	0.46	0.42	xxxxxxxxxxxxxxx	27	0.45(0.0) 5
13(52)	0.28	0.42	xxxxxxxxxxxxxxxxxxxxxxxx	4 25	0.15(0.0) 2-2
12(66)	0.11	0.42	xxxxxxxxxxxxxxxxxxxxxxxxxxxxxx		
11(84)	-0.07	0.43	xxxxxxxxxxxxxxxxxxxxxxxxxxxxxxxxxxxxxxx	20	-0.13(0.0) -6
10(94)	-0.26	0.43	xxxxxxxxxxxxxxxxxxxxxxxxxxxxxxxxxxxxxxxxxxxx		
9(104)	-0.45	0.44	xxxxxxxxxxxxxxxxxxxxxxxxxxxxxxxxxxxxxxxxxxxxxxxx		
8(146)	-0.65	0.46	xxxxxxxxxxxxxxxxxxxxxxxxxxxxxxxxxxxxxxxxxxxxxxxxxxxxxxxxxxxxxxxx		
7(192)	-0.86	0.47	xxxxxxxxxxxxxxxxxxxxxxxxxxxxxxxxxxxxxxxxxxxxxxxxxxxxxxxxxxxxxxxxxxxxxxxxxxxxxxxxxx		
6(208)	-1.10	0.50	xxxxxxxxxxxxxxxxxxxxxxxxxxxxxxxxxxxxxxxxxxxxxxxxxxxxxxxxxxxxxxxxxxxxxxxxxxxxxxxxxxxxxxxx	9	-1.12(0.0) -8
5(186)	-1.36	0.53	xxxxxxxxxxxxxxxxxxxxxxxxxxxxxxxxxxxxxxxxxxxxxxxxxxxxxxxxxxxxxxxxxxxxxxxxxxxxxxxx		
4(214)	-1.67	0.57	xxxxxxxxxxxxxxxxxxxxxxxxxxxxxxxxxxxxxxxxxxxxxxxxxxxxxxxxxxxxxxxxxxxxxxxxxxxxxxxxxxxxxxxxxx		
3(198)	-2.03	0.64	xxxxxxxxxxxxxxxxxxxxxxxxxxxxxxxxxxxxxxxxxxxxxxxxxxxxxxxxxxxxxxxxxxxxxxxxxxxxxxxxxxxxxx		

Figure 4–7. Variable map for the Behavioral scale.

 the model expects a response of "1," a response more
consistent with the person's responses to the remaining five items. The
discrepancy between the actual and expected response results is a standardized residual value of 1. Person 171 exceeded his or her expected response for both Items 27 and 29. Person 196 exhibited an interesting but
extreme pattern—either "never" or "always". While it is noted that with
only six items one large unexpected response can inflate the fit statistic,
the responses to Items 27 and 29 are fairly consistent (i.e., low-scoring
students who respond "always"). In a later section, we will illustrate how
the standardized residuals can be examined to see if they are explained by
item structure or person characteristics.

In summary, the use of such techniques as factor analysis, correlations, and alpha reliability will assist in the instrument-development process, but the shortcomings of these procedures have been illustrated in this section. It was found that approaching a factor or variable definition problem with factor-analytic techniques can result in a derived factor that is conceptually meaningful and accounts for a sufficient amount of variation. Further, proper levels of alpha reliability (i.e., above .75) lent support to adequate sampling of items from the intended domain of content. The findings presented in this section suggest that these classical procedures, while necessary, may not be sufficient, and could, in fact, lead one to a false sense of the adequacy of variable definition. Without adequate variable definition, the validity of meaningful score interpretations is in question.

It is obvious that well-thought-out decisions that are grounded in the literature and judgments of experts need to be made during the content-validation process. When the targeted variables are conceptually identified and then operationally defined through the item-writing process, instrument developers need to place greater emphasis on spanning the underlying psychological continuum for a targeted variable. Systematic expert judgments need to be gathered, using appropriate rating procedures, to examine the estimated item placement along the underlying psychological continuum prior to gathering actual respondent data. In addition to classical techniques, a latent trait rating-scale model should also be employed to test the developer's original conception of the variable for consistency with respondent score patterns.

Understanding Rasch-Model Residuals Through Analysis of Person Characteristics and Item Structure

In the previous section we examined item and person fit statistics to reveal potential item-content ambiguity. Unexpected patterns of standardized residuals for persons not fitting the Rasch model can also be studied in the context of the characteristics of the persons and of the structure of the items (see Gable, Ludlow, and Wolf, 1990). Given adequate information about the people and a clear understanding of item content, these essentially descriptive and graphic analyses can contribute greatly to a better understanding of the data, informed test revisions, and more meaningful inferences from test scores.

An analysis of the standardized residuals for 1039 students in grades 5, 7, and 9 was undertaken for one of the misfitting items described in the earlier section:

29.: "I try to get attention by acting silly in class."

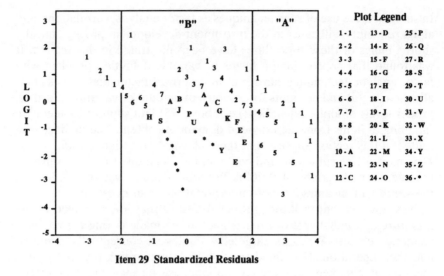

Figure 4–8.   Plot of standardized residuals against person stress level estimates partitioning typical and atypical groups.

The analysis was undertaken for the purpose of revealing unexpected person-by-item response interactions. The overall fit statistic for the item (3.96) indicated that there were unexpected responses made by numerous students. As is often the case with a misfitting item, it was unclear whether some systematic characteristics of the students were responsible or whether the item structure had provoked the unexpected responses. The next section explores these two areas.

Person Characteristics.   The first series of steps consisted of plotting the standardized residuals against the person estimates. These plots revealed whether unexpected responses were coming from high-scoring or low-scoring students. The plot of standardized residuals for item 29 against person estimates (i.e., logits) is presented in Figure 4–8. The first definition of the atypical (i.e., higher agreement than expected, $N = 43$) group is depicted in section A of the plot, where standardized residuals are ≥2.0; the typical group is depicted in section B where standardized residuals are between −2.0 and 2.0 ($N = 875$). The date were disaggregated further as depicted in Figure 4–9. The definition of the typical and atypical groups was restricted to low-scoring people with a logit score less than −1.0 (see sections C and D). Section D in Figure 4–9 identifies the primary target

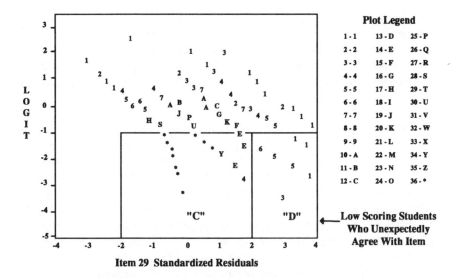

Figure 4–9. Plot of standardized residuals against person stress level estimates partitioning low stress typical and atypical groups.

group for the study, 22 low-scoring (i.e., less frequent self-perceived behavioral displays) students who were unexpectedly agreeing with the item.

In the first set of analyses, descriptive and inferential tests were generated for the person characteristics. Several exploratory statistical tests were run to see if any of the person characteristics related to the response patterns for the targeted item. Two discriminant-function analyses were run for the (a) atypical versus typical and (b) low-stress atypical versus low-stress typical groups. It was found that the person characteristics (i.e., general anxiety, stress due to teacher interactions, grade level, sex, number of siblings, reading level, and math level) could not significantly separate the groups given the small samples in the atypical group.

There were, however, some non-significant trends in the data. These trends were interesting, as they assist in a better understanding of the unexpected person-by-item response interaction for the statement, "I try to get attention by acting silly in class." Here we have a group of students who gave low ratings to the other items on the Behavioral-Manifestations scale. That is, they perceived that they do not tend to manifest such behaviors as getting into fights, talking in class when the should be quiet, picking on other students, yelling at classmates, and talking back to teachers.

But they do indicate that they "get attention by acting silly in class." As compared to the students whose responses are more typical, given their behavioral manifestations of stress members of this group "tended" to be lower achievers in math and reading and to perceive higher levels of source-related stress based on their views of how teachers feel and act toward them.

Item Structure.   At this point the investigation turned to the structure of the item. Given that only a few students were found to be in the low-stress/unexpected agreement (N = 22) and high-stress/unexpected disagreement (N = 9) groups, we know that the item-fit statistic (3.96) was created by additional factors. First, the factor-analysis results for the total group of 1038 students reported by Helms and Gable (1989) were examined. While the structure of the Behavioral-Manifestations factor was reliable (alpha = .75) and stable across the three grade levels, our targeted item always correlated the lowest with the derived factor. Inspection of the structure of the item suggests a situation of perceived double meaning in the content. Some students may try to get attention in class by acting silly. Others may try to get attention in other ways or just act silly. It appears that the potential double meaning in the item has contributed to the lower correlations with the remaining five items defining the scale, and may contribute to the unexpected person-by-item response interactions for a subset of students. This may be especially true for the students in the low-stress atypical group who tended to have lower reading scores.

In summary, this section has illustrated the use of descriptive/graphic and inferential techniques to analyze residual patterns (i.e., difference between observed and expected responses) generated under the Rasch rating scale model. The use of exploratory techniques to analyze person characteristics and item structure was illustrated to provide a better understanding of unexpected person-by-item response patterns. Such explorations are deemed important for instrument development and analysis activities, since they assist in providing finer score interpretations—the crux of the validity construct issue.

Finally, we note an application of examining the variable-definition aspect of construct validity for a curriculum-evaluation activity appropriate for school or corporate environments. Masters and Hyde (1984) administered a 25-item attitude-toward-school measure to grade-3 and grade-4 students in 10 different schools and used the Rasch-latent-trait model to examine the invariance of item-scale values (i.e., difficulty of agreeing with a particular item) across schools. Many researchers would pursue such an analysis from a purely psychometric basis to examine the model's assumption of invariance of the item-parameter estimates for different samples of respondents. The feature of Masters and Hyde's study is the use of the latent trait procedure in the realm of school evaluation. Operationally, they were studying the construct validity or definition of the attitude variable for the 10 different respondent groups. While, overall, the attitude data fit the Rasch latent trait model, two items were identified as functioning differently across the 10 schools. This finding had potential practical significance for school evaluation in that the two items were used in discussions of school characteristics and programs for the particular schools. For example, in a particularly disadvantaged school where special efforts were aimed at promoting self-confidence, self-esteem, and cooperation among students, a higher than expected agreement was found with the item: "I like speaking in front of the class." Across all 10 schools , this item, which was the most difficult with which to agree, turned out to have a high item-misfit statistic, probably due to the atypical response pattern found in one school in relation to the pattern expected from the latent trait model. It was also found that in one school many students found it more difficult to agree than expected with the item: "Physical education is fun." It would be interesting to follow up this situation with an evaluation of the physical education program using qualitative-research techniques, such as class observations and interviews of teachers and students. While not causal in nature, these two examples of items with atypical response patterns could be related to aspects of school-program efforts and could contribute to program-evaluation discussions.

Item Bias

The study of item bias for cognitive measures has received considerable attention (see Cole, 1981; Berk, 1982; Hambleton and Swaminathan, 1984). Techniques available for detecting item bias clearly frame the investigations in the validity domain. This is consistent with Cronbach's (1971) statement that "validation examines the soundness of all the interpretations of a test" (p. 433).

For affective measures, therefore, it is appropriate to study bias in the internal structure of the affective instrument (i.e., construct bias). According to Reynolds;

> Bias exists in regard to construct validity when a test is shown to measure different hypothetical traits (psychological constructs) for one group than another or to measure the same trait but with differing degrees of accuracy. (Reynolds, 1982a, p. 194)

The important role of factor analysis in studying the internal structure of an affective measure should be clear. Until the mid-1980s, though, the factor-analytic approaches used to study bias in internal-test structure (i.e., compare factor structures) focused mainly upon cognitive measures (Reynolds, 1982b). Jensen (1980) and Cole (1981) have reviewed these approaches and conclude that, for the cognitive measures studied, similar factor structures tended to be found for Blacks and Whites and for low and high socioeconomic groups.

Since the mid 1980s, there has been an increasing number of studies comparing factor structures of affective measures across subgroups. There is a widespread reluctance among researchers, however, to use the terms "item bias" and "test bias" when referring to affective instruments, reflecting a belief that these terms have connotations appropriate only in relation to cognitive instruments. Most of these studies, therefore, are said to deal with the operational terms "factorial invariance" and "differential response patterns" or "differential item functioning," rather than test or item bias. The purpose remains to test the invariance of factor structure and/or item uniqueness across various groups in order to determine whether the instruments are measuring the same characteristics or traits with the same amount of accuracy across these groups. Only when equality is determined can the groups appropriately be compared or combined. The ability of instrument developers to determine this equality statistically has been enhanced by computer programs which allow simultaneous multi-group CFA and provide measures of model fit both for the total group and for the individual subgroups. LISREL is the most commonly used of these programs.

One of the earlier studies in this area was unusual in that it identified itself as dealing with item bias in affective instruments. This was Benson's (1982) work, in which the response patterns of Hispanic, White, and Black grade-8 students were studied for a 32-item self-concept and social-attitudes instrument. Simultaneous multi-group confirmatory factor-analysis using the LISREL IV program was employed to statistically compare the groups on the factor structure identified for Hispanics by a classical factor-analysis and varimax rotation. After identifying the factor structure for the Hispanic group, three issues were addressed across the three groups, namely the number of factors derived for each group, correlations between the factors, and the errors in measurement. The data clearly supported the existence of bias and identified items for further review. Many other studies have tested the factorial invariance of affective measures across groups which differ by culture, gender, age, and various other demographic characteristics (Wilson, Moore, and Bullock, 1987; Idaszak, Bottom, and Drasgow, 1988; Byrne, 1988). These sorts of analyses have become an important addition to the ongoing investigation of the construct validity of these instruments.

Another method of analysis which has been widely used to examine item bias in the cognitive domain is Item-Response Theory. While there have been far fewer studies applying this technique to the affective domain, the authors compared a method using Item Response Theory with one using multiple-group confirmatory factor analysis when examining item bias on the School-Situation Survey (Wolf and Gable, 1991). The study indicated that the two methods, while different both methodologically and theoretically, produced very similar results.

Known Groups

Construct validity can also be examined by showing that the instrument successfully distinguishes between a group of people who are known to possess a given characteristic and a group (or groups) who do not have high levels of the trait. The key to this analysis is that the existence of the trait in the groups has to be clearly documented with some external criterion. The groups are then administered the new instrument, and an analysis such as the t-test is used to test whether the instrument has successfully described the known differences between the groups.

Two general examples will clarify the known-groups technique. In the early development of some paper-and-pencil-anxiety measures, groups of high-anxiety and low-anxiety people were formed. The participants' palms were wired for the skin-sweating response (i.e., galvanic skin response), and then an anxiety-provoking situation was presented so that physical levels of anxiety could be documented. The high-anxiety and low-anxiety groups were then administered the anxiety instrument. If the resulting group means were significantly different, the researcher could argue that the instrument measures the anxiety construct.

In the area of personality measures, researchers have used a clinical team of experts to diagnose a group of individuals as having a certain personality trait. A personality measure purporting to assess the same trait was then administered to the target group and to a group judged to be normal. Significant differences between the groups in the predicted direction supported the construct validity of the instrument.

Criterion-Related Validity

Criterion-related validity addresses the question: *"What is the relationship between scores on the instrument and some external criterion that provides a more direct measure of the targeted characteristic?"* Depending upon the time frame employed in the validity inference, two types of criterion-related validity studies are possible: concurrent and predictive.

Evidence of Concurrent Validity

In studying concurrent validity, the instrument is administered, and then, at *approximately the same time*, date are obtained from another instrument or through observation techniques (i.e., the criterion), so that the relationship between the instrument and the criterion can be established and analyzed with respect to the theory underlying the instrument and the criterion. The most frequent statistic employed is the simple correlation coefficient.

For example, we could administer the *Gable-Roberts Attitude Toward Teacher Scale to* a class of students as part of a teacher-evaluation project. Concurrently, the principal could observe several classes and rate the teacher on the same scale. The validity of the student perceptions as an accurate assessment of the teacher's behaviors could be ascertained by correlating the student and the principal ratings on the three *GRATTS* attitude scales (Presentation of Subject, Interest in Job and Students, and Teaching Techniques). If the correlation was near .90, we could conclude that the *GRATTS* possesses criterion-related validity for estimating the principal ratings. If this was the case, we could *substitute* the student ratings, gathered in a brief 10-minute scale administration, for the principal ratings, which entailed several time-consuming observations of the class.

Readers may feel that this is really an example of construct validity. It is true that the data analysis is the same, but note that the research question is different. Whereas, in an analysis of construct validity, we are studying the existence of underlying concepts or constructs to explain variation among items or scales, the criterion-related validity study addresses the viability of substituting a quick student-rating procedure for a time-consuming principal-observation procedure.

Another example from the cognitive domain will further illustrate the nature of concurrent validity. A test manual from an IQ measure contains a correlation of .90 between the long and short form administered concurrently to a sample of students. The criterion-related (concurrent) validity of the short form is then supported as an estimate of the scores from the long form, so that practitioners can confidently use the short form in the midst of testing time constraints.

Evidence of Predictive Validity

In other situations, the instrument may be designed to *predict* a future characteristic or behavior. The instrument is administered, and then, at some later time, measures are obtained on some external criterion. Correlational analyses (simple correlations, regression analyses, or discriminant-function analysis) are most often employed as the primary statistical technique. If the prediction is successful, future users of the instrument could administer the instrument and then estimate the student's status regarding the criterion variable.

An example of establishing the criterion-related (predictive) validity for an attitude scale is found in a study by McCook (1973). A 36-item attitude scale entitled the *McCook Alternative Programming Scale* (MAPS) was developed as a means of predicting potential school dropouts (i.e., the criterion). Responses from 108 grade-12 nondropouts and 39 actual school dropouts were submitted to a factor analysis (construct validity) which resulted in 10 attitude scales (e.g., Parental Involvement in School, Attitude Toward Education, Importance of Peer Group Relations, and Stimulation of the School Environments). A discriminant-function analysis was then run to ascertain to what extent the attitude scales (predictors) could successfully classify the dropouts and nondropouts into their respective groups (i.e., the criterion). Seventy-four percent (74%) of the nondropouts and 94% of the dropouts were successfully assigned. Thus, the criterion-related validity of the MAPS was supported.

Criterion-related validity studies are essential for cognitive instruments used in the area of personnel selection (see American Psychological Association, 1975). Since these studies rarely include affective measures, we will not detail them in this volume. We will, however, refer to them to further illustrate criterion-related validity. In the personnel field, it is common for the selection measures used to assess aspects of the actual job content. Included are tasks, activities, or responsibilities needed to successfully carry out the particular job. The assessment instrument is administered as a selection measure on the logic that the people with the higher scores would perform better in the actual job. The criterion-related validity study necessary to support use of the instrument in this manner could be carried out as follows: A pool of applicants is administered the selection measure. Ideally, most of the applicants would, in this validity study, be admitted to the job class so that at a later time their peers and supervisors could rate their on-the-job performance (i.e., the criterion). The performance ratings would then be correlated with scores on the selection instrument, and high correlations would be supportive of the criterion-related (predictive) validity of the instrument. In practice, it is often difficult to admit most of those tested to the job class. In this situation, the selection measure is administered to current employees in the job class so that their scores can be correlated with on-the-job performance ratings. Naturally, those already on the job are a previously selected group, which tends to restrict the range of scores on both variables. Thus, although these studies are used as predictive studies, they are not always accepted as good evidence of criterion-related validity. Since proper criterion-related studies are difficult to carry out in the personnel area, the content-validation study, which carefully specifies the correspondence of the job specifications with the items and domains on the instrument, takes precedence in the validation process.

A criterion-related validity study from the affective area of interest clearly illustrates the predictive nature of the validity question. One measure of a successful use of an interest inventory is its ability to predict future actual-job choices. To support the criterion-related (predictive) validity of the interest measures, researchers typically administer the interest inventory in high school, and then follow the students for a few years to find out the actual areas of their job choice. For example, Silver and Barnett (1970) reported evidence for the criterion-related validity of the *Minnesota Vocational Interest Inventory* (MVII) by examining job choices (e.g., building trades, electrical, and machine shop) made by high-school graduates who completed the *MVII* in grade 9. Similarly, Campbell (1973) has presented supportive criterion-related (predictive) validity for the *Strong Vocational Interest Blank for Men* (SVIB), indicating that approximately 75% of various samples of college graduates wound up in jobs that were compatible with their high-school (grade 12) *SVIB* profiles.

Summary

In this chapter, we have examined the issue of the validity of instruments for measuring affective characteristics. In general terms, the validity issue pertained to gathering judgmental and empirical evidence regarding what affective characteristic is assessed by the instrument. The interpretations of data were based upon inferences made from the operational definitions (item stems) derived from the conceptual (construct) definitions underlying the instrument.

Three types of validity, as well as appropriate judgmental and empirical evidence, were described, focusing on evidence that would contribute to finer interpretations of the characteristics measured (i.e., that would rule out alternate interpretations). Each type of validity addressed a particular question. Studies of *content validity* asked: "To what extent do the items on the instrument adequately sample from the intended universe of content?" Studies of *construct validity* asked: "To what extent do certain explanatory concepts (constructs) explain covariation in the responses to the instrument items?" Finally, studies of *criterion-related validity* asked: "What is the relationship between scores on the instrument and some external criterion that provides a more direct measure of the targeted characteristic?"

It should be clear that the three types of validity are not independent considerations. All three types share the need for a clearly stated theoretical rationale underlying the targeted affective characteristic—it is on the basis of this rationale that validity is examined, and the interpretations of the data from the instrument are refined. The types of validity differ in the nature of the validity question asked. Two researchers may both employ correlations in their study of validity, but one may be examining construct validity and the other criterion-related validity.

All developers of affective instruments need to place great emphasis on establishing content validity. The intended use of the instrument will dictate the type and amount of construct and criterion-related validity evidence necessary. For example, measures of self-concept, attitude, and values will most likely emphasize construct validity; interest inventories will emphasize criterion-related validity.

Notes

1. Later we will note that an oblique rotation results in a factor-pattern matrix containing regression weights.

2. To be technically correct, we should use the term principal-component analysis when 1's are in the diagonal and indicate that we have derived components instead of factors. In this volume, we will loosely use the term factor analysis instead of component analysis.

3. Readers should recall that the 1's in the diagonal of a correlation matrix represent the variances for each variable. While the items may initially have different variances, their covariances are normalized in generating the correlation matrix so that the items all have equal variance of 1. Otherwise, we could not compare the off-diagonal correlations between the variables. Actually, all of the items are represented by vectors in a geometric space. The 1's in the diagonal of R indicate that we have given each vector a length of 1 and now proceed to examine the angles between the vectors. These angles reflect the correlations between the vectors on the basis of the cosine function. (See the discussion of rotating factors in the illustration provided later in this section.)

4. Include "FORMAT-SORT/" on the rotation procedure line to obtain sorted items by ranked loadings.

5. Readers should note that plotting the data for an oblique rotation is a little tricky in that the coordinates are located as parallel projections from the point to the line. That is, the

coordinate for the *x* axis is obtained by dropping a line parallel to the *y* axis from the point to the *x* axis, which results in a regression weight. In a varimax rotation, perpendicular or parallel projections are identical and result in correlations. In an oblique rotation, perpendicular projections yield correlations in the FACTOR-STRUCTURE matrix: these should be ignored.

6. The correlations represent the cosine of the angle between the two factors. Noting that the cosine curve can be used to calculate angles for various correlations, readers may wish to estimate the actual angle between axes. For example, when the correlation is zero, the angle is 90° (varimax). In our example, the correlation between Factors I and II is .47, so the angle between the axes in Figure 4–2 is estimated to be 75°.

Cosine Curve

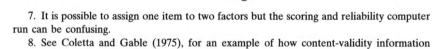

7. It is possible to assign one item to two factors but the scoring and reliability computer run can be confusing.

8. See Coletta and Gable (1975), for an example of how content-validity information assisted in finer interpretations of the derived factors.

9. Only selected scales from the *KUD, SIV,* and *SOV* were used for two reasons. First, the scales were theoretically important to the study; and second, at least one scale from each measure was deleted because the measures were ipsative in nature (i.e., all respondents obtain the same total score). Chapter 3 discussed the implications of ipsative instruments.

10. Special appreciation is extended to David Andrich for his comments in this area.

Additional Readings

Content Validity

Aiken, L.R. (1980). Content validity and reliability of single items or question-naires. *Educational and Psychological Measurement*, 40, 955–959.

Benson, J. (1981). A redefinition of content validity. *Educational and Psychological Measurement*, 41, 793–802.

Fitzpatrick, A.R. (1983). The meaning of content validity. *Applied Psychological Measurement*, 7, 3–13.

Guion, R.M. (1977). Content validity—the source of my discontent. *Applied Psychological Measurement*, 1, 1–10.

Kreitler, S., and Kreitler, H. (1981). Test item content: Does it matter? *Educational and Psychological Measurement*, 41, 635–642.

Yalow, E.S., and Popham, W.J. (1983). Content validity at the crossroads. *Educational Researcher*, 12(8), 10–14.

Construct Validity: Correlations

Byrne, B.M., and Carlson, J.E. (1982). Self-concept and academic achievement: A causal modeling approach to construct validation using a multiple-indicator structural equation model. Paper presented at the meeting of the American Educational Research Association, New York, 1982.

Cronbach, L.J., and Meehl, P.E. (1955). Construct validity in psychological tests. *Psychological Bulletin*, 52, 281–302.

Falender, C.A., and Mehrabian, A. (1980). The emotional climate for children as inferred from parental attitudes: A preliminary validation of three scales. *Educational and Psychological Measurement*, 40, 1033–1042.

Franklin, M.R., Duley, S.M., Rousseau, E.W., and Sabers, D.L. (1981). Construct validation of the Piers-Harris children's self-concept scale. *Educational and Psychological Measurement*, 41, 439–443.

Gable, R.K., Roberts, A.D., and Owens, S.V. (1977). Affective and cognitive correlates of classroom achievement. *Educational and Psychological Measurement*, 37, 977–986.

Hanna, G.S., and Neely, M.A. (1978). Discriminant validity of career maturity inventory scales in grade 9 students. *Educational and Psychological Measurement*, 38, 571–574.

Johnson, B.W., Redfield, D.L., Miller, R.L., and Simpson, R.E. (1983). The Coopersmith self-esteem inventory: A construct validation study. *Educational and Psychological Measurement*, 43, 907–913.

Karmos, A.H. (1979). The development and validation of a nonverbal measure of self-esteem. *Educational and Psychological Measurement*, 39, 479–484.

Loevinger, J. (1979). Construct validity of the sentence completion test of ego development. *Applies Psychological Measurement*, 3, 281–311.

Lunneborg, P.W. (1979). The vocational interest inventory: Development and validation. *Educational and Psychological Measurement*, 39, 445–451.

Omizo, M.M., and Michael, W.B. (1983). Relationship of COP System interest inventory scales to vocational preference inventory (VPI) scales in a college sample: Construct validity of scales based on professed occupational interest. *Educational and Psychological Measurement*, 43, 595–601.

Platten, M.R., and Williams, L.R. (1981). Replication of a test retest factorial validity study with the Piers-Harris children's self-concept scale. *Educational and Psychological Measurement*, 41, 453–462.

Schmeck, R.R., and Ribich, F.D. (1978). Construct validation of the inventory of learning processes. *Applied Psychological Measurement*, 2, 551–562.

Construct Validity: Multitrait-Multimethod

Avison, W.R. (1978). Auxiliary theory and multitrait-multimethod validation: A review of two methods. *Applied Psychological Measurement*, 2, 433–449.
Beck, M.D., and Beck, C.K. (1980). Multitrait-multimethod validation of four personality measures with a high-school sample. *Educational and Psychological Measurement*, 40, 1005–1011.
Byrne, B.M. (1985). Validation of Stephen's Social Behavior Assessment (revised): A multitrait-multimethod analysis. Paper presented at annual meeting of the American Educational Research Association, Chicago, 1985.
Lomax, R.G., and Algina, J. (1979). Comparison of two procedures for analyzing multitrait-multimethod matrices. *Journal of Educational Measurement*, 16, 177–186.
Marsh, H.W. (1983). Multitrait-multimethod analysis: Distinguishing between items and traits. *Educational and Psychological Measurement*, 43, 351–358.
Marsh, H.W., and Butler, S. (1984). Evaluating reading diagnostic tests: An application of comfirmatory factor analysis to multitrait-multimethod data. *Applied Psychological Measurement*, 8(3), 307–320.
Marsh, H.W., and Smith, I.D. (1982). Multitrait-multimethod analyses of two self-concept instruments. *Journal of Educational Research*, 74, 430–440.
Ray, M.L., and Heeler, R.M. (1975). Analysis techniques for exploratory use of the multitrait-multimethod matrix. *Educational and Psychological Measurement*, 35, 255–265.
Roshal, S.M., Frieze, I., and Wood, J.T. (1971). A multitrait-multimethod validation of measures of student attitudes toward school, toward learning, and toward technology in sixth grade children. *Educational and Psychological Measurement*, 31, 999–1006.
Schriesheim, C.A. (1981). Leniency effects on convergent and discriminant validity for grouped questionnaire items: A further investigation. *Educational and Psychological Measurement*, 41, 1093–1099.
Shavelson, R.J., Hubner, J.J., and Stanton, G.C. (1976). Self-concept: Validation of construct interpretations. *Review of Educational Research*, 46(3), 407–441.
Turner, C.J. (1981). Convergent and discriminant validity of measures: Sources of self-esteem in the classroom. *Educational and Psychological Measurement*, 41, 445–452.
Webb, S.C. (1973). Convergent-discriminant validity of a role oriented interest inventory. *Educational and Psychological Measurement*, 33, 441–451.
Widaman, K.F. (1985). Hierarchically nested covariance structure models for multitrait-multimethod data. *Applied Psychological Measurement*, 9(1), 1–26.

Construct Validity: Known Groups

Hattie, J., and Cooksey, R.W. (1984). Procedures for assessing the validities of tests using the "known groups" method. *Applied Psychological Measurement*, 8(3), 295–305.

Construct Validity: Factor Analysis

Aransky, N.K., Covert, R., and Westler, L. (1972). Factor structure of the Pummer studies of attitude patterns. *Educational and Psychological Measurement*, 32, 1119–1123.

Athanson, J.A., O'German, J., and Meyer, E. (1981). Factorial validity of the vocational interest scales of the Holland vocational preference inventory for Australian high school students. *Educational and Psychological Measurement*, 41, 523–527.

Bunting, C.E. (1981). The development and validation of the educational attitudes inventory. *Educational and Psychological Measurement*, 41, 559–565.

Cascio, W.F. (1976). An empirical test of factor structure stability in attitude measurement. *Educational and Psychological Measurement*, 36, 847–854.

Chodzinski, R.T., and Radhewa, B.S. (1983). Validity of Career Maturity Inventory. *Educational and Psychological Measurement*, 43, 1163–1173.

Choroszy, M., Powers, S., and Douglas, P. (1984). The factorial validity of the mathematics attribution scale. *Educational and Psychological Measurement*, 44, 739–742.

DoBoeck, P. (1978). Validity of a cognitive processing model for response to adjective and sentence type inventories. *Applied Psychological Measurement*, 2, 563–570.

Elterick, R. and Gable, R.K. (1972). The factorial dimensions of the Comparative Guidance and Placement Tests for three freshmen curricula groups. *Educational and Psychological Measurement*, 32, 1061–1067.

Fernandes, L.M., Michael, W.B., and Smith, R.A. (1978). The factorial validity of three forms of the dimensions of self-concept measure. *Educational and Psychological Measurement*, 38, 537–545.

Frary, R.B., and Ling, J.L. (1983). A factor-analytic study of mathematics anxiety. *Educational and Psychological Measurement*, 43, 985–993.

Gable, R.K. (1973). The effect of scale modifications on the factorial dimensions and reliability of Super's Work Values Inventory. *Journal of Vocational Behavior*, 3, 303–322.

Gable, R.K., and Pruzek, R.M. (1971). Super's Work Values Inventory: Two multivariate studies of interim relationships. *Journal of Experimental Education*, 40, 41–50.

Gable, R.K., and Roberts, A.D. (1983). An instrument to measure attitude toward school subjects. *Educational and Psychological Measurement*, 43, 289–293.

Gable, R.K., LaSalle, A., and Cook, W. (1973). Dimensionality of self-concept: Tennessee Self-Concept Scale. *Perceptual and Motor Skills*, 36, 551–560.

Green, K., and Harvey, P. (1983). Cross-cultural validation of the attitudes toward mainstreaming scale. *Educational and Psychological Measurement*, 43, 1255–1261.

Gressard, C.P., and Loyd, B.H. (1985). Validation studies of a new computer attitude scale. Paper presented at the annual meeting of the American Educational Research Association, Chicago, 1985.

Ireland-Coleman, M.M., and Michael, W.B. (1983). The relationship of a measure of the fear of success construct to scales representing the locus of control and sex-role orientation constructs for a community college sample. *Educational and Psychological Measurement*, 43, 1217–1225.

Keller, R.T., and Holland, W.E. (1978). A cross-validation study of the Kirton adaptation-innovation inventory in three research and development organizations. *Applied Psychological Measurement*, 2, 563–570.

Kerlinger, F.M. (1972). The structure and content of social attitude referents: A preliminary study. *Educational and Psychological Measurement*, 32, 623–630.

Kim, J., and Muller, C.W. (1978a). *Introduction to factor analysis: What it is and how to do it.* Beverly Hills: Sage.

Kim, J., and Mueller, C.W. (1978b). *Factor analysis: Statistical methods and practical issues.* Beverly Hills: Sage.

Lester, P.E. (1987). Development and factor analysis of the teacher job satisfaction questionnaire (TJSQ). *Educational and Psychological Measurement*, 47, 223–231.

Marsh, H.W., and Hocevar, D. (1983). Confirmatory factor analysis of multitrait-multimethod matrices. *Journal of Educational Measurement*, 20, 231–248.

McGuire, B., and Tinsley, H. (1981). A contribution to the construct validity of the Tennessee Self-Concept Scale: A confirmatory factor analysis. *Applied Psychological Measurement*, 5, 449–457.

McIntire, W.G., and Drummond, R.J. (1976). The structure of self-concept in second and fourth grade children. *Educational and Psychological Measurement*, 36, 529–536.

Michael, J.J., Plass, A., and Lee, Y.B. (1973). A comparison of the self-report and the observed report in the measurement of the self-concept: Implications for construct validity. *Educational and Psychological Measurement*, 33, 433–439.

Michael, W., and Smith, R.A. (1976). The development and preliminary validation of three forms of a self-concept measure emphasizing school-related activities. *Educational and Psychological Measurement*, 36, 521–528.

Michael, W.B., Smith, R.A., and Michael, J.J. (1978). Further development and validation of a self-concept measure involving school-related activities. *Educational and Psychological Measurement*, 38, 527–535.

Michael, W.B., and Bachelor, P. (1990). Higher-order structure-of-intellect creativity factors in divergent production tests: A re-analysis of a Guiford data base. *Creativity Research Journal*, 3, 58–74.

Michael. W.B., and Bachelor, P. (1991). Higher-order factors of creativity within Guiford's structure-of-intellect model: A re-analysis of a fifty-three variable data base. *Creativity Research Journal*, 4, 157–175.

Michael, W.B., and Bachelor, P. (1992). First-order and higher-order creative ability factors in structure-of-intellect measures administered to sixth-grade children. *Educational and Psychological Measurement*, 52, 261–273.

Moran, M., Michael, W.B., and Derubo, M.H. (1978). The factorial validity of three frequently employed self-report measures of self-concept. *Educational and Psychological Measurement*, 38, 547–563.

Murphy, C.A., and Gable, R.K. (1988). Validity and reliability of the original and abridged role conflict and ambiguity scales. *Educational and Psychological Measurement*, 48, 743–751.

Nugent, J., Covert, R., and Chansky, N. (1973). Factor analysis of the Runner studies of attitude patterns interview form (1970 revision). *Educational and Psychological Measurement*, 33, 491–494.

Piotrowski, C., Dunn, B.R., Sheery, D., and Howell, W.L. (1983). Factor structure on the adult Nowicki-Strickland I-E Scale in a college population. *Educational and Psychological Measurement*, 43, 1211–1218.

Pound, R.E., Hansen, J.C., and Putnam, B.A. (1977). An empirical analysis of the Tennessee Self-Concept Scale. *Educational and Psychological Measurement*, 37, 545–551.

Powers, S., and Rossman, M.H. (1983). The reliability and construct validity of the Multidimensional-Multiattributional Causality Scale. *Educational and Psychological Measurement*, 43, 1227–1231.

Powers, S., Douglas, P., and Choraszy, M. (1984). A reliability and validity investigation of the mathematics attribution scale. *Educational and Psychological Measurement*, 44, 733–737.

Rachman, D., Amernic, J., and Aranya, N. (1981). A factor-analytic study of the construct validity of Holland's Self-Directed Search Test. *Educational and Psychological Measurement*, 41, 425–437.

Reece, M., and Gable, R.K. (1982). The development and validation of a measure of general attitudes toward computers. *Educational and Psychological Measurement*, 42, 913–916.

Renzulli, J.S., and Gable, R.K. (1976). A factorial study of the attitudes of gifted students toward independent study. *Gifted Child Quarterly*, Spring (20), 91–99.

Shoemaker, A.K. (1980). Construct validity of area specific self-esteem: The Hare Self-Esteem Scale. *Educational and Psychological Measurement*, 40, 495–501.

Sirois, H., and Gable, R.K. (1979). A factor analytic validity study of the Blumberg-Amidon Teacher Perceptions of Supervisory-Teàcher Conferences Instrument. *Education*, 99(3), 298–302.

Tabachnick, B.G., and Fidell, L.S. (1983). *Using multivariate statistics*. New York: Harper & Row.

Vidoni, D.O. (1977). Factor analytic scales of the adjective checklist replicated across samples: Implications for validity. *Educational and Psychological Measurement*, 37, 535–539.

Walters, L.H., and Klein, A.E. (1980). A cross-validated factor analysis of the Nowicki-Strickland Locus of Control Scale for Children. *Educational and Psychological Measurement*, 40, 1059–1064.

Watson, J.M. (1983). The Aiken Attitude Toward Mathematics Scales: Psychometric data on reliability and discriminant validity. *Educational and Psychological Measurement*, 43, 1247–1253.

Woolley, R.M., and Hakstian, A.R. (1992). An examination of the construct validity of personality-based and overt measures of integrity. *Educational and Psychological Measurement*, 52, 475–489.

Criterion-Related Validity

Campbell, J.B., and Chun, K. (1977). Inter-inventory predictability and content overlap of the 16PF and the CPI. *Applied Psychological Measurement*, 1, 51–63.

Claudy, J.G. (1978). Multiple regression and validity estimation in one sample. *Applied Psychological Measurement*, 2, 595–607.

Davidson, M.L., and Robbins, S. (1978). The reliability and validity of objective indices of moral development. *Applied Psychological Measurement*, 2, 389–401.

DeBoeck, P. (1981). Individual differences in the validity of a cognitive processing model for responses to personality inventories. *Applied Psychological Measurement*, 5, 481–492.

Goldberg, L.R. (1977). What if we administered the "wrong" inventory? The prediction of scores on personality research form scales from those on the California Psychological Inventory, and vice versa. *Applied Psychological Measurement*, 1, 339–354.

Goldberg, L.R., Norman, W.T., and Schwartz, E. (1980). The comparative validity of questionnaire data and objective test data in predicting five peer rating criteria. *Applied Psychological Measurement*, 4, 183–194.

Hansen, C.J., and Zytowski, D.G. (1979). The Kuder Occupational Interest Inventory as a moderator of its predictive validity. *Educational and Psychological Measurement*, 39, 107–118.

Jensen, J.M., Michael, J.J., and Michael, W.B. (1976). The concurrent validity of the Primary Self-Concept Scale for a sample of third grade children. *Educational and Psychological Measurement*, 35, 1011–1016.

Keller, R.T., and Holland, W.E. (1978). A cross-validation study of the Kirton Adaption-innovation Inventory in three research and development organizations. *Applied Psychological Measurement*, 2, 563–570.

Knapp, R.R., Knapp, L., and Michael, W.B. (1979). The relationship of clustered interest measures and declared college major: Concurrent validity of the COP-System Interest Inventory. *Educational and Psychological Measurement*, 39, 939–945.

Omizo, M.M., Hammett, L., and Loffredo, D.A. (1981). The dimensions of self-concept (DOSC) as predictors of academic achievement among Mexican-American junior high school students. *Educational and Psychological Measurement*, 41, 835–842.

Prediger, D.J. (1977). Alternatives for validating interest inventories against group membership criteria. *Applied Psychological Measurement*, 1, 275–280.

5 THE RELIABILITY OF AFFECTIVE INSTRUMENTS

In the previous chapter we examined the validity question: "Does the instrument measure what it is supposed to measure?" We now turn to the issue of reliability, which is concerned with the question: "Does the instrument provide us with an accurate assessment of the affective characteristics?" By "accurate assessment," we mean scores that are *internally consistent* upon one administration of the instrument, as well as *stable* over time, given two administrations (see Stanley, 1971). In this chapter we will explore the measurement theory underlying reliability and the evidence needed to support its internal consistency and stability. Following this, we will summarize the factors affecting the level of reliability and discuss the relationship between reliability and validity. The chapter will conclude with a presentation of an analysis of SPSS computer output pertaining to the reliability of the *Gable-Roberts Attitude Toward Teacher Scale*. All readers should review Kuder's (1991) article entitled "Comments Concerning the appropriate Use of Formulas for Estimating the Internal Consistency Reliability of Tests."

Reliability Theory

Any time we administer an affective instrument, we obtain scores on the scales (item clusters) contained in the instrument. Recall that these scores are most often the sums of the responses to a set of items that have been written to operationally define the affective characteristic. Inferences are then made from these scores back to the original conceptual definition of the characteristic. Obviously, these inferences are only as good as the amount of true-score variance in the observed score. That is, any individual's observed total score (X_{TOT}) actually consists of a true-score component (X_{TRUE}) and an error component (X_E) such that

$$X_{TOT} = X_{TRUE} + X_E \tag{5.1}$$

The first part, X_{TRUE}, reflects the portion of the individual's total score that is associated with a true reflection of the affective characteristic. That is, indeed, a hypothetical component, since it reflects the individual's score obtained by a perfect measurement instrument under perfect conditions. Kerlinger (1973) notes that this score can be considered the mean of the individual's scores under repeated administrations, assuming no learning took place. Quite obviously, we never see an individual's true score; we can only *estimate* the portion of the total score that is true. At the same time, each individual's total score includes an error component (X_E), which reflects the portion of the total score that we cannot explain. The raw score formula can also be written in terms of variance components as

$$V_{TOT} = V_{TRUE} + V_E \tag{5.2}$$

While it would be nice to be able to measure an affective characteristic with precise measurement tools, we know that the instruments we use lead to some errors in measurement. In assessing the reliability of an instrument, we attempt to estimate the amount of error in the scores, so that we can estimate the amount of true variance in the total score—the less error involved, the more reliable the measurement.

Following Guilford's (1954) traditional conception of reliability, Kerlinger (1973, p. 446) lists two definitions of reliability as follows:

1. Reliability is the proportion of the "true" variance to the total variance of the data yielded by a measuring instrument:

$$rel = \frac{V_{TRUE}}{V_{TOT}} \tag{5.3}$$

2. Reliability is the proportion of error variance to the total obtained variance yielded by a measuring instrument subtracted from 1.00, the index 1.00 indicating perfect reliability:

$$\text{rel} = 1 - \frac{V_E}{V_{TOT}} \qquad (5.4)$$

The first formula is certainly a theoretical formula since we never actually measure the true variance. The second formula, though, is practical in that it suggests that the empirical route for estimating the reliability of an instrument is to separate the amount of error variance from the total variance.

Nunnally (1978) presents a description of this measurement error in the context of a domain-sampling model. This model is consistent with our description of an instrument in Chapter 2, as a sampling of items from a well-defined domain or universe of content. In fact, defending this sampling was the basis for establishing content validity.

According to Nunnally (1978), an individual's true score is the score the person would hypothetically obtain over the entire domain of items. Thus, reliability can be conceptualized as the correlation between an individual's scores on the sample of items and their true scores. For any one item, the correlation between the item and the true score equals the square root of the average intercorrelation of item 1 with all of the other items (j) in the domain as follows (Nunnally, 1978, p. 198):

$$r_{1_{TRUE}} = \sqrt{\bar{r}_{1j}} \qquad (5.5)$$

Since the average correlation of an item with all other items in the domain is the reliability coefficient, then the square root of the reliability coefficient equals the correlation of the item with true scores in the domain (i.e., the sum of all items in the domain) such that

$$r_{1_{TRUE}} = \sqrt{\text{rel}} \qquad (5.6)$$

By squaring both sides of equation 5.6, we can also state that the reliability coefficient equals the square of the correlation between an item and true scores such that

$$r^2_{1_{TRUE}} = \text{rel} \qquad (5.7)$$

Recalling that squared correlations indicate the proportion of shared variance, we can extend this to a cluster of items defining a scale on an instrument and state that, conceptually, *the reliability coefficient indicates what percentage of variance in the scale scores can be considered "true" variance.*

For example, if the reliability of a scale is found to be .90, we can infer that 90% of the total variance in the scale scores is true.

Nunnally's development of measurement error (1978) clearly shows the importance of employing reliable instruments in any research project. Unfortunately, some researchers do not take the issue of reliability seriously enough and later find the results of their study to be confusing and disappointing.

Sources of error: Generalizability theory

The previous section described the theory underlying reliability. It became clear that the vehicle for studying reliability was the estimation of the amount of error in the measurement. In this section we will explore the possible sources of error in the context of selecting appropriate procedures for establishing reliability.

We know that the more reliable an instrument, the less the error in the measurement. But where do errors come from? Actually there are several different sources of error depending on the nature of the test and how it is employed. According to Nunnally (1978), the major source of error within an instrument is due to *inadequate sampling of items*. This is consistent with our domain-sampling approach for establishing content validity. Given an adequate sampling of items from the domain, each individual theoretically has a given probability of agreeing with each item, and this probability can be generalized to establish the expected number of agreements within the particular sample of items. The source of error, then, comes from inadequate sampling of items from the domain, which results in low probability-agreement tendencies. This situation is directly reflected in the average interitem correlation, which would tend to be lower when inadequate sampling is present. In the next section, we will discuss the reliability-estimation procedure (i.e., Cronbach's alpha) appropriate for addressing this source of error.

Administration of the same instrument on two *different occasions* is another source of error. Without some intervention we expect that most affective characteristics are fairly stable across a time period of, say, approximately three weeks. If we administer the same instrument to a sample of individuals and find that their scores are not stable, we could conclude that the variability in individual responses over time has contributed to an unreliable assessment.

Another source of possible error is present when parallel *forms* of an instrument have been developed, and the developer wishes to quantify the extent to which the items on both forms assess the same concepts.

Acknowledging the form of the instrument as a source of error will not be emphasized, since such parallel forms are not often developed for affective measures.

Several other sources of error, which are difficult to quantify, can be labeled *situational factors*. For instruments measuring affective characteristics, the most common sources, as described by Isaac and Michael (1981, p. 126), are: (a) individual response variation due to such factors as fatigue, mood, or motivation, which could lead to random or careless responses; (b) variation in administration procedures (i.e., across time for two administrations or across classrooms during one administration) to include physical factors such as temperature and noise and psychological factors such as unclear instructions or lack of test time pressures; and, (c) errors in hand or computer scoring of the responses (e.g., failure to properly address missing data, which leads to zero scores on a 1–5 Likert scale).

It should be clear, though, that reliability like validity is a generic term that refers to different research questions and types of evidence. When reporting reliability data, researchers must clearly state the type of reliability addressed, since it points to the sources of error being studied. For most affective measurement applications, the first two sources of error, **items** and **occasions**, are the most important to assess. Several writers (e.g., Brennan, 1992; Shavelson and Webb, 1991; Shavelson, Webb, and Rowley, 1989; Webb, Rowley, and Shavelson, 1988) have pointed out that classical test theory allows us to quantify the sources of error one at a time. Thus, Cronbach's alpha coefficient would provide us with information regarding item sampling, but we would then need to administer the instrument on a second occasion to examine the error due to occasions or stability reliability. By considering only one definition and source of error at a time, the researcher can not simultaneously examine the relative importance of various sources of error. In fact, it is quite puzzling if one of the separately generated coefficients is high and the other is low.

Generalizability theory, as described by the authors noted above, allows us to estimate the magnitute of these multiple sources of error. Using generalizability theory we could simultaneously examine the homogeneity of the items and the stability of the responses over time, as well as the interaction of these two sources of error. Appendix C contains material developed by S.V. Owen that presents an overview of the purposes of generalizability theory. In addition, example data are presented in a simple instructional manner to illustrate how the generalizability theory coefficients are determined and interpreted. Our appreciation is extended to Professor Owen for the sharing of his work. We will now turn to the two major types of reliability evidence: internal consistency and stability.

Types of Reliability Coefficients

Internal Consistency

The alpha internal-consistency reliability coefficient is deduced directly from the domain-sampling theory of measurement error (Nunnally, 1978). As such, it addresses the important source of error due to the sampling of items, as well as the situational factors described earlier, where a single administration of the instrument is used. The formula is so important that Nunnally states: "It is so pregnant with meaning that it should routinely be applied to all new test" (p. 214). The equation reads as follows:

$$\text{rel}_\alpha = \frac{K}{K-1}\left(1 - \frac{\sum \sigma_i^2}{\sigma_y^2}\right) \tag{5.8}$$

where k = the number of items, $\sum \sigma_i^2$ = the sum of the item variances, and σ_y^2 = the variance of the total (scale) scores. Reference to formula (5.6) also suggests that the *square root of coefficient alpha is the estimated correlation of the scale scores with errorles true scores*. Nunnally (1978) also notes that alpha represents the expected correlation of one instrument with an alternative form containing the same number of items, which further clarifies the association of alpha with the domain-sampling theory of measurement error.

The ideal way to generate alpha reliabilities is to use a computer, which will also generate several other item- and scale-level statistics. Readers should be aware, however, that alpha can be estimated quite quickly using a hand calculator. A simple example will be used to illustrate this point and to further develop the concept of internal consistency of individuals' responses.

Consider the following four attitude-toward-school items taken from a larger set of items:

> I like school.
> School is really fun.
> I enjoy going to school.
> School makes me happy.

Assume that 200 grade-6 students responded to these four items on a 5-point Likert scale ranging from "strongly disagree", (1) to "strongly agree" (5). Rather than generating the applicable variances specified in equation 5.8, the alpha reliability can be estimated by using the interitem

Table 5–1.   Interitem Correlations for Attitude Toward School Items

		1	*2*	*3*	*4*
	1	—			
Items	2	.40	—		
	3	.50	.55	—	
	4	.55	.40	.40	—

correlations (see Cronbach, 1951) calculated when the factor analysis was run to examine construct validity. Table 5–1 contains hypothetical interitem correlations. The alpha reliability coefficient is generated in two steps. First, calculate the average interitem correlation, which is .47 for our example. This average interitem correlation is important in that low levels reflect both a high incidence of error in the sampling of items from the domain of content and the possible existence of situational factors that would influence the responses to the items.

It is important to note that, in essence, calculating the average of the correlations estimates the reliability of a one-item scale. Therefore, it is necessary to estimate the reliability of the four-item scale by using the general form of the Spearman-Brown Prophecy Formula:

$$\text{rel} = \frac{K\bar{r}}{1 + (K - 1)\bar{r}} \tag{5.9}$$

where K represents the number of times one wishes to increase the length of the instrument, and $\bar{r}$ represents the average interitem correlation. Inserting $K = 4$ (i.e., the original number of items) and $\bar{r} = .47$ into the formula for our example yields an alpha of .78. Based upon this reliability coefficient, we can then say that 78% of the variance in the scale scores (i.e., sum of four items) can be considered true variance, and that the estimated correlation of the scales with errorless true scores is the square root of .78 or .88 (see Equation 5.6).

Readers should note that a common error made using this procedure for estimating alpha is to set K at the number of interitem correlations instead of the number of items. In fact, only for a three-item scale will the number of correlations and the value of K be equal. Another common error is to forget to reverse score-negative item stems prior to generating the correlations. Failure to do this will result in negative correlations that appear to lower the alpha reliability. Reverse scoring in the beginning of the analysis will alleviate the need to keep track of which items are negative stems. If you have not reverse scored the items, simply ignore the negative signs when averaging the correlations. If you did reverse score the negative items and still get negative correlations, you will get and, indeed, deserve to get a low alpha.

Also check to see that you have recorded the proper number of interitem correlations if you are taking the values from a correlation matrix for a larger number of items. A handy check is to calculate the number of correlations you need as the "number of combinations of K (items) things taken two at a time," as follows:

$$\frac{K!}{2!\,(K-2)!} \qquad (5.10)$$

where K represents the number of items, and 2 indicates you are correlating two items at a time.[1] For our four-item example, the number of combinations is figured to be

$$\frac{4!}{2!\,2!} = 6$$

For a six-item scale, the number of combinations grows quickly to be

$$\frac{6!}{2!\,4!} = 15$$

Again, recall that figuring the number of correlations you need to average can be done with Equation 5.10, but the K in Equation 5.9 represents the original number of items in your scale. Using the value of K from Equation 5.10 in 5.9 will result in a greatly inflated alpha coefficient. In the short run, you will be quite pleased, but soon reality will set in, and the proper alpha value will be lower. During the pilot testing of a new instrument, this type of error could be quite serious.

In this section, we have illustrated the procedure suggested by Cronbach (1951) to estimate an alpha reliability based upon interitem correlations. A final example using the four attitude-toward-school items listed earlier will further clarify the concept of internal consistency. The question that we pose, in this connection, is: Just what is it about individual response patterns that leads to high alpha internal-consistency reliabilities? We answer this question by considering the two small hypothetical data sets contained in Table 5–2. Example 1 illustrates internally consistent responses across the four items defining the scale. Note that some of the individuals tend to consistently "agree" with the items—i.e., like school—while other students appear not to like school—they consistently "disagree" with the items. Picture two hypothetical students who really do like school (e.g.,

Table 5–2. Response Patterns Leading to High and Low Alpha Reliabilities[a]

		Example 1				Example 2			
		Items				Items			
		1	2	3	4	1	2	3	4
	A	5	4	4	5	2	2	1	2
	B	2	1	2	3	4	1	4	1
	C	1	1	2	1	5	1	4	3
	D	4	5	5	4	2	4	3	2
	E	5	5	5	5	2	4	1	2
Individuals	F	5	3	4	5	4	5	4	5
	G	2	3	1	2	2	1	5	2
	H	3	2	4	1	1	2	5	2
	I	5	2	2	5	4	3	3	1
	J	2	5	5	4	2	2	5	2

[a]Item Stems: 1. I like school.
2. School is really fun.
3. I enjoy going to school.
4. School makes me happy.
Response format: 5 = Strongly agree
4 = Agree
3 = Undecided
2 = Disagree
1 = Strongly disagree

individuals A and D). When these individuals processed these four item stems, they perceived content similarities so that they responded in a similar and consistent manner by tending to "agree" with the statements. Readers will recall that the items represent operational definitions for a concept called "attitude toward school." To the extent that we observe internally consistent responses, we have found some reliability evidence that can be reported along with our validity evidence.

Example 2 illustrates response patterns that are not internally consistent across the four items. Some individuals (e.g., B and C) when processing these four item stems did not perceive similar meaning and thus supplied inconsistent responses. For example, individual C "strongly agreed" with the item "I like school," but "strongly disagreed" with the item "School is really fun."

The effect of internally consistent and inconsistent response patterns on alpha reliability is illustrated in Table 5–3. For each data set, the interitem correlations are presented, and the alpha internal consistency reliability

Table 5–3. Interitem Correlations and Estimated Alpha Reliabilities

		Example 1					*Example 2*		
		Item					*Item*		
		1	2	3	4	1	2	3	4
	1	—	.43	.44	.81	—	−.06.	.06	−.12
Interitem	2		—	.77	.57		—	−.39	.30
Correlations	3			—	.45			—	.33
	4				—				—

$\bar{r} = .58$ $\bar{r} = .02$

Estimated Alpha Reliabilities

$$\text{rel} = \frac{4(.58)}{1 + 3(.58)} = \boxed{.85} \qquad \text{rel} = \frac{4(.02)}{1 + 3(.02)} = \boxed{.08}$$

is estimated using Cronbach's (1951) technique. Note that the average interitem correlation ($\bar{r} = .58$) is higher for example 1, which the domain-sample model attributes to a more adequate sampling of items from the "attitude toward school" domain. In Example 2, we noted that respondents perceived different meanings for the item stems than were anticipated during the content-validation stage. Thus, the domain-sampling model suggests that these items are not representative or well sampled from the domain and therefore result in a lower average interitem correlation ($\bar{r} = .02$). The effect of this situation on the alpha reliabilities is evident, as Example 1 has an alpha of .85 and Example 2, of .08. If the items and data from Example 2 were part of a pilot test of a new instrument, we could only say that 8% of the observed variance in attitudes toward school can be considered true variance and that the estimated correlation between scale scores formed from these items and true scores is .28 (see Equation 5.5). Example 2, then, sends us back to step one where we reanalyze the operational definitions of the content domain and conduct a new content-validity study.

The *split-half* technique has also been used to examine internal-consistency reliability. In this procedure, the instrument or a scale on the instrument is randomly split into two equivalent sets of items which represent two samples of items from the content domain. The correlation of the scores from the two halves is then entered into a special form of the Spearman-Brown Prophecy Formula, which follows from Equation 5.9, to generate the reliability of the whole instrument as follows:

$$\text{rel} = \frac{2r_{12}}{1 + r_{12}} \qquad\qquad (5.11)$$

where 2 = the factor that indicates that the instrument is really twice as long, and r_{12} = the correlation between the two half-instruments.

The major problem with this technique is its dependence on obtaining a proper split of the whole instrument on the basis of item content. Given that computer programs can readily produce Cronbach's alpha, which represents the average of *all possible splits* of the instrument, it is rare that one would want to use the split-half technique.

Stability Reliability. The measures of internal consistency discussed in the previous section do not address an important source of error—error due to fluctuations in individual responses over time. If one is using an affective instrument in a pre/post program evaluation model, we would like to assume that the differences between the pre- and post-scores are due to a treatment effect and not due to a lack of stability reliability in the instrument. On the basis of the affective trait being measured, we need to first theoretically establish that the trait should be stable for, say, a three-week period in the absence of a treatment designed to change the trait. We then administer the instrument to an applicable sample and correlate the test/retest scores to establish its stability reliability.

There are some cautions for planning a stability reliability study. First, we need to be aware that high stability reliability does not address the item-sampling issue from the domain-sampling model (see Nunnally, 1978, ch. 7). That is, an inadequate sample of items could result in an average interitem correlation near zero, which would yield a very low alpha internal-consistency reliability. These same items, though, could be found to have a very high stability reliability, since the two types of reliability address different sources of error. Thus, we should always first establish the alpha reliability and then, if appropriate, generate the stability reliability coefficient. An instrument with a low alpha and a high stability reliability should not be considered reliable.

A second caution pertains to the effect of learning from the first test. It is important to carefully think through the nature of the concept measured by the particular operational definitions (items) selected. If the time between the test and retest is too short (i.e., a few days), respondents may merely repeat their recalled responses.

Third, we should note that the tendency to respond with extreme ratings ("strongly agree") for many items, or attempts to fake or give socially desired responses, can yield stable response patterns. Finally, we note that graduate students often report any form of reliability located in a journal article or test manual without carefully thinking through and defending the nature of the reliability evidence needed for their particular use of the instrument. Another common error is to report reliability data for samples that have little in common (e.g., grade level) with the samples to be employed in the proposed research.

It should be clear that reliability is a generic term, which necessitates different methods (i.e., internal consistency and stability) of generating reliability evidence to account for different sources of error. Clearly designed and labeled reliability evidence should be present prior to using any instrument.

Factors Affecting Reliability

The reliability of a set of items is affected by several factors: the characteristics of the sample, the homogeneity of the item content, the number of items, and the response format. It is essential that instrument developers understand how these areas potentially affect the reliability of a set of items. In this section, we will discuss each area, noting that they are not independent, but most likely interact with each other to affect especially the internal-consistency reliability level.

Sample Characteristics

In pilot testing a set of items, the selection of the sample is crucial. The goal is to select a sample that exhibits the same level of variability in the affective characteristic as that existing in the target population. For example, if a set of attitude-toward-secondary-school items is to be administered, the sample of high-school students should reflect the entire high-school population. It would be an error to administer the items to four easily available grade 9–12 honors classes. Since these students would most likely exhibit generally positive attitudes toward school, the variance in their responses would be less than that for the total high-school population. It is a well-known statistical fact that lowering the level of variance in either or both variables involved in a correlation necessarily reduces the size of the correlation. Thus, two particular items on the scale may actually correlate quite well, but the sample characteristics have, in effect, put a ceiling on the level of correlation. As a result, the average interitem correlation for the set of items will be low, as will the alpha internal-consistency reliability. The domain-sampling model will then lead the developer to conclude erroneously that the sampling of items from the universe of items is inadequate, when in fact the sampling of items may have been quite adequate, but the sampling of people inadequate. The moral is then to be sure that pilot samples always include representative individuals who will produce a variability in responses similar to that in the target population.

This lack of variability will also be found when respondents tend to exhibit extreme responses which result in either high or low means. Items with high or low means and associated low variability will contribute little to the reliability of the set of items. Also, it should be noted that such items stand little hope of contributing much to the study of construct validity using factor analysis, since the factor-analysis model is based upon correlations and shared variance among items. Again, these items will not exhibit much variance that can be shared with the other items.

A final comment regarding how the sample relates to sample size is in order. To help ensure representative samples with adequate variability in responses, developers should use large samples. The question then becomes how large is large? During the instrument-development process, it is quite likely that an item-level factor analysis will be run to examine construct validity. This complex procedure necessitates a safe sample size of about 6–10 times the number of people as items. While smaller samples will suffice for most factor-analytic models, the factor structure for a sample with small people-to-item ratios will not be conceptually clear or stable if the analysis is repeated on another sample.

Homogeneity of Item Content. During the process of establishing content validity the conceptual definitions are operationalized by developing several item stems. As discussed in Chapter 2, it is necessary to develop careful transformations of the targeted item stem, so that the resulting set of items defining a scale share similar content meaning. While this similar content meaning is in the minds of the developer and content experts during the examination of content validity, the homogeneity of the items as they are processed through the minds of the actual respondents is what leads to the necessary alpha internal-consistency reliability. If the items assigned to a particular scale are homogeneous in content, it is more likely that the item/scale correlations and interitem correlations will be higher, which in turn will lead to higher alpha reliabilities.

Number of Items. It is well known that the number of items on a scale relates to the reliability of the scale. Actually, the more items on a scale, the greater the potential for adequate sampling of the content universe and the development of variability in the resulting scale scores. While this is true, the key to the reliability level lies in the average interitem correlation. A few items with a high average interitem correlation will have a

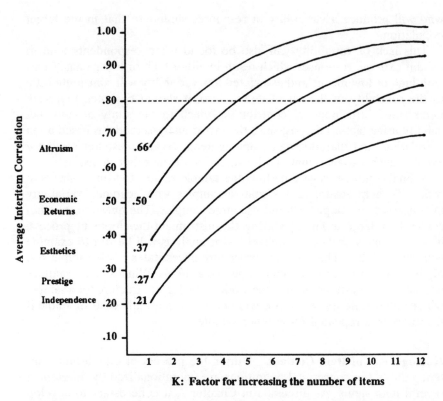

Figure 5–1. Average interitem correlations and alpha reliabilities estimated by increasing the number of items by a factor of K.

higher alpha reliability than a lot of items with a low interitem correlation. To illustrate this point, consider again Equation 5.9:

$$\text{rel} = \frac{K\bar{r}}{1 + (K-1)\bar{r}}$$

where K = the number of items on the scale or the number of times you wish to increase the number of items and $\bar{r}$ = the average interitem correlation. Figure 5–1 contains reliability information generated using Equation 5.9 for selected scales from Super's (1970) *Work Values Inventory* (WVI). The vertical axis indicates the average interitem correlations for five of the *WVI* 3-item scales based upon a sample of 200 high-school sophomores (Gable, 1969). The horizontal axis contains the various values of K. Note that for the value $K = 1$, the average interitem correlations are indicated. By inserting the average correlations into Equation 5.9 and incrementing K progressively, we see how the estimated alpha-reliability value increases as the number of items is increased. Since the original *WVI* instrument contains three items per scale, the plotted values at $K = 3$ represent the alpha reliabilities for the *WVI*, and the values for $K > 3$ represent estimated alpha reliabilities if the number of items on the scales were to be increased in future editions of the instrument.

Returning to our original point, it is clear that a few items with a high average r can have a higher alpha reliability than a lot of items with a smaller average r. For example, for the Altruism scale $\bar{r} = .66$ ($K = 1$), and the 3-item scale has an alpha of .83; for the Independence scale $\bar{r} = .21$, the 3-item scale has an alpha of .43, and the estimated alpha for a 12-item scale is .73. Since the *WVI* contains 15 scales at 3 items each, it would be difficult to revise all of the scales to have adequate reliabilities, since half of the scales had average interitem correlations below .40 and would need a total of about 8 items per scale (i.e., 5 new items) to result in scales with alphas above .80. Typically, good affective measures have average interitem correlations in the .30–.40 range. Therefore, it usually takes 8–10 items to generate alpha-reliability levels in the .80 vicinity. The result of such revisions would clearly lead to an instrument with too many items for an appropriate time period for administration. See Gable and Pruzek (1971) and Gable (1969) for a discussion of how factor analysis and scale revisions could address this problem.

In addition to Equation 5.9, the following equation can also be used to estimate the alpha reliability of a scale if the number of items were increased by a factor of K.

$$\text{rel} = \frac{K\text{rel}}{1 + (K - 1)\text{rel}} \tag{5.12}$$

Actually, 5.9 and 5.12 are the same in that the average interitem correlation in 5.9 is the reliability, in this case for a 1-item scale. To illustrate Equation 5.12, assume we have a 10-item scale with an alpha of .60, and 10 new items are added from the same domain. Since the 10-item scale is now twice as long as the original scale, the estimated reliability ($K = 2$) for the new scale would be .75.

A final equation is available to assist in determining the number of items needed on a scale to generate an adequate internal-consistency reliability level.

$$K = \frac{\text{rel}_{\text{DES}} (1 - \text{rel}_{\text{EX}})}{\text{rel}_{\text{EX}} (1 - \text{rel}_{\text{DES}})} \tag{5.13}$$

where rel$_{DES}$ = desired reliability,
    rel$_{EX}$ = existing level of reliability, and
      K = number of times the scale needs to be increased to yield rel$_{DES}$.

This formula is useful in that it allows one to calculate directly the number of items needed, instead of inserting various values of K into 5.9 or 5.12 on a trial-and-error basis. For example, if we have a 3-item scale with a reliability of .64, we would calculate the factor of K to reach a level of .80 in the following manner:

$$K = \frac{.80(1 - .64)}{.64(1 - .80)} = 2.25$$

A common error in using this formula is to conclude that K represents the number of items to add to the scale. Note carefully that K represents the factor by which the original number of items should be multiplied to lengthen the original scale. In our example, the original 3-item Esthetics scale should be increased by a factor of 2.25. To be safe, we round the factor upward and conclude that we need 3×3 or a total of 9 items (i.e., 6 new items). Reference to Figure 5–1 indicates that the 9-item scale would have an estimated alpha above .80. Once again we see, as Nunnally (1978) points out, that scales with low average interitem correlations (e.g., *WVI* Esthetics in Figure 5–1, $\bar{r}$ = .37) will need several items to reach an acceptable reliability level.

Before leaving this topic, we should note that the items added to an existing scale to enhance reliability should clearly parallel the *best items* on the existing scale. The best items are those with the highest item/scale correlations. Simply look at the content of the item, and write a parallel item.

Acceptable Levels of Reliability

The level of reliability considered to be acceptable for affective measures depends in part on the use for which the instrument is intended. Before levels appropriate for particular users are suggested, some overall comments can be made. In general, affective measures are found to have slightly lower reliability levels than do cognitive measures. Apparently, this is the case because cognitive skills tend to be more consistent and stable than most affective characteristics. Thus, it is typical for good cognitive measures to have alpha and stability reliabilities in the high .80s or low .90s, where even good affective instruments frequently report reliabilities as low as .70.

The difference in the reliability-criterion level also reflects the nature of the decisions to be made based upon the obtained scores. Several crucial programming decisions (e.g., special-education placement and college admissions) are often based upon the results of cognitive achievement measures. On the other hand, many researchers feel that the data resulting from affective measures will be used only for descriptive purposes. While the criterion level for affective measures can be reasonably set at a minimum of .70, there are situations and considerations where higher levels may be necessary. Consider, for example, a researcher who compared two methods of teaching social studies on the dependent variable "attitude toward social studies," measured by an instrument with a reliability of .50. Employing a t-test, the researcher found no differences between the groups. It could well be that 50% of the variance was error variance, which greatly increased the estimated error in the sampling distribution of mean differences (i.e., the denominator of the t-test). This would have concealed the large treatment effect that was really present.[2] Thus, the use of unreliable affective instruments as dependent variables in a program-evaluation study could readily result in what statisticians call a "Type II error"—failure to reject a false null hypothesis (i.e., the program really worked and you say it did not). Consider also a similar problem encountered in the use of affective measures in a regression analysis. The purpose of the analysis is to explain variation in the dependent variable using a set of independent variables. We often forget that if the dependent variable is not highly reliable, we are trying to explain the unexplainable. Unreliable predictors compound the problem even further. The result will be a small multiple correlation and a frustrated researcher who concludes that the independent variables were not well selected. It could be that the variables were theoretically sound but not accurately measured.

An even more serious problem develops when unreliable affective measures are used to make decisions about individuals. Recall that in Chapter 4 we discussed the criterion-related (predictive) validity of the *McCook Alternative Programming Scale* (McCook, 1973). This attitude scale was designed to estimate the probability that future students could be expected to drop out of school. Using discriminant-function analysis during the development of the instrument, a regression equation was developed which was found to be quite accurate in classifying groups of existing dropout and nondropout students. The resulting classification equation could then be applied to individuals currently in school to identity those in need of supportive services. Clearly, the credibility of the equation and the merits of its future use depended largely on the reliability of the predictors in the classification equation. Inappropriate classification could lead to individuals not being identified for needed services.

The point is that no research will be successful when the measurement of the variables is not reliable. We cannot measure affective variables with precise 12-inch rulers. Before we proceed into any research project, we must be certain that the scores will contain only small levels of error variance, or our inferences from the operational to the conceptual definitions of the affective characteristics will be inaccurate and misleading.

The Relationship of Reliability to Validity

In this chapter we have described reliability as an indication of the proportion of variation in test scores, which could be considered true variance as opposed to error variance. Further, we noted that evidence of the reliability of a measure could be in the form of the internal consistency of responses upon one testing or the stability of scores across time. But is a reliable instrument always a valid instrument? The answer is clearly no!

It is commonly stated that "reliability is a necessary but not a sufficient condition for validity." By this statement, we mean that it is clearly possible for an instrument to have high internal consistency and stability reliability but low validity. For example, we could administer a set of 20 items to a sample of students and find that the internal consistency and stability (upon a retest) reliability of the responses were quite high. The validity of the instrument depends upon what we claim the items measure. If we claim that the 20 items reflect attitudes toward school, can we offer validity evidence to support this claim? Assume that you look at the items and conclude that the item content reflects self-concept and has little reference to school situations. You are, in fact, questioning the content and construct validity of the items. It would be appropriate to examine the construct validity in the light of correlations with other known instruments or possibly a factor analysis. Note, though, that the factor analysis could only be as clear as the item content would allow.

The point is that a reliable instrument may or may not be valid. But a valid instrument is usually reliable. Why is this generally the case? Well, if an instrument is carefully developed so that (1) clear judgmental evidence exists to support the correspondence of the operational and conceptual definitions and (2) the empirical evidence based upon actual response data correlations with other known measures or factor analysis is supportive, the instrument should be reliable. If the instrument contained a large portion of error variance such that the responses fluctuated erratically, the correlations with other known instruments would not have been high nor would the factors be meaningful during the construct-validity studies. That is, meaningful correlations during the construct-validity study should in almost all cases result only between items or variables that share reliable variation. Thus, evidence of reliability is important in instrument development— it is, however, a necessary but not a sufficient condition for validity.

Finally, consider how reliability sets a ceiling on the magnitude of the validity coefficient:

$$\text{maximum validity} = \sqrt{\text{rel}(\text{test A}) \times \text{rel}(\text{crit. B})}$$

Suppose that we have a new instrument (A) and a known instrument or a criterion measure(B). If the reliability of both instruments is .81, the maximum validity possible is .81. Consider the situation where the reliability of both instruments is as low as .49, and the maximum validity is, therefore, .49. It is not uncommon for researchers to conclude that a new instrument is not valid on the basis of a lower than theoretically expected correlation with a known measure, when the real problem was a lack of reliability. That is, the theory was great, but so was the amount of error variance in the data from each instrument.

In this section we have discussed the relationship between reliability and validity. Reliability is always important, but validity remains as the ultimate question. Researchers should be aware that some instrument manuals present the more easily obtained evidence of reliability and then try and argue that validity follows. Meaningful validity evidence may be somewhat more difficult to obtain, but must be present in all technical manuals before users can confidently make meaningful score interpretations.

Computer Output: Reliability

In this chapter we have emphasized the importance of the alpha internal-consistency reliability coefficient and noted that its square root represented the estimated correlation of the score with errorless true scores. Recall that Nunnally (1978) even stated that coefficient alpha "is so pregnant with meaning that it should routinely be applied to all new tests" (p. 214). In light of its importance, we have attempted to develop an understanding of the concept of internal consistency by illustrating how responses were internally consistent and how to estimate alpha using interitem correlations. In the process of developing a new instrument or studying an existing one, much more statistical information is needed in addition to the actual alpha coefficient. Basically, this information reflects item-level statistics which contribute to the level of alpha.

In this section we will illustrate how the excellent SPSS Reliability program (SPSS Update 7–9 or SPSS^X) can be used to generate the necessary item analysis and reliability information (SPSS Inc., 1983). For the illustration, we will use the SPSS^X program for the *Gable-Roberts Attitude Toward Teacher* data gathered from 695 grade-11 students responding to the 22-item scale listed in Table 4–6.

In Chapter 4, the construct validity of the attitude scale was examined and the results of both varimax and oblique rotations of the derived factors were reported in Tables 4–10 and 4–11. The alpha reliabilities of both solutions were generated and will be compared later in this section. First, we will begin with an annotation of the reliability output for the varimax solution, which is presented in Table 5–4.

Procedure Lines. The first page of the output lists the reliability procedure lines, which specity the names of the derived scales, the item/scale assignments, and the statistics desired. Note that all of the negative item stems (see Table 4–6) were reverse scored earlier in the program.

Readers should note that setting up the procedure lines in this manner is efficient, but could reduce the sample sizes included in the analyses. Since all 22 variables are specified on the "Variables" line, any subject with one item missing will be deleted from all three scale reliability calculations. While seemingly inefficient, the specification of separate pairs of "Variables" and "Scale" lines for each scale will allow the maximum number of complete sets of data to be included for each scale.

Descriptive Statistics. The item-level means and standard deviations for the eight items defining Factor I, Presentation of Subject, are presented next. High or low means with associated low standard deviations would target items for possible review. This does not appear to be a problem for these data.

Correlations. The item-level intercorrelations are listed on pages 221–222. These are particularly important, since we know that alpha reliability and the adequacy of the sampling of item content in the domain-sampling

Table 5–4. SPSS^x Alpha-Reliability Output

```
33   RELIABILITY   VARIABLES = V1 TO V22/
34                 SCALE(VARI) = V15,V10,V18,V1,V13,V5,V11,V14/
35                 SCALE(VARII) = V2,V4,V6,V19,V21,V7,V3/
36                 SCALE(VARIII) = V9,V22,V16,V8,V12,V17,V20/
37                 MODEL = ALPHA/
38   STATISTICS 1 3 9
```

* METHOD 2 (COVARIANCE MATRIX) WILL BE USED FOR THIS ANALYSIS *

THERE ARE   84584 BYTES OF MEMORY AVAILABLE.
THE LARGEST CONTIGUOUS AREA HAS   84584 BYTES.

************ 2912 BYTES OF SPACE REQUIRED FOR RELIABILITY ************

RELIABILITY ANALYSIS—SCALE (VARI)

1.	V15	PRESENTS SUBJECT . . . CAN BE UNDERSTOOD
2.	V10	DOES NOT MAKE LEARNING FUN
3.	V18	FAILS TO STIMULATE INTEREST IN SUBJECT
4.	V1	MOTIVATES STUDENTS TO LEARN
5.	V13	IS NOT INTERESTING TO LISTEN TO
6.	V5	IS SUCCESSFUL IN GETTING POINT ACROSS
7.	V11	IS GENERALLY CHEERFUL AND PLEASANT
8.	V14	HAS A SENSE OF HUMOR

		MEAN	STD DEV	CASES
1.	V15	3.7151	1.1284	695.0
2.	V10	3.5986	1.2732	695.0
3.	V18	3.6791	1.1647	695.0
4.	V1	3.5540	1.1348	695.0
5.	V13	3.6878	1.2699	695.0
6.	V5	3.7842	1.1025	695.0
7.	V11	3.8043	1.1782	695.0
8.	V14	3.9827	1.0559	695.0

CORRELATION MATRIX

	V15	V10	V18	V1	V13
V15	1.0000				
V10	.5401	1.0000			
V18	.5476	.5407	1.0000		
V1	.5162	.5281	.4890	1.0000	
V13	.5020	.5391	.4875	.4211	1.0000
V5	.5922	.4709	.4251	.5287	.4386
V11	.5054	.5345	.4424	.4411	.4502
V14	.5425	.4611	.4149	.4000	.4602

Table 5–4.   (Cont.)

	V5	V11	V14
V5	1.0000		
V11	.4710	1.0000	
V14	.4250	.5822	1.0000

OF CASES = 695.0

RELIABILITY ANALYSIS—SCALE (VARI)
ITEM-TOTAL STATISTICS

	SCALE MEAN IF ITEM DELETED	SCALE VARIANCE IF ITEM DELETED	CORRECTED ITEM- TOTAL CORRELATION	SQUARED MULTIPLE CORRELATION	ALPHA IF ITEM DELETED
V15	26.0906	36.8434	.7199	.5400	.8628
V10	26.2072	35.7668	.6954	.4964	.8650
V18	26.1266	37.5171	.6381	.4283	.8708
V1	26.2518	37.8745	.6311	.4238	.8708
V13	26.1180	36.7180	.6268	.4052	.8725
V5	26.0216	38.1105	.6356	.4459	.8711
V11	26.0014	37.2291	.6511	.4636	.8695
V14	25.8230	38.6790	.6231	.4407	.8724

RELIABILITY COEFFICIENTS   8 ITEMS
ALPHA = .8839   STANDARDIZED ITEM ALPHA = .8845

RELIABILITY ANALYSIS—SCALE (VARII)

1.	V2	LIKES JOB
2.	V4	IS WILLING TO HELP STUDENTS INDIVID.
3.	V6	IS INTERESTED IN STUDENTS
4.	V19	IS NOT INTERESTED IN THEIR WORK
5.	V21	LIKES STUDENTS
6.	V7	LACKS ENTHUSIASM
7.	V3	IS FAIR IN DEALING WITH STUDENTS

		MEAN	STD DEV	CASES
1.	V2	4.0317	1.0181	695.0
2.	V4	3.9252	1.0001	695.0
3.	V6	3.9108	1.0273	695.0
4.	V19	4.0518	1.0884	695.0
5.	V21	3.9698	1.0819	695.0
6.	V7	4.0144	1.1001	695.0
7.	V3	3.8863	1.1171	695.0

Table 5–4. (Cont.)

	CORRELATION MATRIX			
	V2	V4	V6	V19	V21
V2	1.0000				
V4	.4495	1.0000			
V6	.4573	.6541	1.0000		
V19	.4836	.4166	.5041	1.0000	
V21	.4352	.5359	.6613	.5079	1.0000
V7	.4190	.4777	.5532	.4591	.4519
V3	.4086	.5728	.5687	.4125	.5670

	V7	V3
V7	1.0000	
V3	.4586	1.0000

OF CASES = 695.0

RELIABILITY ANALYSIS—SCALE (VARII)
ITEM-TOTAL STATISTICS

	SCALE MEAN IF ITEM DELETED	SCALE VARIANCE IF ITEM DELETED	CORRECTED ITEM-TOTAL CORRELATION	SQUARED MULTIPLE CORRELATION	ALPHA IF ITEM DELETED
V2	23.7583	24.6360	.5710	.3407	.8654
V4	23.8647	23.7857	.6824	.5089	.8516
V6	23.8791	22.9335	.7575	.6095	.8416
V19	23.7381	23.8535	.6024	.3877	.8619
V21	23.8201	23.0411	.6962	.5232	.8493
V7	23.7755	23.6902	.6110	.3855	.8609
V3	23.9036	23.1795	.6522	.4529	.8553

RELIABILITY COEFFICIENTS   7 ITEMS
ALPHA = .8733   STANDARDIZED ITEM ALPHA = .8741

RELIABILITY ANALYSIS—SCALE (VARIII)

1.	V9	ASSIGNS TOO MUCH HOMEWORK
2.	V22	TESTS TOO FREQUENTLY
3.	V16	IS TOO STRUCTURED
4.	V8	TRIES TO COVER TOO MUCH IN A SHORT TIME
5.	V12	DISCIPLINES TOO STRICTLY
6.	V17	IS TOO BUSY TO SPEND TIME WITH STUDENTS
7.	V20	DOES NOT EVALUATE STUDENT WORK FAIRLY

224   INSTRUMENT DEVELOPMENT IN THE AFFECTIVE DOMAIN

Table 5–4.   (Cont.)

		MEAN	STD DEV	CASES
1.	V9	4.1324	1.1821	695.0
2.	V22	4.1007	1.1469	695.0
3.	V16	3.8115	1.1314	695.0
4.	V8	3.5122	1.2860	695.0
5.	V12	4.0460	1.0632	695.0
6.	V17	3.8273	1.0918	695.0
7.	V20	3.7683	1.1220	695.0

CORRELATION MATRIX

	V9	V22	V16	V8	V12
V9	1.0000				
V22	.5003	1.0000			
V16	.4593	.4466	1.0000		
V8	.5117	.4525	.4002	1.0000	
V12	.5340	.5267	.4265	.4275	1.0000
V17	.3917	.4005	.3679	.3484	.5232
V20	.4153	.4179	.3980	.3760	.4716

	V17	V20
V17	1.0000	
V20	.4401	1.0000

OF CASES = 695.0

RELIABILITY ANALYSIS—SCALE (VARIII)
ITEM-TOTAL STATISTICS

	SCALE MEAN IF ITEM DELETED	SCALE VARIANCE IF ITEM DELETED	CORRECTED ITEM-TOTAL CORRELATION	SQUARED MULTIPLE CORRELATION	ALPHA IF ITEM DELETED
V9	23.0662	24.4481	.6498	.4393	.8156
V22	23.0978	24.9126	.6300	.4055	.8189
V16	23.3871	25.6641	.5668	.3253	.8284
V8	23.6863	24.5009	.5724	.3463	.8290
V12	23.1525	25.1496	.6716	.4726	.8136
V17	23.3712	26.0551	.5558	.3435	.8299
V20	23.4302	25.7066	.5692	.3332	.8280

RELIABILITY COEFFICIENTS   7 ITEMS
ALPHA = .8447   STANDARDIZED ITEM ALPHA = .8461

theory (see Sources of Error discussion earlier in this chapter) are based upon the magnitude of the average interitem correlation. For these items, we observe that all of the correlations are positive and range from .40 to .59 in magnitude. As a result, the average correlation of .49 is quite high and supportive of the internal consistency of the responses to the set of items. It is not uncommon, however, to find correlations in this matrix that are near zero or even negative, which would certainly lower the alpha level. All such items should be targeted for review.

Reliability Statistics.   The next section of the output presents the item and scale-level reliability statistics. The *scale mean if item deleted* column contains the scale mean that would result if the particular item was deleted from the scale. The *scale variance if item deleted* column indicates the amount of variance the scale would have if the particular item were deleted. Items that contribute to greater variation in scale scores, when they are deleted, should be considered for review. The next column labeled *corrected item-total correlation* is crucial to the study of reliability as it represents the correlation of the particular item with the remaining items on the scale. Do not be mislead by the label "item-total correlation," which suggests a total score on the instrument; the statistics actually reflect item-scale correlations. Items correlating less than .20 with their respective scale should be targeted for review. The next column is labeled *squared multiple correlation* and contains the correlation between the particular item and a linear composite of the remaining items defining the scale. This value is calculated using multiple regression where the target item is the criterion and the remaining items are the predictors. These data are not particularly useful, since the values will, for all practical purposes, relate highly to the item-scale correlations in the previous column. The final column, *alpha if item deleted*, is extremely important, as it indicates the level of alpha reliability present if the particular item is deleted from the scale. Finally, we note that below these columns two values of alpha are presented. The first value labeled "alpha" is the alpha-reliability coefficient generated using Equation 5.8. The second alpha labeled "standardized item alpha" represents the estimate of alpha generated through the correlation technique as specified in equation 5.9. This technique standardizes each item by dividing it by its respective standard deviation found during the correlation process. The resulting two alpha values will be quite similar; most researchers report the alpha from Equation 5.8.

Now that we have discussed the components of the reliability output, we can suggest a strategy for using the output. As with many canned computer programs, although one has much data available, only certain information will be considered essential. The suggested procedure is as follows:

1. Check the overall alpha reliability (p. 222) noting that you are look-ing for at least a .70 but would be most pleased with a value greater than .80. For these data, we have a value of .88 on Factor I.
2. Return to the means and standard deviations (p. 221) and look for relatively high or low means and associated low standard devia-tions. The data for Factor I look fine.
3. Examine the item intercorrelations to asscertain if you have any low or negatively correlated items. For affective scales, you are hoping for correlations in the .30–.50 range, since about eight of these items will yield a very adequate alpha.
4. For the five columns of item/scale statistics (p. 222) focus directly on two columns: *corrected item-total (scale) correlation* and *alpha if item deleted*. These two columns are loaded with crucial information regarding which items are not contributing to a high reliability level. In general, you will find that deleting items with the lower item/scale correlations will enhance the alpha level. This will be particu-larly true for scales with few items. If a scale has a large number of items (e.g., 15), the deletion of an item with the lowest item-scale correlation may not alter the reliability at all, since there are so many other items on the scale. For the data presented here for eight items defining Factor I, item 14 has the lowest correlation with the remaining seven items on the scale. (Readers should note that item 14 also exhibited the lowest loading on Factor I in Table 4–10). Deleting the item does not increase the overall reliability of .88, generated for the total of eight items. Thus, no changes should be made in the items defining Factor I.

We have examined the reliability data for Factor I. Readers can pro-ceed to examine Factor II (Interest in Job and Students) and Factor III (Teaching Techniques). What decisions would you make?

It should be clear that the *GRATTS* items provided a clear factor structure (see Table 4–9) and quite high alpha reliabilities, mostly due to the simple nature of the items. In practice, many sets of affective items will not yield such high levels of item intercorrelations, item-scale correlations, and alpha reliabilities, especially during the early pilot testing of a new instrument. The information contained in the SPSS^X-Reliability program will be most helpful in refining the instrument.

Table 5–5. Alpha Reliabilities for Attitude-Toward-Teacher Varimax and Oblique Rotations

Factor	Number of Items		Number of Items Common to Both Solutions	Alpha Reliability	
	Varimax	Oblique		Varimax	Oblique
Presentation of Subject	8	8	8	.88	.88
Interest in Job and Students	7	6	6	.87	.86
Teaching Techniques	7	5	5	.84	.81

Varimax and Oblique Factor Solution Reliabilities

Earlier in this section, reference was made to the varimax and oblique rotations following the factor analysis of the *GRATTS* data (see Tables 4–8 and 4–9). With the exception of a few items, the factor structure for both solutions was the same. The reliability output just reviewed represented the factors (scales) derived through the varimax rotation. For illustrative purposes, Table 5–5 contains a summary of the alpha-reliability information for the two solutions. Included in the table are the number of items defining each factor, the number of items common to both solutions, and the alpha reliabilities. It is clear that the varimax and oblique solutions revealed the same factor structures (see Tables 4–10 and 4–11). As usual, the oblique solution tended to clean up the varimax solution slightly by deleting one item from Factor II and two items from Factor III which had the lowest loadings on the varimax solution. Since we know that these items all had moderate interitem correlations and that the number of items relates to the level of alpha, we expect the slight decrease in the level of alpha from the varimax to the oblique solution. In this data set, the solutions are indeed comparable and the associated alpha levels are quite high; either solution could be chosen to describe the factor structure of the items. In other data sets, the factor structures could be rather different. The outcome of inspecting the conceptual interpretation of the factors, as well as the associated alpha reliabilities, could clearly favor one of the solutions.

Now It's Your Turn

In this section, item analysis and reliability information will be presented for a pilot version of a 40-item attitude survey administered to managers in a large corporation (Keilty, Goldsmith, and Boone, 1983). Following a brief description of the survey and the respondents, item-analysis and reliability data will be presented, along with a series of questions to be considered by the reader.

Description of the Instrument

The *Manager Concern Survey* contains 40 situation statements which the respondent rates on a Likert-type scale, ranging from 1 ("almost never") to 5 ("almost always"). Scores are obtained within each of the four basic styles of leader behavior (S1: telling; S2: selling; S3: participating; S4: delegating), in two domains of concern for people (human, 5 items), and concern for tasks (task, 5 items). Responses to the 40 items are reported at the human- and task-domain levels within each of the four styles, yielding a total of eight scores.

Sample

Data were obtained from 88 Self ratings and 277 Other ratings by managers during a series of professional seminars conducted for a large corportion.

Item Analysis/Reliability

Tables 5–6 and 5–7 present the item-analysis and reliability data for the Self and Other forms. The situations or items on the scale have been clustered, based upon their respective domain (i.e., human, task) within each of the four styles (i.e., S1, S2, S3, S4) of leadership. This grouping facilitates analysis of the items and is consistent with the scoring scheme employed for the scale. Presented in the table are the response percentages, means, standard deviations, correlation (r) with the domain, domain reliability if the item is deleted, and the overall domain internal-consistency reliability.

Table 5–6. Manager Concern Survey: Self

(N = 88)

Style 1 Domain	Situation	Response Percentages					Mean	Std. Dev.	r with Domain	Domain Alpha Reliability If Item Deleted	Domain Alpha Reliability
		1	2	3	4	5					
S1 Human	5	1	7	28	41	23	3.77	.92	.31	−.12	
	10	1	8	29	43	19	3.72	.91	.16	.08	
	16		7	33	48	12	3.66	.79	−.20	.42	.20
	37		8	47	34	11	3.49	.80	.02	.23	
	40			32	50	18	3.86	.70	.22	.05	
S1 Task	4	1	4	16	48	31	4.02	.87	.41	.36	
	7		2	34	48	16	3.77	.74	.32	.43	
	23		3	25	55	17	3.85	.74	.05	.59	.51
	33		7	25	54	14	3.75	.78	.35	.41	
	35		3	34	50	13	3.72	.73	.31	.44	
S2 Human	11	8	24	46	19	3	2.86	.94	.12	.28	
	15		2	17	50	31	4.09	.75	.16	.23	
	21		5	19	52	24	3.95	.79	.22	.18	.30
	36		1	15	53	31	4.14	.70	.21	.20	
	39		5	13	54	28	4.07	.77	.01	.36	
S2 Task	3	1	2	16	63	18	3.94	.73	.14	.65	
	17		6	30	49	15	3.73	.78	.44	.50	
	19		7	28	42	23	3.81	.87	.45	.49	.60
	32		9	33	43	15	3.64	.85	.38	.53	
	38		7	30	51	12	3.69	.78	.38	.53	

Table 5–6. (Cont.)

(N = 88)

Style 1 Domain	Situation	Response Percentages					Mean	Std. Dev.	r with Domain	Domain Alpha Reliability If Item Deleted	Domain Alpha Reliability
		1	2	3	4	5					
S3 Human	2		3	14	53	30	4.09	.75	.36	.50	.57
	13		3	19	43	35	4.11	.79	.38	.48	
	22			11	46	43	4.32	.67	.31	.52	
	27			14	50	36	4.23	.67	.33	.51	
	30		1	20	44	35	4.14	.76	.26	.55	
S3 Task	9	1	3	12	57	27	4.06	.79	.30	-.03	.20
	14	3	14	19	38	26	3.69	1.11	-.07	.37	
	20	1	1	21	41	36	4.10	.84	.09	.17	
	28	1	4	14	56	25	3.99	.82	.14	.12	
	31	15	35	33	16	1	2.53	.97	.08	.18	
S4 Human	6		1	23	59	17	3.92	.66	.42	.47	.57
	18		1	26	49	24	3.95	.74	.42	.46	
	24	6	10	31	44	9	3.41	.99	.35	.51	
	25		2	36	47	15	3.74	.73	.40	.47	
	26		11	44	32	13	3.45	.86	.12	.63	
S4 Task	1	1	13	40	29	17	3.49	.96	.08	.24	.24
	8	3	17	32	39	9	3.33	.98	-.07	.40	
	12			5	33	62	4.58	.58	-.08	.33	
	29		8	32	40	20	3.73	.88	.35	-.08	
	34			8	36	56	4.48	.64	.37	.00	

Table 5–7. Manager Concern Survey: Other

(N = 277)

Style 1 Domain	Situation	Response Percentages					Mean	Std. Dev.	r with Domain	Domain Alpha Reliability If Item Deleted	Domain Alpha Reliability
		1	2	3	4	5					
S1 Human	5	1	12	32	37	18	3.61	.94	.16	.12	.30
	10	3	16	32	39	10	3.39	.97	.03	.13	
	16	1	8	30	45	16	3.67	.87	.02	.15	
	37	1	13	36	42	8	3.43	.86	.29	.11	
	40	2	5	20	47	26	3.89	.93	.23	.20	
S1 Task	4		3	19	42	36	4.10	.83	.41	.57	.63
	7	1	3	25	39	32	3.99	.89	.33	.61	
	23	1	4	23	51	21	3.86	.83	.33	.61	
	33		5	23	49	23	3.88	.83	.44	.55	
	35		4	23	50	23	3.92	.79	.43	.56	
S2 Human	11	3	19	44	29	5	3.13	.89	.29	.73	.70
	15	1	9	26	40	24	3.76	.94	.57	.60	
	21		7	33	47	13	3.65	.80	.58	.61	
	36	1	4	31	49	15	3.74	.80	.46	.65	
	39	1	4	20	51	24	3.94	.81	.42	.67	
S2 Task	3	1	8	22	50	19	3.77	.89	.04	.75	.64
	17		7	26	45	22	3.83	.85	.50	.54	
	19	2	6	27	43	22	3.78	.90	.53	.52	
	32	1	10	25	49	15	3.68	.89	.51	.53	
	38		3	25	52	20	3.88	.76	.47	.56	

Table 5-7. (Cont.)

(N = 277)

Style 1 Domain	Situation	Response Percentages					Mean	Std. Dev.	r with Domain	Domain Alpha Reliability If Item Deleted	Domain Alpha Reliability
		1	2	3	4	5					
S3 Human	2	2	7	20	41	30	3.90	.98	.46	.22	.76
	13	1	7	28	42	22	3.77	.89	.57	.36	
	22	1	6	24	48	21	3.82	.87	.59	.36	
	27		4	19	53	24	3.95	.79	.54	.31	
	30	1	6	12	40	41	4.16	.90	.48	.25	
S3 Task	9	1	6	23	50	20	3.82	.84	.20	.06	.26
	14	3	8	30	41	18	3.64	.97	.07	.20	
	20	1	4	10	48	37	4.15	.85	.29	-.03	
	28		6	13	48	33	4.06	.85	.27	-.01	
	31	14	29	29	22	6	2.78	1.12	-.21	.51	
S4 Human	6	2	8	32	43	15	3.62	.90	.60	.72	.78
	18	2	7	31	48	12	3.61	.84	.64	.70	
	24	2	12	42	32	12	3.40	.92	.54	.74	
	25	2	9	36	36	17	3.56	.94	.65	.70	
	26	1	3	20	50	26	3.97	.82	.32	.80	
S4 Task	1	6	16	35	29	14	3.29	1.07	.26	.44	.49
	8	4	12	32	39	13	3.45	.98	.10	.55	
	12		1	12	44	43	4.29	.73	.29	.43	
	29	2	9	26	41	22	3.72	.98	.43	.30	
	34		1	11	43	45	4.32	.71	.32	.41	

Table 5–8. Interitem Correlations for Manager Concern Survey: Other S3-Task Items

Items	9	14	20	28	31
9	—				
14	.25	—			
20	.17	.11	—		
28	.22	.08	.41	—	
31	-.16	-.22	-.06	-.08	—

Research Questions

Considering the data presented in Table 5–6 for the Self data and Table 5–7 for the Other data, how would you answer the following questions?

1. How would you describe the response patterns?
2. How do these response patterns affect the item means and standard deviations.?
3. How are the correlations with the domains (i.e., scales) calculated?
4. Consider the correlations of the items with the domain and the domain alpha reliabilities if an item is deleted. What items would you target for review?
5. (a) How do the correlations of items with the domain explain the domain alpha reliabilities?
   (b) Explain why the S3 Task domain on the Other form has an alpha of only .26, while the S4 Human domain has an alpha of .78 (see Table 5–7).
6. Table 5–8 contains the interitem correlations for the S3-Task items on the Other form. (Assume that appropriate items have already been reverse scored where necessary.) Based upon these intercorrelations and the resulting domain alpha reliability of .26, do/ answer the following:
   (a) Calculate the estimated alpha reliability using Equation 5.9.
   (b) On the basis of all the data presented, discuss how item 31 contributes to the alpha level.
   (c) How many additional items would be needed to raise the alpha level to at least .80?
   (d) Suggest a specific plan for revising the set of items to obtain an alpha of .80.

Notes

1. The symbol! indicates "factorial." For example, $4! = 4 \times 3 \times 2 \times 1$.
2. To illustrate: consider the separate variance model where $t = (\overline{X}_1 - \overline{X}_2)/\sqrt{S_1^2/N_1 + S_2^2/N_2}$. Increased error variance could increase the values of S^2 and reduce the value of t.

Additional Readings

Reliability

Benson, P.G., and Dickinson, T.L. (1983). Mixed standard scale response inconsistencies as reliability indices. *Educational and Psychological Measurement*, 43, 781–789.

Bintig, A. (1980). The efficiency of various estimations of reliability of rating scales. *Educational and Psychological Measurement*, 40, 619–643.

Borhnstedt, G.W. (1970). Reliability and validity assessment in attitude measurement. In G.F. Summer (Ed.), *Attitude measurement*. Chicago: Rand McNally.

Bray, J.H., Maxwell, S.E., and Schneeck, R.R. (1980). A psychometric investigation of the survey of study habits and attitudes. *Applied Psychological Measurement*, 4, 195–201.

Carmines, E.G., and Zeller, R.A. (1979). *Reliability and validity assessment*. Beverly Hills: Sage.

Cowan, G., and Komorita, S.S. (1971). The effects of forewarning and pretesting on attitude change. *Educational and Psychological Measurement*, 31, 431–439.

Cronbach, L.J. (1951). Coefficient alpha and the internal structure of tests. *Psychometrika*, 16, 297–335.

Davidson, M.L., and Robbins, S. (1978). The reliability and validity of objective indices of moral development. *Applied Psychological Measurement*, 2. 389–401.

Feldt, L.S., Woodruff, D.J., and Salih, F.A. (1987). Statistical inference for coefficient alpha. *Applied Psychological Measurement*, 11, 93–103.

Gable, R.K. (1973). The effect of scale modifications on the factorial dimensions and reliability of Super's Work Values Inventory. *Journal of Vocational Behavior*, 3, 303–322.

Huck, S.W. (1978). A modification of Hoyt's analysis of variance reliability estimation procedure. *Educational and Psychological Measurement*, 38, 725–736.

Lumsden, J.L. (1977). Person reliability. *Applied Psychological Measurement*, 1, 477–482.

Marsh, H.W., et al. (1983). Self concept: Reliability stability, dimensionality, validity, and the measurement of change. *Journal of Educational Psychology*, 75, 772–790.

Novick, M., and Lewis, G. (1967). Coefficient alpha and the reliability of composite measurements. *Psychometrika*, 32, 1–13.

Parish, T.S., and Taylor, J.C. (1978a). A further report on the validity and reliability of the Personal Attribute Inventory for Children as a self-concept scale. *Educational and Psychological Measurement*, 38, 1225–1228.

Parish, T.S., and Taylor, J.C. (1978b). The Personal Attribute Inventory for Children: A report on its validity and reliability as a self-concept scale. *Educational and Psychological Measurement*, 38, 565–569.

Putnins, A.L. (1980). Reliability of the Jesness Inventory. *Applied Psychological Measurement*, 4, 127–129.

Roberts, D.M., and Bilderback, E.W. (1980). Reliability and validity of a statistics attitude survey. *Educational and Psychological Measurement*, 40, 235–238.

Taylor, J.B. (1977). Item homogeneity, scale reliability, and the self-concept hypothesis. *Educational and Psychological Measurement*, 37, 349–361.

Watkins, D., and Astilla, E. (1980). The reliability and validity of the Coopersmith Self-Esteem Inventory for a sample of Filipino high school girls. *Educational and Psychological Measurement*, 40, 251–254.

Weiten, W. (1985). Reliability and validity of a scale to measure test-wiseness. Paper presented at the annual meeting of the American Educational Research Association, Chicago, 1985.

Whitely, S.E. (1978). Individual inconsistency: Implications for test reliability and behavioral predictability. *Applied Psychological Measurement*, 2, 571–579.

Zirkel, P., and Gable, R.K. (1977). The reliability and validity of various measures of self-concept among ethnically disadvantaged adolescents. *Measurement and Evaluation in Guidance*, 10(1), 48–54.

6 A REVIEW OF THE STEPS FOR DEVELOPING AN AFFECTIVE INSTRUMENT

Overview

In Chapter 1, we discussed the theoretical basis underlying selected affective characteristics. In Chapter 2, the conceptual definitions were operationalized by developing belief statements, or, in the case of the semantic differential, bipolar adjective pairs. Chapter 3 described the standard techniques for scaling affective characteristics. Techniques described included Thurstone's equal-appearing interval, latent trait, Likert's summated ratings, and Osgood's semantic differential. It was pointed out that all of the techniques share the common goal of locating a person on a bipolar evaluative dimension with respect to a given target object. For each technique, the scaling process resulted in a single affective score arrived at on the basis of responses to a set of belief statements. Similarities and differences among the scaling techniques were presented. Finally, Chapter 3 discussed the practical and psychometric differences between ipsative and normative measures.

Chapters 4 and 5 discussed theory and techniques for examining the validity and reliability of the affective instrument. Emphasis was first placed upon examining the correspondence between the judgmental evidence

INSTRUMENT DEVELOPMENT IN THE AFFECTIVE DOMAIN

Table 6–1. Steps in Affective-Instrument Development

Step	Activity	Chapter
1	Develop Conceptual Definitions	1
2	Develop Operational Definitions	2
3	Select a Scaling Technique	3
4	Conduct a Judgmental Review of Items	4
5	Select a Response Format	3
6	Develop Directions for Responding	
7	Prepare a Draft of the Instrument and Gather Preliminary Pilot Data	
8	Prepare the Final Instrument	
9	Gather Final Pilot Data	
10	Analyze Pilot Data	5
11	Revise the Instrument	
12	Conduct a Final Pilot Study	
13	Produce the Instrument	
14	Conduct Additional Validity and Reliability Analyses	4, 5
15	Prepare a Test Manual	

collected in the content-validity study and the empirical evidence gathered to examine construct validity. Finally, the importance of high alpha internal-consistency reliability was discussed.

Suggested Steps in Affective Instrument Development

In this chapter we will review the steps for developing an instrument to measure affective characteristics. Differences in procedures resulting from the scaling technique selected will be noted as the 15 steps in Table 6–1 are described.

Step 1. Develop Conceptual Definitions (Chapter 1)

The first step in the development of any instrument is to conduct a comprehensive review of the literature, so that conceptual definitions of the affective characteristic can be developed. This is a crucial step in the process, since the development or selection of a conceptual definition for the affective characteristic will provide the important theoretical base underlying the instrument.

Step 2: Develop Operational Definitions (Chapter 2)

After careful consideration of the literature review and the conceptual definitions, operational definitions are developed—these are the *belief statements* to be used in the instrument. For the *Equal-Appearing-Interval* (see Thurstone, 1931a) and *Latent-Trait* (see Wright and Masters, 1982) techniques, the developer attempts to develop statements that span the favorable, neutral, and unfavorable points of the continuum underlying the affective characteristic. On the other hand, the Likert (1932) *Summated-Rating* technique requires statements that can be easily judged to be either favorable (i.e., positive) or unfavorable (i.e., negative) in direction. Neutral statements do not fit the Likert technique. For Osgood's *Semantic Differential* (Osgood et al., 1957), pairs of bipolar adjectives are selected to form the extremes of the favorable or unfavorable continuum. Careful thought needs to be given to selecting the bipolar adjectives from Osgood's suggested evaluative, potency, and activity dimensions. In most studies (e.g., program evaluations), the semantic-differential scales will be comprised of evaluative adjectives, with possibly a few adjectives from the potency and activity dimensions included as anchors to clarify the interpretation of a later factor analysis.

Step 3: Select a Scaling Technique (Chapter 3)

It may seem a little early in the process, but the scaling technique needs to be selected next. All of the techniques described in Chapter 3 are appropriate, with Likert's procedure appearing to be the most popular at the current time, and with the more psychometrically complex latent-trait technique gaining quickly in popularity. The selection of a technique will have implications for how the remaining steps are conducted.

Step 4: Conduct a Judgmental Review of Items (Chapter 4)

In step 4 the issue of content validity is addressed as the statements are reviewed by content experts. For the Thurstone (1931a) *Equal-Appearing-Interval* procedure, two types of judgment are appropriate. First, the judges rate the statements with respect to how much they relate to the conceptual definition of the affective characteristic, keeping in mind the reading level of the target group. If more than one scale is to be included in the instruments the judges should also rate the assignment of items to scale categories. After any necessary revisions based upon this review are made, the second judgment needed in the Thurstone technique is the specific favorable or unfavorable rating by the judges for each item. This rating is used to develop the scale value that locates the statement on the evaluative continuum underlying the affective characteristic. Include several groups of about 20 judges each to ascertain if the scale values are stable across different types of judges. Finally, select items that are nonambiguous and equally spaced along the response continuum using the Criterion of Ambiguity. (See Chapter 3 for a description of these procedures.)

For the *Latent-trait* procedure, the items should also be reviewed to ascertain how well they relate to the conceptual definitions and any categories built into the instrument. For the Likert (1932) *Summated-Rating* procedure, the items should be reviewed to confirm that they are positive or negative in nature. A judgmental rating task (see Chapter 4 under content validity) should also be carried out to rate the extent to which the statements reflect the stated conceptual definition, as well as any categories specified in the instrument.

For Osgood's *Semantic-Differential* (Osgood et al., 1957) technique, the essential judgmental evidence pertains to the selection of bipolar adjectives used to anchor the scales as they relate to the concept to be rated. In Osgood's work the semantic differential was used to measure the semantic meaning of concepts; thus, the bipolar adjectives were often from several dimensions. Users of the technique to measure such affective characteristics as attitudes or self-concept suggest that mostly evaluative adjectives should be used.

For the Thurstone, Likert, and latent-trait techniques, the developer should conduct a formal readability analysis. Procedures available examine word difficulty and the complexity of the sentence structure. Word difficulty is usually based upon the number of syllables in a word and comparisons with known word lists (see Dale and Chall, 1948, for grade 4 and up; Spache, 1953, for elementary grades).

Step 5: Select a Response Format (Chapter 3)

The response format will depend largely on the scaling technique selected. For the *Thurstone* procedure, the respondents will merely select statements that describe the target object being rated. For the *Latent-Trait* and *Likert* techniques, degrees of agreeing, importance, or frequency are recorded, most often using a 5-point scale. Finally, for Osgood's *Semantic Differential,* the bipolar adjectives are listed at the ends of the response continuum for each scale (item). The steps between the two adjectives are generally in-dicated by unlabeled spaces.

Step 6: Develop Directions for Responding

Respondents, especially young students, should never be confused by incomplete or vague instructions. The procedures for responding to the statements, as well as the meaning of the anchor points on the continuum, should be carefully developed and reviewed by your colleagues, as well as a few members of the target group.

Step 7: Prepare a Draft of the Instrument and Gather Preliminary Pilot Data

You are now ready to type a draft of the instrument. Work with a good secretary to design a tentative layout and type a draft of the form. Show the instrument to two or three appropriate teachers and colleagues for final review of such areas as clarity of directions, readability, and ease of responding. Also, administer the instrument to a representative sample of about 10 students and watch them complete the form. Following the ses-sion, discuss the form with them and obtain their reactions to the areas listed above. Listen well and take good notes, since a few perceptive student comments could be of immense importance to the success of your project.

Step 8: Prepare the Final Instrument

How professional the final instrument appears to the respondent is an important consideration. At all costs, avoid an inferior layout and typing job with copies of the form run off on a ditto machine. Take the draft of the instrument to a professional printer and obtain advice regarding such matters as layout., size and color of paper, and type of print to be used. If you cannot afford to have the instrument professionally typeset, find an experienced typist, and prepare several drafts until the layout looks pleas-ing. Then take the original to a printer to be copied on colored paper, or copy the form yourself on a good Xerox machine. If you want the re-spondents to take their job seriously, show them that the project is important by supplying them with a well-designed, easily-read form.

Step 9: Gather Final Pilot Data

Now that the instrument has been produced, you are ready to gather data for the examination of validity and reliability. Locate a representative sample of people the size of which is such that there are 6 to 10 times as many people as there are statements on the instrument (e.g., for a 40-item instrument, use from 240 to 400 people). You may think that this is a large sample for only a pilot study, but keep in mind that the empirical basis of the validity, reliability, and scoring scheme for the instrument will be determined or confirmed using these data. Actually, it is possible to use fewer people than specified above and still run the various item-analysis, reliability, correlation, and factor-analysis procedures. The real issue is not the number of people but the variability and representativeness of the response patterns compared to those of the large population from which you have sampled. We know that restricting the possible variation will lower the correlations among the items on the instrument. Also, if the sample respondents do not produce response patterns similar to those of the population, the factor structure of the pilot data will not be stable across future groups of respondents. That is, the affective characteristics (i.e., constructs) measured will not be clearly defined, and the scales produced will tend to be unreliable from an internal-consistency or stability sense. Therefore, if you pilot the instrument in one school, be sure that the sampling of classrooms or people represents the school and that the school characteristics represent your target population. To be safe, use heterogeneous samples with respect to ability, sex, and curriculum track, as well as several types of schools (e.g., rural, urban, and suburban).

Finally, be aware that the factor structure of the affective characteristic may not be the same across different age groups. If your target population is grades 9–12, you may wish to compare the factor structure for grades 9 and 10 combined with that for combined grades 11 and 12. A common error is to examine the factor structure and calculate the alpha reliability on a middle school grades 6–8 sample and then routinely use the instrument for different grade levels such as grades 3–5. Consideration of the formation of attitudes at the lower grades and the readability of the items may reveal that the instrument does not adequately assess the characteristic at the lower-grade levels.

Step 10: Analyze Pilot Data (Chapter 5)

Analyses of the pilot data employ the techniques of factor analysis, item analysis, and reliability analysis.

(handwritten annotation: 11 items; v 6; 66 # people)

Factor Analysis. If you have responses from 6 to 10 times the number of people as items, you could proceed directly to the factor analysis (see Chapter 4) to examine the response data-generated constructs that explain the variation among the items on the instrument. These empirically derived constructs are then compared with the judgmentally developed categories reviewed previously during the examination of content validity in step 4. If the empirically derived constructs and the judgmentally created categories do not correspond, the conceptual and operational definitions of the affective characteristic (see Chapters 1 and 2) should be reviewed in light of the characteristics of the target group of people.

Item Analysis. An item analysis can be conducted along with or even prior to the factor analysis. If you have too few people in the pilot study, the item analysis can be used to identify items to delete from the instrument prior to running the factor analysis. The item analysis will generate response frequencies, percentages, means, and standard deviations. Items associated with either high or low means and low standard deviations should be reviewed and considered for deletion (see Chapter 5). Also, generate correlations of the items with the appropriate scale or total score for the Likert technique, and between the bipolar adjective scale and the derived concept dimension or total score for the semantic differential. The distinction between a scale and total score for the Likert technique is based upon whether the set of items measures more than one dimension of affect as indicated in the factor analysis. Items should be correlated with the scale score defined by the cluster of items defining the scale (see Chapter 5).

Reliability. The final analysis of the pilot data consists of examining the internal-consistency reliability of the item clusters defining each scale on the Likert instrument, or concept dimensions on the semantic differential. The SPSS Reliability program is recommended for this analysis. For the Thurstone items, the binary response pattern (i.e., 0 = item not selected and 1 = item selected) can also be analyzed using the alpha-reliability formula. In addition to the overall scale- or dimension-reliability coefficient, the SPSS program will indicate the reliability of the cluster of items if each respective item is deleted. If there are only 6–8 items per scale, the deletion of an item with a low item/scale correlation should result in a higher scale reliability for the remaining items (see Chapter 5).

Step 11: Revise the Instrument

Based especially on the information obtained from step 10, the next step is to carry out final revisions of the instrument. Items can be added, deleted, or revised to enhance clarity of the items and the validity and reliability of the instrument.

Step 12: Conduct a Final Pilot Study

If substantial changes are made to the instrument, additional pilot data should be obtained and step 10 repeated. If steps 1–9 are carefully followed, it is likely that this final pilot study can be avoided. When in doubt, carry out the pilot. You have invested too much at this point to just assume the factor structure and reliabilities are appropriate. If you use an unfinished instrument in some later research project, the whole project could be jeopardized by a hasty decision at this point.

Step 13: Produce the Instrument

Production of the final form of the instrument should take into consideration all of the typesetting and copying suggestions stated in step 8.

Step 14: Conduct Additional Validity and Reliability Analyses

Now that you have evidence of the factor structure of the instrument as well as the item-analysis and reliability information, you are ready to extend the examination of validity. Chapter 4 described appropriate procedures to be considered here—these include correlations with other known measures, the multitrait-multimethod correlation display, known groups, and additional factor analyses. These types of information will be necessary for a meaningful interpretation of scores obtained from the new affective instrument. Additional reliability evidence, especially stability reliability, should also be gathered to ascertain if the measured affective characteristic is stable over time, as consistent with theoretical expectations.

Step 15: Prepare a Test Manual

The final step in the process of instrument development is to share your work with other professionals. A short (i.e., 10-page) manual should be

written, documenting such areas as theoretical rationale, the process followed to develop the instrument, scoring procedures, validity, reliability,
and score interpretation. Readers are encouraged to consult the APA publication entitled *Standards for Educational and Psychological Tests* (1985)
for guidelines in preparing the manual.

In summary, developing a good instrument is a lot of hard work. If one
cuts corners and takes the quick and easy route, the product will most
likely reflect the level of effort.

References

Aiken, L.R. (1980). Attitude measurement and research. In D.A. Payne (Ed.),
   Recent developments in affective measurement (pp. 1–24). San Francisco: Jossey-
   Bass.
Allport, G.W. (1935). Attitudes. In C. Murchison (Ed.), *Handbook of social psy-
   chology* (pp. 798–884). Worcester, MA: Clark University Press.
Allport, G.W. (1961). *Pattern and growth in personality.* New York: Holt, Rinehart
   and Winston.
Allport, G.W., Vernon, P.E., and Lindzey, G.A. (1960). *A study of values.* Boston:
   Houghton Mifflin.
American Psychological Association. (1975) *Principles For The Validation And Use
   Of Personnel Selection Procedures,* Washington, DC: The Association.
American Psychological Association. (1985). *Standards for education and psycho-
   logical testing.* Washington, DC: The Association.
Anderson, L.W. (1981). *Assessing affective characteristics in the schools.* Boston:
   Allyn and Bacon.
Andrich, D. (1978a). Application of a psychometric model to ordered categories
   which are scored with successive integers. *Applied Psychological Measurement,*
   21, 581–594.
Andrich, D. (1978b). Rating formulation for ordered response categories. *Psycho-
   metrika,* 43, 561–573.
Andrich, D. (1978c). Scaling attitude items constructed and scored in the Likert
   tradition *Educational and Psychological Measurement,* 38, 665–680.
Arrindell, W.A., and van der Ende, J. (1985). An empirical test of the utility of the
   observations-to-variables ration in factor and components analysis. *Applied
   Psychological Measurement,* 9, 165–178.
Ashford, S.J., and Tsui, A.S. (1991). Self-regulation for managerial effectiveness:
   The role of active feedback seeking. *Academy of Management Journal,* 34, 251–
   280.
Bachelor, P.A. (1989). Maximum likelihood confirmatory factor-analytic investiga-
   tion of factors within Guilford's structure of intellect model. *Journal of Applied
   Psychology,* 74, 797–804.

Bandura, A. (1977). *Social learning theory.* Englewood Cliffs, NJ: Prentice-Hall.

Bandura, A., Adams, N.E., Hardy, A.B., and Howells, G.N. (1980). Tests of the generality of self-efficacy theory. *Cognitive Therapy and Research,* 4, 39–66.

Bandura, A. (1986). *Social foundations of thought and action.* Englewood Cliffs, NJ: Prentice-Hall.

Bandura, A. (1989). Human agency in social cognitive theory. *American Psychologist,* 44, 1175–1184.

Bell, T.H. (1983). *A nation at risk: The imperative for educational reform* (Report of the National Commission on Excellence in Education). *Education Week* (April 27), pp. 12–16.

Benson, J. (1982). Detecting item bias in affective scales. Paper presented at the annual meeting of the American Educational Research Association, New York, March 1982.

Benson, J., and Hocevar, D. (1985). The impact of item phrasing on the validity of attitude scales for elementary children. *Journal of Educational Measurement,* 22(3), 231–240.

Benson, J., and Wilcox, S. (1981). The effect of positive and negative item phrasing on the measurement of attitudes. Paper presented at the annual meeting of the National Council on Measurement in Education. Los Angeles, April 1981.

Bentler, P.M., and Bonett, D.G. (1980). Significance tests and goodness-of-fit in the analysis of covariance structures. *Psychological Bulletin,* 88, 588–606.

Berk, R.A. (Ed.), (1982). *Handbook of methods for detecting item bias.* Baltimore, MD: Johns Hopkins University Press.

Betz, N.E., and Hackett, G. (1981). The relationship of career-related self-efficacy expectations to perceived career options in college women and men. *Journal of Counseling Psychology,* 23, 399–410.

Betz, N.E., and Hackett, G. (1983). The relationship of mathematics self-efficacy expectations to the selection of science-based college majors. *Journal of Vocational Behavior,* 23, 329–345.

Bloom, B.S. (Ed.) (1956). *Taxonomy of educational objectives, handbook 1: Cognitive domain.* New York: McKay.

Bloom, B.S. (1976). Human characteristics and school learning. New York: McGraw-Hill.

Bollen, K.A. (1989). *Structural equations with latent variables.* New York: Wiley.

Boyer, E.L. (1983). *High school: A report on secondary education in America.* New York: Harper & Row.

Brennan, R.L. (Winter, 1992). Generalizability theory. *Educational Measurement: Issues and Practices,* 27–34.

Brookover, W.B., LePere, J.M., Homochek, T.S., and Erickson, E. (1965) *Self-concept of ability and school achievement, II.* Final Report of Cooperative Research Project No. 1636. East Lansing: Michigan State University.

Brophy, J.E., and Good, T.L. (1974). *Teacher-student relationships: Causes and consequences.* New York: Holt, Rinehart and Winston.

Byrne, B.M. and Shavelson, R.J. (1987). Adolescent self-concept: Testing the assumption of equivalent structure across gender. *American Educational Research Journal*, 24, 365–385.

Byrne, B.M. (1988). Measuring adolescent self-concept: Factual validity and equivalency of the SDQ III across gender. *Multivariate Behavioral Research*, 23, 361–375.

Byrne, B.M. (1989). *A primer of LISREL: Basic applications and programming for confirmatory factor analytic models*. New York: Springer-Verlag.

Byrne, B.M. (1990a). Investigating gender differences in adolescent self-concept: A look beneath the surface. *Applied Measurement in Education*, 3, 255–274.

Byrne, B.M. (1990b). Methodological approaches to the validation of academic self-concept: The construct and its measures. *Applied Measurement in Education*, 3, 185–207.

Campbell, D.P. (1973). The Strong Vocational Interest Blank for Men. In D.G. Zytowski (Ed.), *Contemporary approaches to interest measurement* (pp. 20–57). Minneapolis: University of Minnesota Press.

Campbell, D.T. (1950). The indirect assessment of social attitudes. *Psychological Bulletin*, 47, 15–38.

Campbell, D.T. (1977). Recommendations for APA test standards regarding construct, trait, and discriminant validity. *American Psychologist*, 15, 546–553.

Campbell, D.T., and Fiske, D.W. (1959). Convergent and discriminant validation by the multitrait-multimethod matrix. *Psychological Bulletin*, 56, 81–105.

Campbell, N., and Grissom, S. (1979). Influence of the item direction on student responses in attitude measurement. Paper presented at the annual meeting of the American Educational Research Association, San Francisco, April 1979. (ERIC Document Reproduction Service No. ED 170 366.)

Campion, M.A. (1991). Meaning and measurement of turnover: Comparison of alternative measures and recommendations for research. *Journal of Applied Psychology*, 76, 199–212.

Carmines, E.G., and Zeller, R.A. (1979). *Reliability and validity assessment*. Beverly Hills, CA: Sage Publications.

Carmines, E.G., and McIver, S.P. (1981). Analyzing models with unobserved variables: Analysis of covariance structures. In G.W. Bohrnstedt and E.F. Borgatta (Eds.), *Social measurement: Current issues* (pp. 65–115). Beverly Hills, CA: Sage.

Carver, C.S., and Scheier, M.F. (1981). *Attention and self-regulation: A control-theory approach to human behavior*. New York: Springer-Verlag.

Cattell, R.B. (1944). Psychological measurement: Ipsative, normative and interactive. *Psychological Review*, 51, 292–303.

Cattell, R.B. (1966). The meaning and strategic use of factor analysis. In R.B. Cattell (Ed.), *Handbook of multivariate experimental psychology*. Chicago: Rand-McNally.

Cattell, R.B. (1978). *The scientific use of factor analysis*. New York: Plenum Press.

Clark, K.E., and Campbell, D.P. (1965). *Manual for the Minnesota Vocational Interest Inventory*. New York: Psychological Corporation.

Clemans, W.V. (1966). An analytical and empirical examination of some properties of ipsative measures. *Psychometric Monographs*, No. 14. Princeton: Psychometric Corporation.

Cole, N.S. (1981). Bias in testing. *American Psychologist* 36(10), 1067–1077.

Coletta, A.J., and Gable, R.K. (1975). The minicourse: Where the affective and cognitive meet. *Phi Delta Kappan*, 54, 621–623. Reprinted in *Introduction to the Foundations of American Education: Readings*. Boston: Allyn and Bacon, 1975.

Collins, J.L. (1982, March). Self-efficacy and ability in achievement behavior. Paper presented at the annual meeting of the American Educational Research Association, NY.

Comrey, A.L. (1978). Common methodological problems in factor analytic studies. *Journal of Consulting and Clinical Psychology*, 46(4), 648–659.

Comrey, A.L., and Montag, I. (1982). Comparison of factor analytic results with two choice and seven choice personality item formats. *Applied Psychological Measurement*, 6(3), 285–289.

Coopersmith, S. (1967, 1989). *The antecedents of self-esteem*. San Francisco: Freeman.

Coover, D., and Delcourt, M.A.B. (1992). Construct and criterion-related validity of the adult-attitudes toward computers survey for a sample of professional nurses. *Educational and Psychological Measurement*, 52, 653–661.

Cronbach, L.J. (1946). Response sets and test validity. *Educational and Psychological Measurement*, 6, 475–494.

Cronbach, L.J. (1950). Further evidence on response sets and test design. *Educational and Psychological Measurement*, 10, 30–31.

Cronbach, L.J. (1951). Coefficient alpha and the internal structure of tests. *Psychometrika*, 16. 297–334.

Cronbach, L.J. (1971). Test validation. In R.L. Thorndike (Ed.), *Educational Measurement* (2nd ed.). Washington, DC: American Council on Education.

Cronbach, L.J. and Meehl, P.E. (1955). Construct validity in psychological tests. *Psychological Bulletin*, 52, 281–302.

Crowne, D.P., and Marlowe, D. (1960). A new scale of social desirability independent of psychopathology. *Journal of Consulting Psychology*, 24, 349–354.

Dale, E., and Chall, J. (1948). A formula for predicting reliability. *Educational Research Bulletin*, 27 (January), 11–20.

Davidson, H.H., and Lang, G. (1960). Children's perceptions of their teachers' feelings toward them related to self-perception, school achievement and behavior. *Journal of Experimental Education*, 29, 107–118.

Dawis, R.V. (1980). Measuring interests. In D.A. Payne (Ed.), *Recent developments in affective measurement* (pp. 77–92). San Francisco: Jossey-Bass.

D'Costa, A., Odgers, J.G., and Koons, P.B. (1969). *Ohio Vocational Interest Survey*. New York: Harcourt Brace Jovanovich.

Deal, T.E., and Kennedy, A.A. (1982). *Corporate cultures*. Reading, MA: Addison-Wesley.

Dixon, P.N., Bobo, M., and Stevick, R.A. (1984). Response differences and preferences for all-category-defined and end-category-defined Likert formats. *Educational and Psychological Measurement*, 44, 61–66.

Dolan, L.S., and Enos, M.M. (1980). *School attitude measure.* Glenview, IL: Scott. Foresman.

Douglas, J.D., and Rice, K.M. (1979). Sex differences in children's anxiety and defensiveness measures. *Developmental Psychology,* 15, 223–224.

Doyle, K.A. (1975). *Student evaluation of instruction.* Lexington, MA: Lexington Books, D.C. Heath.

DuBois, B., and Burns, J.A. (1975). An analysis of the meaning of the question mark response category in attitude scales. *Educational and Psychological Measurement,* 35, 869–884.

DuBois, P.H. (1970). *A history of psychological testing.* Boston: Allyn and Bacon.

Edwards, A.L. (1957). *Techniques of attitude scale construction.* New York: Appleton-Century-Crofts.

Edwards, A.L. (1959). *Manual for the Edwards Personal Preference Schedule.* New York: Psychological Corporation.

Elkind, D. (1981). *The hurried child: Growing up too fast too soon.* Reading, MA: Addison-Wesley.

Everitt, B.S. (1975). Multivariate analysis: The need for data, and other problems. *British Journal of Psychiatry,* 126, 237–240.

Field, G.R.H., and Abelson, M.A. (1982). Climate: A reconceptualization and proposed model. *Human Relations,* 35(3), 181–201.

Finn, R.H. (1972). Effects of some variations on the means and reliabilities of ratings. *Educational and Psychological Measurement,* 32, 255–267.

Fishbein, M., and Ajzen, I. (1975). *Belief, attitude, intention and behavior: An introduction to theory and research.* Reading, MA: Addison-Wesley.

Fisher, C.D., and Locke, E.A. (1992). The new look in job satisfaction research and theory. In Cranny, C.J., Smith, P.C., and Stone, E.F. *Job Satisfaction.* New York: Lexington.

Fitts, W.H. (1965). *A manual for the Tennessee Self-Concept Scale.* Nashville, TN: Counselor Recordings and Tests.

Froman, R.D., and Owen, S.V. (1991, April). High school students' perceived self-efficacy in physical and mental health. *Journal of Adolescent Research,* 6(2), 181–196.

Gable, R.K. (1969). A factor analysis of Super's Work Values Inventory. Paper presented at the annual meeting of the Northeastern Educational Research Association, Ellenville, NY, October 1969.

Gable, R.K. (1970). A multivariate study of work value orientations. Unpublished doctoral dissertation, State University of New York at Albany.

Gable, R.K., LaSalle, A., and Cook, W. (1973). Dimensionality of self-concept: Tennessee Self-Concept Scale. *Perceptual and Motor Skills,* 36, 551–560.

Gable, R.K., and Pruzek, R.M. (1971). Super's Work Value Inventory: Two multivariate studies of interim relationships. *Journal of Experimental Education,* 40, 41–50.

Gable, R.K., and Pruzek, R.M. (1972) Methodology for instrument validation: An application to attitude measurement. Paper and Symposia Abstracts of 1972

Annual Meeting. American Educational Research Association, Ellenville, NY, October 1972.

Gable, R.K., and Roberts, A.D. (1982). *The Gable-Roberts Attitude Toward Teacher Scale.* Unpublished manuscript, University of Connecticut, Storrs.

Gable, R.K., and Roberts, A.D. (1983). An instrument to measure attitude toward school subjects. *Educational and Psychological Measurement, 43,* 289–293.

Gable, R.K., Ludlow, L.H., and Wolf, M.B. (1990). The use of classical and Rasch latent trait models to enhance the validity of affective measures. *Educational and Psychological Measurement, 50,* 869–878.

Garmezy, N. (1983). Stressors of childhood. In N. Garmezy and M. Rutter (Eds.), *Stress, coping, and development in children* (pp. 43–84). New York: McGraw Hill.

Garner, W.R. (1960). Rating scales, discriminability, and information transmission. *Psychological Review, 67,* 343–352.

Getzels, J.W. (1966). The problem of interests: A recommendation. In H.A. Robinson (Ed.), *Reading: Seventy-five years of progress.* Supplementary Monographs, 66, 97–106.

Gist, M.E. (1987). Self-efficacy: Implications for organizational behavior and human resource management. *Academy of Management Review, 12,* 472–485.

Gist, M.E., and Mitchell, T.R. (1992). Self-efficacy: A theoretical analysis of its determinants and malleability. *Academy of Management Review, 17,* 183–211.

Glass, G.V., and Maguire, T.O. (1966). Abuses of factor scores. *American Educational Research Journal, 3,* 297–304.

Glover, J., and Archambault, F.X. (1982). An investigation of the construct validity of the Coopersmith Self-Esteem Inventory for mainland and island Puerto Ricans. Paper presented at the annual meeting of the Northeastern Educational Research Association, Ellenville, NY, October 1982.

Glick, W.H. (1985). Conceptualizing and measuring organizational and psychological climate: Pitfalls in multilevel research. *Academy of Management Review, 10* (3), 601–616.

Goldsmith, M. (1992). *The impact of feedback and follow-up on leadership effectiveness* (Report No. 17). La Jolla, CA: Keilty, Goldsmith & Company.

Good, T.L., and Brophy, J.E. (1978). *Looking in classrooms* (2nd ed.). New York: Harper & Row.

Gordon, L.V. (1960). *SRA manual for Survey of Interpersonal Values.* Chicago: Science Research Associates.

Green, B.F. (1954). Attitude measurement. In G. Lindzey (Ed.), *Handbook of Social Psychology* (pp. 335–369). Reading, MA: Addison-Wesley.

Gressard, C.P., and Loyd, B.H. (1986). Validation studies of a new computer attitude scale. *Association for Educational Data Systems Journal, 18,* 295–301.

Griswold, P.A. (1983). Some determinants of computer awareness among education majors. *Association for Educational Data Systems Journal, 16,* 92–103.

Guilford, J.P. (1952). When not to factor analyze. *Psychological Bulletin, 49,* 31.

Guilford, J.P. (1954). *Psychometric methods.* New York: McGraw-Hill.

Gulo, E.V. (1975). Measuring dimensions of teaching effectiveness with the semantic differential. Unpublished manuscript, Northeastern University, Boston.

Guttman, L. (1944). A basis for scaling qualitative data. *American Sociological Review*, 9, 139–150.

Guttman, L. (1953). Image theory for the structure of quantitative variates. *Psychometrika*, 18, 277–296.

Hackett, G., and Betz, N.E. (1981). A self-efficacy approach to the career development of women. *Journal of Vocational Behavior*, 18, 326–339.

Hambleton, R.K., and Swaminathan, H. (1984). *Item response theory: Principles and applications*. Boston: Kluwer-Nijhoff.

Hansen, G.S., and Wernerfelt, B. (1989). Determinants of firm performance: The relative importance of economic and organizational factors. *Strategic Management Journal*, 10, 399–411.

Helms, B.J. (1985). A study of the relationship of child stress to demographic, personality, family and school variables. Unpublished doctoral dissertation, University of Connecticut.

Helms, B.J., and Gable, R.K. (1989). *School Situation Survey Manual*. Palo Alto: Consulting Psychologists Press.

Hetherington, E.M. (1979). Divorce: A child's perspective. *American Psychologist*, 34, 851–858.

Hicks, L.E. (1970). Some properties of ipsative, normative, and forced-choice normative measures. *Psychological Bulletin*, 74(3), 167–184.

Hively, W. (1974). Introduction to domain-referenced teaching. *Educational Technology*, (June), 5–10.

Hocevar, D., Zimmer, J., and Strom, B. (1984). The confirmatory factor analytic approach to scale development and evaluation. Paper presented at the annual meeting of the National Council on Measurement in Education, New Orleans, April 1984.

Hoffman, L.W. (1979). Maternal employment: 1979. *American Psychologist*, 34, 859–865.

Hogan, T.P. (1975). *Survey of school attitudes*. New York: Harcourt Brace Jovanovich.

Holland, J.L. (1975). *Manual for the Vocational Preference Inventory*. Palo Alto, CA: Consulting Psychologists Press.

Iaffaldano, M.R., and Muchinsky, P.M. (1985). Job satisfaction and job performance: A meta-analysis. *Psychological Bulletin*, 97, 251–273.

Idaszak, J.R., Bottom, W.P., and Drasgow, F. (1988). A test of the measurement equivalence of the revised job diagnostic survey: Past problems and current solutions. *Journal of Applied Psychology*, 73, 647–656.

Isaac, S., and Michael, W.B. (1981). *Handbook in research and evaluation* (2nd ed.). San Diego, CA: Edits publishers.

Jackson, D.W. (1977). *Jackson vocational Interest Survey Manual*, London, Ontario: Research Psychologists Press.

James, L.R., and Jones, P. (1979). Psychological climate: Dimensions and relationships of individual and aggregated work environment perceptions. *Organizational Behavior and Human Performance*, 23, 201–250.

Jenkins, G.D., and Taber, T.D. (1977). A Monte Carlo study of factors affecting three indices of composite scale reliability. *Journal of Applied Psychology*, 62, 392–398.

Jensen, A.R. (1980). *Bias in mental testing*. New York: Free Press.

Joe, V.C., and John, J.C. (1973). Factor structure of the Rotter I-E scale. *Journal of Clinical Psychology*, 29, 66–68.

Johnson, W.J., Dixon, P.N., and Ryan, J.M. (1991, April). Factorial and Rasch analysis of the Charles F. Kettering Ltd. school climate profile. Paper presented at the meeting of the American Educational Research Association, Chicago, IL.

Jöreskog, K.G., and Sörbom, D. (1984). *LISREL: Analysis of structural relationships by the method of maximum likelihood, Version VI* (2nd edition). Chicago: National Educational Resources.

Jöreskog, K.G. and Sörbom, D. (1989). *LISREL 7: A guide to the program and applications* (2nd edition). Chicago: SPSS Inc.

Kahn, H. (1974). Instructor evaluation using the Thurstone technique. Unpublishd manuscript, University of Connecticut, Storrs.

Kaiser, H. (1958). The varimax criterion for analytic rotation in factor analysis. *Psychometrika*, 23, 187–200.

Katzell, R.A., Thompson, D.E., and Grizzo, R.A. (1992). How job satisfaction and job performance are and are not linked. In Cranny, C.J., Smith, P.C., and Stone, E.F. *Job Satisfaction*. New York: Lexington.

Keilty, J., Goldsmith, M., and Boone, R. (1983). *Leadership Practices Inventory*. La Jolla, CA: Keilty, Goldsmith & Boone.

Kenny, D.A. (1976). An empirical application of confirmatory factor analysis to the multitrait-multimethod matrix. *Journal of Experimental Social Psychology*, 12, 247–252.

Kenny, D.A. (1979). *Correlation and causality*. New York: Wiley-Interscience.

Kerlinger, F.N. (1973). *Foundations of Behavioral Research* (2nd ed.). New York: Holt, Rinehart and Winston.

Kiesler, C.A., Collins, B.E., and Miller, N. (1969). *Attitude change*, New York: Wiley.

Koch, W.R. (1983). Likert scaling using the graded response latent trait model. *Applied Psychological Measurement*, 7(1), 15–32.

Komorita, S.S. (1963). Attitude content, intensity, and the neutral point on a Likert scale. *Journal of Social Psychology*, 61, 327–334.

Komorita, S.S., and Graham, W.K. (1965). Number of scale points and the reliability of scales. *Educational and Psychological Measurement*, 25(4), 987–995.

Krathwohl, D.R., Bloom, B.S., and Masia, B. (1964). *A taxonomy of educational objectives, handbook II: The affective domain*. New York: McKay.

Kuder, F. (1951). *Kuder Preference Record-Vocational-CH*. Chicago: Science Research Associates.

Kuder, F., and Diamond, E.E. (1979). *Kuder DD Occupational Interest Survey general manual* (2nd ed.). Chicago: Science Research Associates.

Kuder, F. (Winter, 1991). Comments concerning the appropriate use of formulas for estimating the internal consistency reliability of tests. *Educational and Psychological Measurement*, 51(4).

Land, K.C. (1969). Principles of path analysis. In E.J. Borgatta (Ed.), *Sociological methodology* (pp. 3–37). San Francisco: Jossey-Bass.

Latham, G.P., and Saari, L.M. (1979). Application of social learning theory to training supervisors through behavioral modeling. *Journal of Applied Psychology*, 64, 239–246.

Leithwood, K. (1992)., The move toward transformational leadership. *Educational Leadership*, 49(5), 8–12.

Leithwood, K., Jantzi, D., and Dart, B. (in press). *Toward a multi-level conception of policy implementation processes based on commitment strategies*. New York: JAI Press.

Lindia, S.A., and Owen, S.V. (April, 1991). A computer-intensive program as a moderator of group and gender differences in sex-role socialization, self-efficacy, and attitudes toward computers. Paper presented at the annual meeting of the New England Educational Research Organization, Portsmouth, N.H.

Lindia, S.A. (1992). Effects of a computer-intensive program on self-efficacy, sex-role socialization, and attitudes toward computers with sixth-grade students. (Doctoral dissertation, University of Connecticut, 1992).

Likert, R. (1932). A technique for the measurement of attitudes. *Archives of Psychology*, 140, 152.

Locke, E.A. (1976). The nature and causes of job satisfaction. In M.D. Dunnette (Ed.), *Handbook of industrial and organizational psychology* (1st ed., pp. 1297–1349). Chicago: Rand McNally.

Lord, R.G., and Hanges, P.J. (1987). A control system model of organizational motivation: Theoretical development and applied implications. *Behavioral Science*, 32, 161–179.

Lynch, M.D. (1973). Multidimensional measurement with the D statistic and the semantic differential. Unpublished manuscript, Northeastern University, Boston.

Mahoney, M.J., and Thoreson, C.E. (1974). *Self-control: Power to the person*. Monterey, CA: Brooks/Cole.

Marsh, H.W. and Hocevar, D. (1985). Application of confirmatory factor analysis to the study of self-concept: First- and higher-order factor models and their invariance across groups. *Psychological Bulletin*, 97, 562–582.

Marsh, H.W. (1987). The factorial invariance of responses by males and females to a multidimensional self-concept instrument: Substantive and methodological issues. *Multivariate Behavioral Research*, 22, 457–480.

Marsh, H.W. (1989). Confirmatory factor analyses of multitrait-multimethod data: Many problems and a few solutions. *Applied Psychological Measurement*, 13, 325–362.

Marsh, H.W., and Bailey, M. (1991). Confirmatory factor analysis of multitrait-multimethod data: A comparison of alternative models. *Applied Psycholgical Measurement*, 15, 47–70.

Masters, G.N. (1980). A Rasch model for rating scales. Unpublished doctoral dissertation, University of Chicago.

Masters, G.N., Wright, B.D., and Ludlow, L.H. (1981). *SCALE: A Rasch program for rating scale data*. MESA Psychometric Laboratory, University of Chicago.

Masters, G.N., and Hyde, N.H. (1984). Measuring attitude to school with a latent trait model. *Applied Psychological Measurement*, 8(1), 39–48.

Matell, M.S., and Jacoby, J. (1971). Is there an optimal number of alternatives for Likert scale items? Study I: Reliability and validity. *Educational and Psychological Measurement*, 31, 657–674.

Mayberry, P.W. (1984). A study of item bias for attitudinal measurement using maximum likelihood factor analysis. Paper presented at the annual meeting of the National Council on Measurement in Education, New Orleans, April 1984.

McCook, W.M. (1973). Predicting potential dropouts in the inner-city: The development of an attitude scale. Unpublished doctoral dissertation, University of Connecticut, Storrs.

McKelvie, S.G. (1978). Graphic rating scales: How many categories? *British Journal of Psychology*, 69(2), 185–202.

McMorris, R. (1971). Normative and ipsative measures of occupational values. Paper presented at the annual meeting of the Northeastern Educational Research Association, Ellenville, NY, November 1971.

Melnick, S.A., and Gable, R.K. (1990a). The use of the neutral point on a 5-point Likert scale: What does it really mean? Paper presented at the annual meeting of the New England Educational Research Organization, Rockport, Maine.

Melnick, S.A., and Gable, R.K. (1990b). The use of negative item stems: A cautionary note. *Educational Research Quarterly*, 14(3), 31–36.

Melnick, S.A. (in press). The effects of item grouping on the reliability and scale scores of an affective measure. *Educational and Psychological Measurement*.

Michael, W.B., Bachelor, P., Bachelor, P., and Michael, J. (1988). The convergence of the results of exploratory and confirmatory factor analysis in the latent structure of a standardized affective measure. *Educational and Psychological Measurement*, 48, 341–354.

Mobley, W.H. (1977). Intermediate linkages in the relationship between job satisfaction and employee turnover. *Journal of Applied Psychology*, 62, 237–240.

Mulaik, S.A., James, L.R., Van Alstine, J., Bennett, N., Lind, S., and Stillwell, C.D. (1989). Evaluation of goodness-of-fit indices for structural equation models. *Psychological Bulletin*, 105, 430–445.

Murphy, C.A., Coover, D, and Owen, S.V. (1989). Development and validation of the Computer Self-Efficacy Scale. *Educational and Psychological Measurement*, 49, 893–898.

Norton, K. (1984). Sports plus: A treatment intended to improve attitudes of gifted, normal, and special populations toward physical education. Unpublished doctoral dissertation, University of Connecticut, Storrs.

Nunnally, J.C. (1978). *Psychometric theory* (2nd ed.). New York: McGraw-Hill.

Ory, J.C. (1982). Item Placement and Wording Effects on overall ratings. *Educational and Psychological Measurement*, 42, 767–775.

Ory, J.C., and Wise, S.L. (1981). Attitude change measured by scales with 4 and 5 response options. Paper presented at the meeting of the National Council on Measurement in Education, Chicago.

Osgood, C.E. (1952). The nature and measurement of meaning. *Psychological Bulletin*, 49, 197–237.

Osgood, C.E., Suci, C.J., and Tannenbaum, P.H. (1957). *The measurement of meaning*. Urbana: University of Illinois Press.

Owen, S.V., and Froman, R.D. (1988). Development of a college academic self-efficacy scale. Paper presented at the annual meeting of the National Council On Measurement in Education, New Orleans.

Owen, S.V., Smith, A.L., and Froman, R.D. (1989, October). Sex differences in social skills self-efficacy. Paper presented at the annual meeting of the New England Psychological Association, Framingham, MA.

Owen, S.V. (1989). Building self-efficacy instruments. Presentation at the 17th annual Nursing Research Conference, Tucson.

Owen, S.V., and Ramirez, M.O. (1991). Factorial validation of the study skills self-efficacy scale. Paper presented at the annual meeting of the Eastern Educational Research Association, Boston.

Owen, S.V., and Froman, R.D. (1992). Academic self-efficacy in at-risk elementary students. *Journal of Research in Education*, 2, 3–7.

Pannu, P.S. (1974). A conceptual and empirical analysis of anxiety inducing elementary school situations. Unpublished doctoral dissertation, The University of Texas, Austin.

Pappalardo, S.J. (1971). An investigation of the efficacy of "in-basket" and "role-playing" variations of simulation technique for use in counselor education. Unpublished doctoral dissertation, State University of New York at Albany.

Pedhazur, E.J. (1982). *Multiple regression in behavioral research: Explanation and prediction* (2nd ed.). New York: Holt, Rinehart & Winston.

Phillips, D.J. (December, 1990). The price tag on turnover. *Personnel Journal*.

Piers, E.V., and Harris, D.A. (1964). Age and other correlates of self-concept in children. *Journal of Educational Psychology*, 55, 91–95.

Pilotte, W.J., and Gable, R.K. (1990). The impact of positive and negative item stems on the validity of a computer anxiety scale. *Educational and Psychological Measurement*, 50, 603–610.

Pilotte, W.J. (1991). The impact of mixed item stems on the responses of high school students to a computer anxiety scale. (Doctoral Dissertation, University of Connecticut, Storrs).

Podsakoff, P.M., and Williams, L.J. (1986). The relationship between job performance and job satisfaction. In E.A. Locke (ed.), *Generalizing from laboratory to field settings* (207–253). Lexington, MA: Lexington.

Porras, J.L., Hargis, K., Patterson, K.J., Maxfield, D.G., Roberts, N., and Bies, R.J. (1982). Modeling-based organizational development: A longitudinal assessment. *Journal of Applied Behavioral Science*, 18, 433–446.

Psychological Corporation. (1982). *Differential apptitude test*. New York: The Corporation.

Purkey, W.W. (1970). *Self-concept and school achievement*. Englewood Cliffs, NJ: Prentice-Hall.

Rasch, G. (1966). An item analysis which takes individual differences into account. *British Journal of Mathematical and Statistical Psychology*, 19, 49–57.

Reece, M.J., and Owen, S.V. (1985). Proximity effects among rating scale items. Paper presented at the annual meeting of the National Council on Measurement in Education, Chicago, April 1985.

Rentz, R.R., and White, W.F. (1967). Factors of self-perception in the Tennessee Self-concept Scale. *Perceptual and Motor Skills*, 24, 118.

Reynolds, C.R. (1982a). The problem of bias in psychological assessment. In C.R. Reynolds and T.B. Gutkin (Eds.), *The handbook of school psychology* (pp. 178–208). New York: Wiley.

Reynolds, C.R. (1982b). Methods for detecting construct and predictive bias. In R.A. Berk (Ed.), *Handbook of methods for detecting test bias* (pp. 199–227). Baltimore, MD: Johns Hopkins University Press.

Rezmovic, E.L., and Rezmovic, V. (1981). A confirmatory analysis approach to construct validation. *Educational and Psychological Measurement*, 41, 61–72.

Rokeach, M. (1968). *Beliefs, attitudes, and values: A theory of organization and change*. San Francisco: Jossey-Bass.

Rokeach, M. (1973). *The nature of human values and value systems*. New York: Free Press.

Rorer, L.G. (1965). The great response style myth. *Psychological Bulletin*, 63, 129–156.

Rosenthal, T.L., and Bandura, A. (1978). Psychological modeling: Theory and practice. In S.L. Garfield and A.E. Bergin (Eds.), *Handbook of psychotherapy and behavior change: An empirical analysis* (2nd ed.) (pp. 621–658). New York: Wiley.

Rummel, R.J. (1970). *Applied factor analysis*. Evanston, IL: Northwestern University Press.

Samejima, F. (1969). Estimation of latent ability using a response pattern of graded scores. *Psychometrika Monograph Supplement*, 17.

Schlesinger, L.A., and Heskett, J.L. (1991). The service-driven service company. *Harvard Business Review*, September–October, 71–81.

Schmeck, R., Ribich, F., and Ramanaiah, N. (1977). Development of a self-report inventory for assessing individual differences in learning process. *Applied Psychological Measurement*, 1, 413–431.

Schmitt, N., and Stults, D.M. (1986). Methodology review: Analyses of multitrait-multimethod matrices. *Applied Psychological Measurement*, 10, 1–22.

Schneider, B. (1975). Organizational climates: An essay. *Personnel Psychology*, 28(4), 447–480.

Schrieshiem, C.A., and Hill, K.D. (1981). Controlling acquiescence response bias by item reversals: The effects on questionnaire validity. *Educational and Psychological Measurement*, 41, 1101–1114.

Schunk, D.H. (1981). Modeling and attributional effects on children's achievement: A self-efficacy analysis. *Journal of Educational Psychology*, 73(1), 93–105.

Schurr, K.T., and Henriksen, L.W. (1983). Effects of item sequencing and grouping in low-inference type questionnaires. *Journal of Educational Measurement*, 20, 379–391.

Scott, W.A. (1968). Comparative validities of forced-choice and single-stimulus tests. *Psychological Bulletin*, 70(4), 231–244.

Sears, P.S. (1973). Self-concept in the service of educational goals. *California Journal for Instructional Improvement*, 6, 3–12.

Severy, L.J. (1974). *Procedures and issues in the measurement of attitudes* (TM Report 30). Washington, DC: National Institute of Education.

Shavelson, R.J., Bolus, R., and Keesling, J.W. (1980). Self-concept: Recent developments in theory and methods. In D.A. Payne (Ed.), *Recent developments in affective measurement* (pp. 25–43). San Francisco: Jossey-Bass.

Shavelson, R.J., Hubner, J.J., and Stanton, J.C. (1976). Self-concept: Validation of construct interpretations. *Review of Educational Research*, 46, 407–441.

Shavelson, R.J., Webb, N.M., and Rowley, G.L. (June, 1989). Generalizability theory. *American Psychologist*, 922–932.

Shavelson, R.J., and Webb, N.M. (1991). *Generalizability theory*. Newbury Park, CA: Sage.

Shaw, M., and Wright, J.M. (1967). *Scales for the measurement of attitudes*. New York: McGraw-Hill.

Silver, H.A., and Barnette, W.L., Jr. (1970). Predictive and concurrent validity of the Minnesota Vocational Interest Inventory for vocational high school boys. *Journal of Applied Psychology*, 34, 436–440.

Slocumb, E.M. (1989). An examination of factors influencing early adolescent development: An analysis using latent variable structural equation modeling. (Doctoral dissertation, University of Connecticut, 1989).

Smircich, L. (1983). Concepts of culture and organizational analysis. *Administrative Science Quarterly*, 28, 339–358.

Smist, J.M. (1993, October). Science self-efficacy among high school students. Paper presented at the annual meeting of the Northeastern Educational Research Association, Ellenville, NY.

Snider, J.G., and Osgood, C.E. (Eds.). (1969). *Semantic differential technique: A sourcebook*. Chicago: Aldine.

Spache, G. (1953). A new readability formula for primary grade reading materials. *Elementary School Journal*, 53, 410–413.

SPSS, Inc. (1983). *SPSS-X users guide*. New York: McGraw-Hill.

Stanley, J.C. (1971). Reliability. In R.L. Thorndike (Ed.), *Educational Measurement* (2nd ed.) (pp. 356–442). Washington, DC: American Council on Education.

Steers, R.M., and Lee, T.W. (1983). Facilitating effective performance appraisals: The role of employee commitment and organizational climate. In F. Landry, S. Zedeck, and J. Cleveland (Eds.), *Performance Measurement and Theory* (pp. 75–93). Hillsdale, NJ: Lawrence Erlbaum.

Stevens, D.J. (1980). How educators perceive computers in the classroom. *Association for Educational Data Systems Journal*, 221–232.

Stevens, D.J. (1982). Educators' perceptions of computers in education: 1979 and 1982. *Association for Educational Data Systems Journal*, 145, 1–15.

Super, D.T. (1970). *Manual for the Work Values Inventory*. Boston: Houghton-Mifflin.

Tabachnick, B.G., and Fidell, L.S. (1983). *Using multivariate statistics.* New York: Harper & Row.

Tenopyr, M.L. (1968). Internal consistency of ipsative scores: The "one reliable scale" phenomenon. Paper presented at the 76th annual convention of the American Psychological Association, San Francisco, September 1968.

Thurstone, L.L. (1927). A law of comparative judgment. *Psychological Review*, 34, 273–286.

Thurstone, L.L. (1928). Attitudes can be measured. *American Journal of Sociology*, 33, 529–554.

Thurstone, L.L. (1931a). The measurement of attitudes. *Journal of Abnormal and Social Psychology*, 26, 249–269.

Thurstone, L.L. (1931b). The measurement of change in social attitudes. *Journal of Social Psychology*, 2, 230–235.

Thurstone, L.L. (1946). Comment. *American Journal of Sociology*, 52, 39–40.

Thurstone, L.L., and Chave, E.J. (1929). *The measurement of attitude.* Chicago: University of Chicago Press.

Triandis, H.C. (1971). *Attitudes and attitude change.* New York: Wiley.

Tyler, R.W. (1973). Assessing educational achievement in the affective domain. *Measurement in Education*, 4(3), 1–8.

Ulosevich, S.N., Michael, W.B., and Bachelor, P. (1991). Higher-order factors in structure-of-intellect (SOI) aptitude tests hypothesized to portray constructs of military leadership: A re-analysis of an SOI data base. *Educational and Psychological Measurement*, 51, 15–37.

Ulrich, D., Halbrook, R., Meder, D., Stuchlik, M., and Thorpe, S. (1991). Employee and customer attachment: Synergies for competitive advantage. *Human Resource Planning*, 14(2), 89–103.

Vance, R.J., MacCallum, R.C., Coovert, M.D., and Hedge, J.W. (1988). Construct validity of multiple job performance measures using confirmatory factor analysis. *Journal of Applied Psychology*, 73, 74–80.

Veiga, J.F. (1991). The frequency of self-limiting behavior in groups: A measure and an explanation. *Human Relations*, 44, 877–895.

Velicer, W.F., and Stevenson, J.F. (1978). The relation between item format and the structure of the Eysenck Personality Inventory. *Applied Psychological Measurement*, 2, 293–304.

Velicer, W.F., DiClemente, C., and Corriveau, D.P. (1979). Item format and the structure of the Personal Orientation Inventory. Paper presented at the annual meeting of the Eastern Psychological Association. Philadelphia, April 1979.

Wagner, R.V. (1969). The study of attitude change: An introduction. In R.V. Wagner and J.J. Sherwood (Eds.), *The study of attitude change* (pp. 1–18). Belmont, CA: Brooke Cole.

Warner, W., Meeker, M., and Eells, K. (1949). *Social class in America.* Chicago: Science Research Associates.

Webb, N.M., Rowley, G.L., and Shavelson, R.J. (July, 1988). Using generalizability theory in counseling and development. *Measurement and Evaluation in Counseling and Development*, 21, 81–90.

Welsh, M., Bachelor, P., Wright, C.R., and Michael, W.B. (1990). The exploratory and confirmatory factor analyses of the latent structure of the study attitudes and methods survey for a sample of 176 eighth-grade students. *Educational and Psychological Measurement*, 50, 369–376.

Wheaton, B., Muthen, B., Alwin, D.F., and Summers, G.F. (1977). Assessing reliability and stability in panel models. In D.R. Heise (Ed.), *Sociological methodology, 1977* (pp. 84–136). San Francisco: Jossey-Bass.

Wicker, W.A. (1969). Attitudes versus actions: The relationship of verbal and overt behavioral responses to attitude objects. *Journal of Social Issues*, 25, 41–78.

Widaman, K.F. (1985), Hierarchically tested covariance structure models for multitrait-multimethod data. *Applied Psychological Measurement*, 9, 1–26.

Wiener, Y. (1988). Forms of value systems: A focus on organizational effectiveness and cultural change and maintenance. *Academy of Management Review*, 13(4), 534–545.

Wiley, D. (1967). Latent partition analysis. *Psychometrika*, 32, 183–193.

Wilson, M.J., Moore, A.D., and Bullock, L.M. (1987). Factorial invariance of the behavioral dimensions rating scale. *Measurement and Evaluation in Counseling and Development*, 11–17.

Wolf, M.B., and Gable, R.K. (1991, April). *A comparison of confirmatory factor analysis and item response theory for detecting item bias on an affective instrument*. Paper presented at the meeting of the American Educational Research Association, Chicago, IL.

Woodrow, E.J. (1991). A comparison of four computer attitude scales. *Journal of Educational Computing Research*, 7(2), 165–187.

Wright, B.D., and Masters, G.N. (1982). *Rating scale analysis*. Chicago: Mesa Press.

Wright, B.D., and Stone, M.H. (1979). *Best test design*. Chicago: Mesa Press.

Zimmerman, B.J. (1989). A social cognitive view of self-regulated academic learning. *Journal of Educational Psychology*, 81, 329–339.

Zytowski, D.G. (1973). *Contemporary approaches to interest measurement*. Minneapolis: University of Minnesota Press.

APPENDIX A

SEMANTIC DIFFERENTIAL: ME AS A COUNSELOR DEVELOPED BY SALVATORE J. PAPPALARDO

INSTRUCTIONS

The purpose of this study is to measure the MEANINGS of certain things to various people by having them judge them against a series of descriptive scales. In taking this test, please make your judgments on the basis of what these things mean TO YOU. On each page of this booklet you will find a different concept to be judged and beneath it a set of scales. You are to rate *the concept* on each of these scales in order. Here is how you are to use these scales:

If you feel that the concept at the top of the page is VERY CLOSELY RELATED to the one end of the scale, you should place your check mark as follows:

fair_X_:___:___:___:___:___:____unfair

or

fair____:___:___:___:___:___:_X_unfair

If you feel that the concept is QUITE CLOSELY RELATED to one or the other end of the scale (but not extremely), you should place your check mark as follows:

weak____:___:___:___:___:___:____strong

or

weak____:___:___:___:___:_X_:____strong

If the concept seems ONLY SLIGHTLY RELATED to one side as opposed to the other side (but is not really neutral), then you should check as follows:

active____:___:_X_:___:___:___:____passive

or

active____:___:___:___:___:_X_:____passive

The direction toward which you check, of course, depends upon which of the two ends of the scale seems more ·characteristic of the thing you're judging.

If you consider the concept to be NEUTRAL on the scale, both sides of the scale EQUALLY ASSOCIATED with the concept, or if the scale is COMPLETELY IRRELEVANT, unrelated to the concept, then you should place your check mark in the middle space:

safe____:___:___:_X_:___:___:____dangerous

IMPORTANT: Place your check marks IN THE MIDDLE OF SPACES, not on the boundaries.

Be sure you check every scale for every concept. DO NOT OMIT ANY.

Never put more than one check mark on a single scale.

DO NOT LOOK BACK AND FORTH through the items. Do not try to remember how you checked similar items earlier in the test. MAKE EACH ITEM A SEPARATE AND INDEPENDENT JUDGMENT. It is your first impressions, the immediate "feelings" about the items, that we want. On the other hand, please do not be careless, because we want your true impressions. THANK YOU.

NAME_____ SEX____ DATE_____

CONCEPT: ME AS GUIDANCE COUNSELOR

1.	CARELESS	__:__:__:__:__:__ CAREFUL
2.	CONFIDENT	__:__:__:__:__:__ UNCERTAIN
3.	UNFAIR	__:__:__:__:__:__ FAIR
4.	CONVENTIONAL	__:__:__:__:__:__ IMAGINATIVE
5.	SHALLOW	__:__:__:__:__:__ DEEP
6.	OPTIMISTIC	__:__:__:__:__:__ PESSIMISTIC
7.	KIND	__:__:__:__:__:__ CRUEL
8.	VALUABLE	__:__:__:__:__:__ WORTHLESS
9.	INSENSITIVE	__:__:__:__:__:__ SENSITIVE
10.	SUSPICIOUS	__:__:__:__:__:__ TRUSTING
11.	ACCEPTANT	__:__:__:__:__:__ REJECTING
12.	OBSTRUCTIVE	__:__:__:__:__:__ HELPFUL
13.	WARM	__:__:__:__:__:__ COLD
14.	UNPLEASANT	__:__:__:__:__:__ PLEASANT
15.	COWARDLY	__:__:__:__:__:__ BRAVE
16.	SHARP	__:__:__:__:__:__ DULL
17.	TENSE	__:__:__:__:__:__ RELAXED
18.	HONEST	__:__:__:__:__:__ DISHONEST
19.	HUMBLE	__:__:__:__:__:__ ASSERTIVE
20.	ACTIVE	__:__:__:__:__:__ PASSIVE
21.	WEAK	__:__:__:__:__:__ STRONG
22.	GOOD	__:__:__:__:__:__ BAD
23.	RELIABLE	__:__:__:__:__:__ UNRELIABLE
24.	RESERVED	__:__:__:__:__:__ EASYGOING
25.	UNIMPORTANT	__:__:__:__:__:__ IMPORTANT

APPENDIX B

OCCUPATIONAL VALUES INVENTORY: NORMATIVE FORM DEVELOPED BY ROBERT MCMORRIS

DIRECTIONS FOR PART N: For each of the following statements regarding work values, please indicate how important you think it is for people generally. Indicate your choice in the columns to the right of the statement by marking an X.

	Unimportant	Moderately Important	Very Important
People want a job where they			
1. are favored by the boss	___ ___	___ ___	___
2. don't have to think	___ ___	___ ___	___
3. receive kickbacks	___ ___	___ ___	___
4. need little training	___ ___	___ ___	___
5. can pilfer things on the job	___ ___	___ ___	___
6. are a relative of the owner	___ ___	___ ___	___
7. can expect financial favors	___ ___	___ ___	___
8. are given political favoritism	___ ___	___ ___	___
9. let others make decisions	___ ___	___ ___	___

OCCUPATIONAL VALUES INVENTORY: IPSATIVE FORM DEVELOPED BY ROBERT MCMORRIS

DIRECTIONS FOR PART I: For each of the following sets of three statements regarding work values, please pick the one which you think is *most* important to people generally and the one which is *least* important. Indicate your choices in the columns to the right of the statements by marking an X.

	Most	Least
People want a job where they		
10. are favored by the boss	____	____
11. don't have to think	____	____
12. receive kickbacks	____	____
People want a job where they		
13. need little training	____	____
14. can pilfer things on the job	____	____
15. are a relative of the owner	____	____
People want a job where they		
16. can expect financial favors	____	____
17. are given political favoritism	____	____
18. let others make decisions	____	____

	Unimportant	Moderately Important	Very Important
19. To what extent is social acceptability important?	____ ____	____ ____	____

APPENDIX C: Example of Generalizability Study and Decision Study, by Steven V. Owen, Bureau of Educational Research, University of Connecticut, Storrs, CT 06269

Imagine a scale administered twice. The data allow estimates of two sources of measurement error: among items on the scale (i.e., coefficient alpha), and across occasions (i.e., test-retest coefficient). The classical test theory approach is to estimate the two error sources separately, and then report both. If both estimates show small error, great. But if the two reliability estimates differ widely, it is difficult to reconcile the two definitions of measurement error. However, a generalizability study (*G*-study) can combine the two sources of error, and also can study their interaction. The *G*-study is easily adapted to as many sources of measurement error as the researcher is willing to consider. For example, in a single *G*-study, one might investigate parallel test forms, multiple raters or observers, homogeneity among items, and stability over occasions.

Our *G*-study example involves a 15-item measure given to 35 persons twice over a 4-week interval. To get the *G*-study data, we can run a program specifically designed for generalizability analysis (e.g., GENOVA), or use a canned statistical package that will produce estimates of variance components (e.g., BMDP-8V or SAS-VARCOMP). The data we have are arranged as a 3-way ANOVA: Subjects (35 levels) by items (15 levels) by occasions (2 levels). This is a repeated measures design, because each subject will have a score on each occasion, for each item. Unlike the typical ANOVA design, subjects in a *G*-study are an explicit factor, with as many levels as there are persons. That is because the variance component attributed to subjects represents "real" variation, that is, genuine individual differences among respondents. The more variation attributable to subjects, the better. All of the remaining variance components represent some form of measurement error. Before continuing, it might be helpful for you to draw a model of the ANOVA, so the source table below will make sense.

On the printout, the ANOVA source table is arranged just as you would suspect (I've omitted information irrelevant to the *G*-study, such as sums of squares, *df*, etc.).

	ESTIMATES OF
SOURCE	*VARIANCE COMPONENTS*
SUBJECTS (S)	.1259
ITEMS (I)	.0532
OCCASIONS (O)	−.0028
S × I	.0631
S × O	−.0069
I × O	.0405
S × I × O	.3006

The last term—S × I × O—is actually a combination of the 3-way interaction, plus all variance unaccounted for (that is, residual). Also, because variances cannot be negative, it is conventional to replace any negative variance estimates with zeros.

As a thought problem, it will be useful for you to describe the meaning of each of these ANOVA effects. For example, a large variance component on the S × I term means that subjects' rank ordering varies according to what item they are responding to. That is not good news. If the scale items are meant to be homogeneous and are properly sampled from the domain, then you should want a person with a lot of the attribute to show a high score on *each* item.

From here, it is a simple matter of combining variance components to get the big picture: the *G*-coefficient. Actually, there are two types of *G*-coefficient, depending on how you intend to use the measure. If your aim is criterion referencing (How much of this attribute does the person show?), then you will calculate $G_{absolute}$. If you are interested in a norm-referenced approach (How do persons rank order on the attribute?), then you want to estimate $G_{relative}$.

To get the variance component for $G_{absolute}$:

$$\sigma^2_{abs} = \frac{\sigma^2_i}{n_i} + \frac{\sigma^2_o}{n_o} + \frac{\sigma^2_{si}}{n_i} + \frac{\sigma^2_{so}}{n_o} + \frac{\sigma^2_{io}}{n_i n_o} + \frac{\sigma^2_{sio}}{n_i n_o}$$

where σ^2_{abs} = total amount of measurement error for absolute decisions
σ^2 = a variance component from the ANOVA source table
n = the number of contributors to the variance component (e.g., σ^2_i has 15 item contributors, so $n_i = 15$).

Notice that we are combining all the components, except the one for subjects. All of the components in the equation represent sources of measurement error, so we hope that the total, σ^2_{abs}, is not too large.

Next, we adapt a formula straight out of classical test theory to get the *G*-coefficient:

reliability = true variance/(true variance + error variance)

The overall question is, What proportion of the total variance is true? Using the language of generalizability theory, the formula is

generalizability (absolute) = $\sigma^2_s/(\sigma^2_s + \sigma^2_{abs})$

Plugging in numbers (remember that we replaced the negative components):

$$\sigma^2_{abs} = \frac{.0532}{15} + \frac{.0000}{2} + \frac{.0631}{15} + \frac{.0000}{2} + \frac{.0405}{30} + \frac{.3006}{30}$$
$$= .019$$
$$G_{abs} = .1259/(.1259 + .019)$$
$$= .869$$

Now, if we want to calculate $G_{relative}$, the formula is simpler, because we are interested solely in variance having to do with rank ordering of subjects. Thus,

$$\sigma^2_{rel} = \frac{\sigma^2_{si}}{n_i} + \frac{\sigma^2_{so}}{n_O} + \frac{\sigma^2_{sio}}{n_i n_O}$$

$$= \frac{.0631}{15} + \frac{.0000}{2} + \frac{.3006}{30}$$

$$= .014$$

The formula for G_{rel} changes slightly:

generalizability (relative) $= \sigma^2_s / (\sigma^2_s + \sigma^2_{rel})$

$$G_{rel} = .1259/(.1259 + .014)$$
$$= .900$$

You should expect G_{abs} to be smaller than G_{rel}, because G_{abs} incorporates more components representing error. In other words, G_{abs} has more error variation in its denominator, which makes its value smaller.

The G-coefficients above were calculated on the basis of **two** administrations of the scale. If you want to estimate what happens under other circumstances, you would go forward into a Decision study (*D*-study). For example, if you are curious about what the generalizability is predicted to be for only **one** measurement occasion, all you have to do is change the number of contributors to the occasion variance (in the denominators). Thus, $n_O = 1$ instead of 2. Applying this simple change, we get

$$G_{abs} = .805 \text{ and}$$
$$G_{rel} = .838.$$

These are still adequate generalizability estimates, but they show that the error variance attributable to occasion was not negligible. Perhaps we could compensate by adding more items? This is another *D*-study, but just as simple as the first example. Doubling the number of items (and assuming proper domain sampling), we once again shift the denominators to reflect that; e.g., $n_i = 30$, instead of 15. Under that assumption,

$$G_{abs} = .892 \text{ and}$$
$$G_{rel} = .946.$$

We see that creating more items is expected to deliver substantially more dependability in our scores. Because increasing the number of items is more economical than adding measurement occasions, that is the route we should take.

SUBJECT INDEX

AUTHOR INDEX

271

274 AUTHOR INDEX

Ory, J.C., 56
Osgood, C.E., 33, 40, 72, 73, 74, 75, 79, 237, 240
Owen, S.V., 5, 8, 16–17, 18, 19, 65, 205, 263

Pannu, P.S., 170
Pappalardo, S.J., 74
Patterson, K.J., 16
Pedhazur, E.J., 172
Phillip, D.J., 10
Piers, E.V., 23
Pilotte, W.J., 59–60, 61–64
Podsakoff, P.M., 9
Porras, J.L., 16
Pruzek, R.M., 100, 215
Purkey, W.W., 23

Ramanaiah, N., 17
Ramirez, M.O., 17, 18
Rasch, G., 65–66, 67, 68, 70, 71, 176–187
Reece, M.J., 8, 65
Rentz, R.R., 134
Reynolds, C.R., 187, 188
Rezmovic, E.L., 168
Rezmovic, V., 168
Ribich, F., 17
Rice, K.M., 170
Roberts, A.D., 8, 31, 33, 34, 50
Roberts, N., 16
Rokeach, M., 19–20, 22
Rorer, L.G., 58
Rosenthal, T.L., 15
Rowley, G.L., 205
Rummell, R.J., 111
Ryan, J.M., 67

Saari, L.M., 16
Samejima, F., 71
Scheier, M.F., 14
Schein, E.H., 10, 21
Schlesinger, L.A., 10
Schmeck, R., 17
Schneider, B., 9
Schriescheim, C.A., 60, 62
Schunk, D.H., 16
Schurr, K.T., 64–65

Scott, W.A., 85
Severy, L.J., 5, 7
Shavelson, R.J., 23, 205
Shaw, M., 7, 50
Silver, H.A., 192
Slocumb, E.M., 174
Smircich, L., 21
Smist, J.M., 18
Smith, A.L., 18
Snider, J.G., 72, 73
Sörbom, D., 61, 106, 159, 162, 163
Spache, G., 240
Stanley, J.C., 201
Stanton, J.C., 23
Steers, R.M., 9
Stevens, D.J., 8
Stevenson, J.F., 56
Stevick, R.A., 57
Stilwell, C.D., 163
Stone, M.H., 66, 176
Strong, E.K., 24
Stuchlik, M., 3, 10, 11, 22
Suci, C.J., 33, 40, 72, 73, 74, 75, 79, 240
Summers, G.F., 160
Super, D.T., 20, 50, 85, 102, 103, 214
Swaminathan, H., 66, 187

Tabachnick, B.G., 108
Taber, T.D., 55
Tannenbaum, P.H., 33, 40, 72, 73, 74, 75, 79, 240
Tenopyr, M.L., 85
Thompson, D.E., 9
Thoreson, C.E., 17
Thorpe, S., 3, 10, 11, 22
Thurstone, L.L., xv, 5, 40, 42–50, 52, 66–67, 79, 80, 239–240, 243
Triandis, H.C., 6, 7
Tsui, A.S., 14, 16
Tyler, R.W., 1, 8, 19–21, 24–25

Ulosevich, S.N., 165
Ulrich, D., 3, 10, 11, 22

Van Alstine, J., 163
Vance, R.J., 168
van der Ende, J., 110